The Beatles:

Having Read the Book

The Beatles:

Having Read the Book

Greg Sterlace

First Edition, February 2016

Second Edition, March 2017

Copyright © 2016 by Gregory James Sterlace

Published in the United States by
Adequate Life Publishing
In conjunction with Lulu.com

ISBN: 978-1-329-53652-4

All Rights Reserved. Without limiting the rights under copyright reserved above, no part of this publication may be reproduced, stored in or introduced into a retrieval system, or transmitted, in any form, or by any means (electronic, mechanical, photocopying, recording, or otherwise) without the prior written permission of the copyright owner of this book.

DEDICATION

To my beautiful wife Paula: There is no one compared with you. We were married in a cemetery on June 1st, naturally.

And to my parents Patricia Van Remmen (writer) and James Ralph Sterlace (sports enthusiast).

Special thanks to Eugene Kelly and Bill Tutton.

FOREWORD

Back when I first became a Beatles fan in the 1970s, it *seemed* like I could count on one hand the number of books I could easily access. Titles like *The Longest Cocktail Party* and *Apple To The Core,* alongside the authorized biography by Hunter Davies, were on the shelves at the local library. Garage sales turned up things like the novelizations of *A Hard Day's Night*, *Help!* and *Yellow Submarine* (as well as a 1964 tome bearing the questionable title, *The True Story of The Beatles*). Eventually, my quest for information took me to bookstores in this pre-digital age, where I came upon a few newly-published works: *The Beatles: An Illustrated Record* and *All Together Now*, as well as *Growing Up With The Beatles* and those hard cover picture books meant to be given as inexpensive gifts.

But even at that time and with my relatively callow reading habits, I was aware enough to recognize that a thoroughly satisfying telling of their story was lacking. The best books covered only one angle or another; it seemed like there was so much more to learn, but most everything I could get my hands on came up short. The landscape changed in 1977 when, as far as I was concerned, Beatle scholarship took a mighty leap forward with the publication of Nicholas Schaffner's *The Beatles Forever*. Here at last was a book that discussed their music *and* history in a readable and coherent fashion, loaded with photos to boot. To say that *that* book (along with aforementioned works by Tyler-Carr and Castleman-Podrazik) left a lifelong impression would be a pretty accurate summation.

In the wake of *The Beatles Forever*'s publication, slowly but steadily the field of Beatles study began to take shape, and by the end of the decade, some memoirs had emerged — from the not yet "Sir" George Martin and from the group's first manager, Alan Williams. Bios of individual Beatles had arrived, as well as a brilliant and knowing satire (roughly coinciding with the TV send-up by The Rutles), *Paperback Writer*. Alongside a number of fanzines also appearing by this time, the vacuum in amassing detailed and factual Beatle information slowly started to fill in.

Things might have reached critical mass on their own but John Lennon's tragic end surely sped up the process, as now the group passed into history (being spoken of in past tense for the first time). Thereafter, books began arriving off the press faster than I could process them. Philip Norman's *Shout!*, for a time, took its place as the successor to Hunter Davies' *Authorized Biography*; deeply flawed as it was, so narrow still was the literary canon at that time that we fans were willing to overlook its considerable shortcomings just for the sake of embracing a fresh and vivid read. An insider tell-all, *The Love You Make*, became a best-seller, regrettably; while a truer-than-we-realized hatchet job, *The Lives of John Lennon*, earned a place in fan infamy. Just on the horizon lay the work of Mark Lewisohn and his essential *The Beatles Recording Sessions*. With that, the era of the Beatles historian had truly arrived.

As the Beatles scholar I've become (and also as a critical thinker), I now know that I was not alone in feeling the influence of *The Beatles Forever*. With the publication of Greg Sterlace's *Having Read The Book*, it's become clear that the impact of this particular volume is still being felt, as it's one of the very few Beatle titles that he's accorded the top grade of A+ to. The need for Greg's book is manifest, given the literally thousands of volumes of Beatle-related tomes populating (and in some cases, littering) the literary landscape currently in existence. *Having Read The Book* cuts through the crap, in much the same way the *Rolling Stone Record Guide* once did for music: with unerring judgment, Greg lays waste to the worthless while extolling the worthy. (As the creator of the FAQ book series, I feel I have pretty good radar when it comes to judging what's worth reading and what isn't. Greg has taken on a monumental task and made it entertaining besides.)

I enjoyed trawling through this work; revisiting some old friends, who — like actual ones in your life, you may find yourself wondering, "Why did I ever think this was cool?" — as well as discovering some overlooked gems that warrant a new look. I also found myself re-experiencing works that I hadn't thought about in years, as well becoming intrigued with Greg's takes and insights. Mostly, this is a fun way to blow a lot of valuable hours: down the rabbit hole and following wherever his droll but spot-on commentary takes you.

Mostly, I consider that if this book or one like it existed back in the day, how much less time would I have squandered on works that went nowhere, were glutted with inaccuracies or were wholly devoid of insights. Thanks, Greg, for doing the heavy lifting for us fans!

Robert Rodriguez
Beatles author and podcaster
www.somethingaboutthebeatles.com

INTRODUCTION

Back in the 1970's I was sitting at home minding my own business when my brother Mark came in the room and handed me a book he had shoplifted from a drug store. It was ostensibly about my favorite pop group (aka rock band) the Beatles. It was a little paperback called *The Longest Cocktail Party* by Richard DiLello published by Hugh Hefner. I thought I would find out all kinds of groovy things about the Beatles. Instead, I found out all kinds of groovy things about DiLello, his boss Derek Taylor, and the wicked fun they had at Apple records as the sun set on England in the late 1960's. The Beatles only made cameo appearances in the text. That didn't stop *Playboy* from marketing the book correctly. *Playboy* made sure to feature a picture of the group with moustaches on the cover circa 1967 (despite the fact the book covered the years 1968-1971). If they had put Derek Taylor on the cover in his moustache it would have really hurt sales. So I had my first Beatles book, albeit actually a book about their self-run business with a photo on the cover that pre-dated the start of said business. My life was now beginning. It was the start of over four decades of reading about John, Paul, George, and their little drummer boy.

Remember those fabulous 70's? The whole band was still alive (Stuart notwithstanding). There wasn't a new book coming out every day. There wasn't a "new" album release every year. No year went by without at least one solo studio album of fresh material although a couple years had slim pickings. 1972 had only John's despised semi flop *SOMETIME IN NEW YORK CITY* and 1977 had only Ringo's despised mega flop *RINGO THE 4th*. It was a glorious time. It was a time before the shooting and the stabbing. A possible reunion was always in the air. The Beatles were still ripe for satire. Lennon had not been changed into

Saint John. He was derided as much as he was praised. McCartney dragged Linda around on tour even though she couldn't play keyboards to save her life. Harrison had lost the good will of his fans with one terrible U.S. tour and a string of sanctimonious records. Starr had lost his bearings and his ability to get on the charts.

There were a slew of humorous takes on the Beatles' legend and their mostly sub-par solo careers:

1. *NATIONAL LAMPOON'S RADIO DINNER* album featured Tony Hendra's devastating parody of *Rolling Stone's Lennon Remembers* interview. Tony utilized Lennon's most ridiculous statements verbatim to show what a fool John could be.
2. Rock critic extraordinaire Lester Bangs ripped the group apart in delightful style in his article "Dandelions in Still Air: The Withering Away of the Beatles" (first printed in *The Real Paper*, reprinted in *Creem*, available currently in *The Mammoth Book of the Beatles*).
3. *National Lampoon* devoted a whole issue to them in which we learned Manson was the fifth Beatle, their second movie was soft core porn, and if we all worked together we could find a cure for Beatlemania.
4. Mark shipper's fantasy novel *Paperback Writer* revealed the first Beatles album was entitled *WE'RE GONNA CHANGE THE FACE OF POP MUSIC FOREVER*.
5. Beatle buddies Neil Innes and Eric Idle concocted the mockumentary *All You Need is Cash* featuring: Yoko as a Nazi, John in seclusion ala Charles Foster Kane, McCartney with his new band Punk Floyd, Harrison played by an Indian who does not speak for he is the quiet Rutle, John Belushi as Allen Klein, Mick Jagger

remembering the famous Che Guevara Stadium show, and their classic animated film *Yellow Submarine Sandwich*. George Harrison gives his seal of approval to the tele-film by appearing as a TV news reporter.

6. Jim Bickhart's sleeve notes for A&M records specially priced compilation *THE BEST OF THE MOVE* puts down the solo years. Bickhart lets us know, "…old Beatle records sound great, but contrastingly, we all have our opinions about current Beatle residues."

Now that John and George are long dead I think it's high time that we bring humor back when writing about the group. After all, the fab four were some of the funniest men in rock, often willing to be self-deprecating. I want to treat the boys from Liverpool like *Creem* magazine always did with love but not reverence. I was inspired by Cosmo Kramer's coffee table book about coffee tables to write this Beatle book about Beatle books. I realized I only had one talent; the ability to meld Beatle minutiae into a cohesive reference book.

I'd like to share something Nicholas Schaffner said in his introduction to *The Beatles Forever:* "Putting together a book such as this one poses a dilemma: how much should the author assume the reader already knows? Or wants to know? Should one cater to those in the beginning, the intermediate, or the advanced stages of Beatlemania? I have tried to include something for all of them, and can only keep my fingers crossed that I don't lose everybody in the process. I hope die-hards will find enough…arcane facts…to keep them happy-and that in turn doesn't cause the 'general reader' to bog down." This states it perfectly for my book as well.

The cottage industry of Beatle publications is more prolific now than it ever was. As the band recedes into the mythic fog of 20th century history we get more and more documentation about their music, their love lives, their personalities, and their finances. I wanted to try to make sense of it by reviewing the best and the worst of the Beatle tomes as they stand side by side in bookstores everywhere. I spent 40 years reading about them knowing that one day I would share my accumulated knowledge with the fans in Pepperland. You're welcome! Having read the book, I'd love to turn you on.

Greg Sterlace
2015

P.S.: When I first started reading Robert Christgau (the Dean of rock critics) in 1975 I was much taken with the format of his Consumer Guide. I thought I would wait 40 years and then use it for my own writing. *Entertainment Weekly* also liked the way he did things and began copying it back in the 90's. Like *EW* my use of this format is in homage to Bob and a tribute to all the men and women who have died in the trenches of Hollywood, Tin Pan Alley, and Las Vegas.

P.P.S.: One of the fun parts of reading a book like this is finding all the mistakes the author made. Hopefully, I've kept mine to a bare minimum but feel free to search for all my fab related screw ups.

CRITICISM, genre of writing that places value judgments on literature, film, visual art, architecture, and other creative endeavors, and which, quite frankly, appears to have been written by an insufferably precocious, attention-starved 9 year old.

The fundamental flaws evident in criticism are simply too numerous to list here, but rest assured, unlucky readers of any part of the collected body of this laughably derivative style of writing will wish they had never been bothered.

Perhaps it's finally time for the entire form of analysis to call it quits and retreat from public view with whatever little dignity it may have remaining.

D-

-Keith Mandrell from *The Onion Book of Known Knowledge* (2012 Little, Brown and Company)

As there are well over 2,000 Beatle books in existence, the author chooses to offer a selection.

ABBEY ROAD/LET IT BE by Peter Doggett (1998 Schirmer)

In case you were looking around for a guide to the last two albums they made together, here you go. You can take your copies of the music and play them as you read along. You'll find out amazing facts like:

1. "Paul donned the mantle of leadership" during the recording of *LET IT BE*.
2. George felt "weird vibes" when with the band in 1969. I'm guessing it was because Paul had donned the mantle of leadership.
3. John's first reaction to making the *Let It Be* movie was, "George and I...we don't want to do the fucker." Probably because Paul had donned the mantle of leadership.
4. "Genius is pain," proclaimed Lennon in 1970. He was probably thinking of Paul donning the mantle of leadership.

The only good thing about this throwaway book is when author Peter Doggett stops with his hackneyed version of things and gives us a bonus chapter featuring the original album reviews from *Rolling Stone, The Times,* and *New Musical Express*. Those are very worthwhile especially the famous pan from NME's Alan

Smith. In a review of *LET IT BE* featuring the headline "New LP shows they couldn't care less," Alan writes "If *LET IT BE* is to be their last it will stand as a cheapskate epitaph, a cardboard tombstone, a sad and tatty end to a musical fusion which wiped clean and drew again the face of pop music." I gather Alan didn't like the album. This despite the fact that it featured two big hit singles (three in America) and a beautiful book of photographs that were suitable for framing (no book included with the American vinyl). Alan "value for money" Smith was sickened by Apple putting out an album with three previously released numbers and then jacking up the price because of "the accompanying book of fab glossy pix." But Alan, the three previously released tracks (*GET BACK, ACROSS THE UNIVERSE*, and *LET IT BE*) are presented in different and better Phil Spector versions. Shouldn't that count for something?   B-

<u>ACROSS THE UNIVERSE WITH JOHN LENNON</u> by Linda Keen (1999 Hampton Roads)

If you thought *Lennon Remembers* and *The Playboy Interviews* were great this book goes where no man has gone before. To heaven, to the other side, call it what you wish. It goes there. When I first picked up this book I thought it was going to be a tie-in to the first *Star Wars* prequel (released the same year). You know, something along the lines of John Lennon telling Julian, "I am your father," right before he cuts the kid's arm off. But it's better than that. Linda Keen interviews dead John Lennon as his spirit slips away across the universe. If there was anybody who could pull this feat off it is Linda Keen. A teacher of psychics and a talented psychic herself, she began tapping into Lennon's post-death consciousness in 1986. Thirteen years of chatting later we get a best of compilation of all the wonderful, magical, and important things Johnny has told her. Just in case you think Linda is making this shit up there is this important message on the back cover, "The lively and irreverent conversations reported here are utterly true to memory." I don't doubt it. Now, a glimpse into the rich tapestry of the after-life you will discover if you are strong enough to take this living practical journey into another part of the being we all comprise. Call it God. Call it love. Call it what you will it to be. This book makes it clear what we already know but still want to hear:

1. John chews gum up in Heaven; in fact, he "chomps" on it.
2. Lennon in an earlier life (pre-1940) was a Druid priest.
3. Linda and John are very old friends. It turns out at the same time she was a Druid priestess.
4. John, "…when people don't appreciate that there's spirit to communicate with, it gets pretty sad in this wonderful place we like to call our Infinite Dwelling."
5. John, "Everybody's been to Heaven; they just can't recall what it's like." Very helpful. Thank you.
6. John, "The soul resides in other dimensions which are places we construct ourselves depending on the kind of reality we believe in." Obviously.
7. On being shot to death by a deranged fan, "At first, I didn't even realize I was dead…I was so confused and angry. I could feel the whole world projecting their sorrow and pain onto me. They didn't understand the process of death and that ultimately there are reasons

for everything." What a relief! I hope Yoko read this book. It would definitely set her mind at ease.
8. Linda, "Were you able to stay spiritually in touch with Yoko?" John, "Yeah, sometimes and with my sons." Great. So it is a happy ending.
9. Linda, "Do you think people are going to buy the idea you were Mozart?" John, "It's irrelevant whether they buy it or not." I agree.

Unfortunately, Linda never gets around to asking John about The Threatles reunion, or what he thinks of Yoko's boyfriends since he's been gone, or if he's embarrassed by the horrible music Julian and Sean have foisted on the public, or if he ever sees Jimi Hendrix or Janis Joplin flying around up there, or if he thinks Chapman should be paroled. But you can't have everything. F +

THE ACT YOU'VE KNOWN FOR ALL THESE YEARS: The Life and Afterlife of Sgt. Pepper by Clinton Heylin (2007 Canongate)

Clinton Heylin wrote 17 books before this one so I'm assuming he was desperately looking around for a new idea and instead hit on this old chestnut: how the Beatles evolved to the point where they could create *SGT. PEPPER* and how it changed the pop music landscape in ways that are still being felt today. It shows how the band's contemporaries were influenced to create some of their best works. We hear from Graham Nash, Brian Wilson, Roy Wood, and John Sebastian all talking about what an incredibly fertile period the late 60's was.

I'm very happy to report that Mr. Heylin is not awash in longing for a magical period that he missed out on but instead tries to put the time into perspective. Bravo! He takes on Beatle scribe Ian MacDonald's assertion that the most exciting time period in popular culture was 1966-1967 and that anyone who missed out on that era is screwed. Heylin points out that "...excitement is rather subjective, and a nostalgia for one's youth, tells us nothing of the milieu, save that they had a good time." Refreshingly the author also has a clear eyed view of *PEPPER's* songs "...some truly great, most simply well-crafted, and a couple of fillers." Like Orson Welles' *Citizen Kane* "It was precisely the fact that *PEPPER* was a clever collage of all the most up-to-date innovations of others that made it sparkle so brightly." It's nice to read a rock music book that compares classic pop albums to legendary cinematic achievements. I always thought rock and roll, films, television, plays, musicals, sculpture, painting, and sports went hand in hand off the cliff of mundane day to day existence. I never felt one form of expression was intrinsically better than another. Different mind expanding drugs for different folks I always say. On the dust cover the *San Antonio Current* calls Clinton Heylin, "The greatest living writer about rock music." I wouldn't go that far. Robert Christgau, Greil Marcus, and Chuck Klosterman would all have something to say about that. But Heylin does have a certain something. Not content with jabbing Ian MacDonald in the eye he rips apart all-time Beatle expert Mark Lewisohn "What Lewisohn knew about cultural or musical context could be written on a postage stamp, and still leave room for the complete works of Wittgenstein. He has burrowed so deep into the Fab Four's forest, he had long forgotten there was a world beyond their woods." Heylin also takes time out for constructive criticism of *Rolling Stone* which called *SGT. PEPPER* the best album of the first 20 years of the periodical's existence (unfortunately, *PEPPER* came out five months before the magazine started) and called the Clash's *LONDON CALLING* best album of the 1980's (unfortunately, it came out December 14, 1979).

As the book winds up Heylin wraps *PEPPER* up in a nice little package "Bathed in its own 129 days of genius myth it was the product of a time so remote, so shrouded in the fog of nostalgia, that it not only transcends most criticism, it has acquired a social conscience the era never actually had." There is nothing more fun for me than a Beatle book that takes on the group's legend and strives to look at it objectively.   A-

ALL THE SONGS: The Story Behind Every Beatle Release by Jean-Michel Guesdon & Philippe Margotin (2013 Black Dog & Leventhal)

A giant sized look at the story behind every Beatles release from *MY BONNIE* to the *LET IT BE* album. With a preface by poet Patti Smith who has always been more of a Stones fan. There's nothing to see here, folks. Move along.

If you want a terrific book about the canon turn to *Revolution in the Head* or you can check out my take on all their original compositions starting with:

LOVE ME DO: How George Martin could choose this clunky little piece of garbage over *P.S. I LOVE YOU* I will never understand. That's not even to mention *I SAW HER STANDING THERE* which would have been a way better choice than either of them.

P.S. I LOVE YOU: The first taste of Paul's ability to write great melodies. It's surprising that their first 45 features McCartney on both sides or maybe it isn't; it was credited to McCartney/Lennon on the label.

PLEASE PLEASE ME: An early example of a pop hit about oral sex or the lack of it. Did teen-age girls of the period know that John was exhorting them to come on and please him that way?

ASK ME WHY: I've heard this many times yet I can never remember how it goes. It must be one of those forgettable B-sides.

FROM ME TO YOU: Usually put down as a holding move between *PLEASE PLEASE* and *SHE LOVES YOU*. I find this to be the early A-side I hum more than any other.

THANK YOU GIRL: A throwaway B-side that hearkens back to the emptiness of *LOVE ME DO*.

I SAW HER STANDING THERE: Their first rock and roll classic, the first song on their first LP, and the last song Lennon sang in concert. Check out the Tubes' version. It's wild!

MISERY: The first glimpse into the way pain aficionado John Winston Lennon felt about life in a tongue in cheek way.

DO YOU WANT TO KNOW A SECRET: It would have been better if John had sung it rather than handing it off to the quiet Beatle.

THERE'S A PLACE: The first lyric to show Lennon's introspective existential side. It's all in the mind. He could have re-recorded this for *PLASTIC ONO BAND* and it would have fit right in.

SHE LOVES YOU: Paul first using his famous distancing technique.

I'LL GET YOU: In the end the love you take is sweeter than the love you make.

I WANT TO HOLD YOUR HAND: The ladies of the night taught them this technique in Hamburg.

THIS BOY: Nice three part harmonies when they played this in Miami in February 1964 (see the *Anthology* DVD). It's like an early prototype of *BECAUSE*.

IT WON'T BE LONG: Issued the morning of the Kennedy assassination.

ALL I'VE GOT TO DO: Lennon, surprisingly, telling his woman he's there for her too.

ALL MY LOVING: This should have been a single. It ended up as the title track of an extended play. The first song Lennon performed in New York City (on 2/9/64) and the song that was playing on Muzak as they brought him into the hospital in New York City (on 12/8/80).

DON'T BOTHER ME: George sums up his life philosophy in three words.

LITTLE CHILD: Abort.

HOLD ME TIGHT: Somehow, this piece of trash was an intake and the original try of *ONE AFTER 909* became an outtake. Is there no justice?

I WANNA BE YOUR MAN: It would have been better if John had sung it rather than handing it off to the uncharismatic Beatle.

NOT A SECOND TIME: John didn't have to give anyone a second chance; girls were lined up at his door.

CAN'T BUY ME LOVE: This was the first Paul dominated A-side. Beware the one legged woman.

YOU CAN'T DO THAT: I bet John thought if Paul can write a song with a contraction I can write a song with a contraction. This is from the legendary *CAN'T* single.

I CALL YOUR NAME: A very early Lennon. There is an excellent version of this by the Mamas and Papas with a terrific lead vocal by Cass Elliott who later died in Beatle buddy Harry Nilsson London apartment. Keith Moon died there too.

A HARD DAY'S NIGHT: I'm glad John couldn't hit the high note. I like the contrast when McCartney swoops in. Is this a sign they're sharing a girl?

THINGS WE SAID TODAY: Knock out early McCartney. This is one of the best B-sides. It's right up there with *REVOLUTION*, *DON'T LET ME DOWN*, and *OLD BROWN SHOE*. Nice version of this on *HOLLYWOOD BOWL*.

I SHOULD HAVE KNOWN BETTER: As a young American I learned of this number, not from their first movie, but from the *HEY JUDE* compilation (AKA *THE BEATLES AGAIN*). It sat out of place next to all the more famous songs culled from British 45's.

IF I FELL: I love how John sings this tender love ballad to sulking Starkey in *A Hard Day's Night*.

I'M HAPPY JUST TO DANCE WITH YOU: Otherwise you might start holding hands and it becomes a slippery slope.

AND I LOVE HER: And who starts a sentence with "and?"

TELL ME WHY: And if I do what's my reward?

ANY TIME AT ALL: Lennon, surprisingly, telling his woman he's there for her too.

I'LL CRY INSTEAD: Some real feeling from the pain aficionado as he struggles to keep up his tough guy facade. This is my favorite early Lennon.

WHEN I GET HOME: My wife thinks this song sucks.

I'LL BE BACK: Can't remember how this one goes either.

I FEEL FINE: Lennon surprisingly feels fine. She must have please pleased him.

SHE'S A WOMAN: I should hope so. Otherwise you've got big problems.

NO REPLY: Lennon sees the light and not for the last time. There would be LSD, Transcendental Meditation, Primal Scream Therapy, and Brandy Alexanders.

I'M A LOSER: What does that make the rest of us?

BABY'S IN BLACK: Not exactly upbeat.

I'LL FOLLOW THE SUN: Resurrected from the archives as they ran out of material for *BEATLES FOR SALE*. It's followed on that album by *MR. MOONLIGHT*.

EIGHT DAYS A WEEK: I believe they meant to say, "I do not have anything but love, girl, seven days a week." You think somebody would have caught this before they embarrassed themselves.

EVERY LITTLE THING: A tribute to the band's favorite new show *The Addams Family*

I DON'T WANT TO SPOIL THE PARTY: More melancholy from the king of sadness.

WHAT YOU'RE DOING: The first part of Paul's Jane-Asher-is-a-pain-in-the-ass trilogy. To be followed by *WE CAN WORK IT OUT* and *I'M LOOKING THROUGH YOU*.

A TICKET TO RIDE: John thinks he's going to be sad. So what else is new?

YES IT IS: Lennon searching for his soul mate. He's tortured again as usual. Earlier his baby was in black. Now she wears red.

HELP!: More anguish from JWL. I'm sensing a pattern developing.

I'M DOWN: Jokey anguish from JPM on the flip side. I first heard this on *RENAISSANCE MINSTRELS VOL. II* and assumed it was part of the *GET BACK* sessions. Live and learn.

THE NIGHT BEFORE: One of many one night stands for the cute one.

YOU'VE GOT TO HIDE YOUR LOVE AWAY: One of the best rock singers imitating one of the worst rock singers.

I NEED YOU: Slight but enjoyable Harrisong.

ANOTHER GIRL: One of many one night stands for the cute one.

YOU'RE GOING TO LOSE THAT GIRL: John stealing somebody's girl just because he can.

IT'S ONLY LOVE: Some people hate this song. But I think it is peachy keen.

YOU LIKE ME TOO MUCH: Slight but unenjoyable Harrisong.

TELL ME WHAT YOU SEE: Not much.

I'VE JUST SEEN A FACE: Classic Paul. Capitol put this at the beginning of the U.S. *RUBBER SOUL* thereby giving American fans the right sense of its importance. Paul brought this to the Wings' set in the mid-70's and performed it with Paul Simon on the SNL 40th anniversary special.

YESTERDAY: John accused Paul of stealing this melody. What an envious guy.

DRIVE MY CAR: Not actually about driving her car.

NORWEGIAN WOOD: George on sitar and allegedly the melody was stolen from Bob "having a sandwich" Zimmerman.

YOU WON'T SEE ME: Paul imagines what it would be like to have a girl blow him off.

NOWHERE MAN: First he's a loser, then he needs help, and now he feels like he's going nowhere. To be followed by knowing what it's like to be dead, being so lonely he wants to die, things going so badly they're going to crucify him, wishing he was a baby, and wishing he was dead. Be careful what you wish for.

THINK FOR YOURSELF: A continuation of George's message to the fans that first manifested itself in *DON'T BOTHER ME*.

THE WORD: John announces that he's going to show everyone the light. If you want to be a hippie just follow him.

MICHELLE: Paul making up a woman. To be followed by Eleanor, Vera, Rita, Madonna, Molly, Magill who called herself Lil though everyone knew her as Nancy, Loretta, and Joan.

WHAT GOES ON: This would slot in perfectly on *BEAUCOUPS OF BLUES*.

GIRL: This dream girl turned out to be Yoko. Some dream girl!

I'M LOOKING THROUGH YOU: Jane, if you don't watch it I'm going to marry an American hussy.

IN MY LIFE: John on lyrics and Paul on melody. They should have followed this formula more often, at least once more.

WAIT: That this is an outtake from *HELP!* should tell you everything you need to know.

IF I NEEDED SOMEONE: George continues his theme of iconoclasm.

RUN FOR YOUR LIFE: From the Wife Beater.

DAY TRIPPER: I'm terribly sorry but we only accept full time hipsters into our little group. People who hide themselves behind a wall of illusion never glimpse the truth. Are you one of them?

WE CAN WORK IT OUT: Jane, you ignorant slut.

PAPERBACK WRITER: Paul as novelist writing boring stories of boring people doing boring things.

RAIN: Yet another psychological torment track from the misery expert.

TAXMAN: Paul Weller went back in time to help George with this one.

ELEANOR RIGBY: I always picture this as a black and white Bergman movie.

I'M ONLY SLEEPING: To quote Ian MacDonald, "...dismisses the empty activity of the mundane world with an indolence that holds the seeds of Lennon's later heroin addiction."

LOVE YOU TO: How Bono hopes you feel.

HERE, THERE, AND EVERYWHERE: A rare love song from McCartney.

YELLOW SUBMARINE: A little ditty aimed at children, which promotes heavy drug use.

SHE SAID SHE SAID: Spiritual disorientation at its finest.

GOOD DAY SUNSHINE: Spiritual orientation at its finest.

AND YOUR BIRD CAN SING: But don't let her, John. I'm begging you, please.

FOR NO ONE: A cold, unfeeling bitch lets our humble narrator down.

DOCTOR ROBERT: An ode to John's dentist who dropped acid in Lennon's coffee, thereby, making the world a better place.

I WANT TO TELL YOU: I prefer O.J.'s second book about the murders, *If I Did It*.

GOT TO GET YOU INTO MY LIFE: This is a little love song that is actually about getting high. John thought it was about acid. Paul clarified that is was about marijuana.

TOMORROW NEVER KNOWS: No one goes there anymore, it's too crowded.

STRAWBERRY FIELDS FOREVER: The first song I ever heard knowing full well it was the Beatles. It was spring 1973 and my brother Mark had just bought a copy of *1967-1970* at Adam, Meldrum, and Anderson's. I think our friend Bill Tutton suggested he do so. Down the needle went on side one track one and we were off to the races. It was kind of perfect for an eight year old boy to hear a song from a man remembering when he was an eight year old boy. At that time there was nothing to get hung about. I happened to be living in my childhood home at 251 Zimmerman Blvd. at the time. Later on I found out John lived as a child at 251 Menlove Avenue. Mere coincidence? Yes.

PENNY LANE: I thought the blue suburban skies were about living on Zimmerman Boulevard in Tonawanda, NY down the street from Adam, Meldrum, and Anderson's. Later on my brother Mark became a Zimmerman fanatic. How did that feel?

SGT PEPPER'S LONELY HEARTS CLUB BAND: Paul can make men up too. Sgt. Pepper and Billy Shears were to be followed by Chuck, Dave, Jude, Desmond, Rocky, Dan, Jo Jo, Maxwell Edison, and Teddy.

WITH A LITTLE HELP FROM MY FRIENDS: I prefer the version they use in *The Wonder Years.*

LUCY IN THE SKY WITH DIAMONDS: Influenced by pedophile Lewis Carroll, not LSD influenced like many thought. Isn't that worse?

GETTING BETTER: Lennon admits to domestic assault on Paul's little ditty.

FIXING A HOLE: You can't get your life together. It's already together.

SHE'S LEAVING HOME: Lennon's Aunt Mimi interjections are priceless. You can't buy love or fun.

BEING FOR THE BENEFIT OF MR. KITE: Just like *FIXING A HOLE* this one is not about heroin use. You're thinking of *COLD TURKEY*.

WITHIN YOU, WITHOUT YOU: Not to be confused with *WITHOUT YOU* or *WITH OR WITHOUT YOU*.

WHEN I'M 64: Why hasn't he lost his hair? His father was bald, which means there should be a great chance that he would go bald. Didn't Ringo even sing about it on *DON'T PASS ME BY*?

LOVELY RITA: Later to be replaced in his affections by the lovely Linda.

GOOD MORNING, GOOD MORNING: A prescient number by Mr. Lennon that clearly foretold his demise.

A DAY IN THE LIFE: Their best recording. Full of war, fatal car crashing, smoking on buses, and counting holes in Blackburn, Lancashire.

ALL YOU NEED IS LOVE: The last Lennon A-side for nearly two years as Paul "Wings" McCartney takes the reins.

BABY YOU'RE A RICH MAN: Two wealthy songwriters let us know that we too can be one of the beautiful people, if we only knew.

HELLO GOODBYE: Smells a mile away, doesn't it?

I AM THE WALRUS: Using the *Spaniard in the Works* part of his brain Lennon concocts a pleasant little snarling little piece of anti-authoritarian anger complete with Edgar Allan Poe, William Shakespeare, Humpty Dumpty, Allen Ginsberg, Eric Burdon, Smoking Jokers, and Lucy in the Sky.

MAGICAL MYSTERY TOUR: What could be more magical than riding in a bus with a bunch of strangers to nowhere in particular?

YOUR MOTHER SHOULD KNOW: I prefer John's *MOTHER*.

FOOL ON THE HILL: Paul's version of *NOWHERE MAN*.

FLYING: No lyrics on this one.

BLUE JAY WAY: Wish there were no lyrics on this one.

LADY MADONNA: Technically a Beatles single. Figuratively, the first hit from Wings. Paul brought it into the Wings' set list as soon as he started adding fab numbers. A travesty that *ACROSS THE UNIVERSE* was left to rot while this and it's equally undistinguished B-side went out to the public.

THE INNER LIGHT: Flip side to their worst 45 ever. With *UNIVERSE* and *HEY BULLDOG* available John was shunted aside to make room for George's first composition on a single. It makes *LOVE YOU TO* and *WITHIN YOU, WITHOUT YOU* sound like *SOMETHING* and *HERE COMES THE SUN*.

HEY JUDE: My all-time favorite McCartney song. My wife doesn't care for it.

REVOLUTION: Way better than *REVOLUTION 1* so it's lucky that Paul and George insisted that Lennon record a fast version. The shoo-be-doo-wops from P and G on the *David Frost Show* take a great song and make it better.

BACK IN THE USSR: Paul advocating communism. McCartney plays drums on this one. I hope you don't miss Starkey's presence too much. I personally never would have known if I hadn't read about it.

DEAR PRUDENCE: John trying to talk Mia "I've had sex with Frank Sinatra and Woody Allen" Farrow's sister out of her bungalow. Paul plays drums on this one, too. I never would have noticed if I hadn't read about it. Interesting that Paul and John put this album in running order and they put two of the Ringo less tracks at the beginning of the album.

Mia starred in *Rosemary's Baby* for Roman Polanski which was shot at the Dakota. She then flew to India to hang with the Beatles and Mike Love. Love then flew home to Los Angeles where the Beach Boys recorded a song by up and coming songwriter Charles Milles Manson called *CEASE TO EXIST*. Beatlemaniac and psychomaniac Manson then listened to *THE BEATLES* and decided that *HELTER SKELTER* (Paul), *PIGGIES* (George) and *REVOLUTION 9* (John) were telling him to kill Roman Polanski's wife. Lennon moved into the Dakota four years later down the street from Mia Farrow's apartment. Mark Chapman claims he saw Mia Farrow near the Dakota during the afternoon of 12/8/80 which Chapman took as an omen to do what he came to do.

GLASS ONION: Little Nicola told John that he was not the walrus. She was right.

OB-LA-DI, OB-LA-DA: Tied with *MAXWELL'S SILVER HAMMER* for most despised Paul song as voted on by John, George, and Ringo.

WILD HONEY PIE: Most despised Paul song as voted on by me. Paul played drums again on this one.

THE CONTINUING STORY OF BUNGALOW BILL: Oh, no! Yoko makes her first appearance on a Lennon recording.

WHILE MY GUITAR GENTLY WEEPS: George asks Eric "sweet tooth" Clapton to come to the studio to play on this one. Therefore, guaranteeing for one evening, that Clapton wouldn't be hitting on George's wife.

HAPPINESS IS A WARM GUN: John's specialty, more zany lyrics that could be misconstrued by the mentally ill.

MARTHA MY DEAR: McCartney advocating house training your dog with drums, yet again, by Paul.

I'M SO TIRED: Best Lennon vocal ever which is saying a lot considering all the stiff competition.

BLACKBIRD: This is the lyrical inspiration for the name of Paul next group.

PIGGIES: An ode to intolerance from mister bad karma.

ROCKY RACCOON: Unfortunately, Paul left his best lyric for this throwaway country number on the cutting room floor: move over doc/let's have none of your cock.

DON'T PASS ME BY: Couldn't they have just left this up on the fridge?

WHY DON'T WE DO IT IN THE ROAD: Quite a funny sex song.

I WILL: No Harrison on this one. He was busy keeping an eye on Clapton.

JULIA: John conflates his beloved mother with his new girlfriend who he took to calling *mother*.

BIRTHDAY: Mine is on April Fools' Day. Please send cash.

YER BLUES: Nothing will make you more suicidal than sitting around for two goddamn months meditating.

MOTHER NATURE'S SON: This sounded great in that margarine commercial. You guessed it, Paul on drums.

EVERYBODY'S GOT SOMETHING TO HIDE EXCEPT ME AND MY MONKEY: Well, I guess it's better than calling her *mother*.

SEXY SADIE: This song is a punk off to the maharishi for having lust in his heart.

HELTER SKELTER: Paul advocating a pleasant summer evening out at the playground riding on a slide.

LONG LONG LONG: A song about Krishna and how pretty he looks in a mini-dress.

REVOLUTION 1: Don't worry, folks. The millionaire in his cracker box palace has assured us that everything will be alright. I hope John was being ironic.

HONEY PIE: Paul advocating entering a pie eating contest.

SAVOY TRUFFLE: Don't eat so many sweets that you end up toothless.

CRY BABY CRY: An eerie evocation of the spirit world. This is the first part of the creepy quartet that ends *THE BEATLES*.

CAN YOU TAKE ME BACK?: Paul adding a touch of sinister childhood reminiscing to the proceedings.

REVOLUTION 9: Don't be fooled by the credits. This is not a Lennon/McCartney song. This is a nightmarish sound collage put together by J&Y with a little help from the Georges while Paul was away in America. Glad it made it onto *THE BEATLES* because it would have been ignored on *TWO VIRGINS*. Then again if Lennon could make this poppy an avant-garde excursion for fab release why couldn't he have done something fun and/or interesting for *UNFINISHED MUSIC No. 1*, *UNFINISHED MUSIC No.2,* or *THE WEDDING ALBUM*. I mean, they did charge full price for those pieces of crud.

If you are in the minority (like me) and you enjoy this track then I recommend you check out the Adam Curtis movie *It Felt Like a Kiss* (2009) which captures the 60's in a crazy collage type way. Block that kiss!

GOODNIGHT: This would slot in perfectly on *SENTIMENTAL JOURNEY*.

ONLY A NORTHERN SONG: George recorded many clunkers in his career. This time he tried to make a bad song on purpose and succeeded.

ALL TOGETHER NOW: Paul advocating simultaneous orgasm.

HEY BULLDOG: An open invitation to the lonely.

IT'S ALL TOO MUCH: George steals from the Merseybeats before he would go on to plunder from James Taylor and the Chiffons.

GIVE PEACE A CHANCE: Timothy Leary sings along before taking John to court over *COME TOGETHER*. Tommy Smothers sings along before Lennon is thrown out of the Smother Brothers reunion show at the Troubador for over the top heckling and waitress punching.

GET BACK: The song that John claimed was Paul's way of telling Yoko to get lost.

DON'T LET ME DOWN: John insists that Yoko treat him better than he is willing to treat others.

THE BALLAD OF JOHN AND YOKO: This simple little topical, therefore dated, rock and roll number is my favorite Beatles song. Not sure why. Is it because it's John and Paul alone (McCartney plays drums) at the end of their tether? Is it sheer catchiness? Is it because I adore song titles that feature the name Yoko? It can't be that. I hate *DEAR YOKO*. This was the last Beatles A-side recorded specifically for the singles market.

OLD BROWN SHOE: Fantastic song by George! Harrison was fed up with John not playing on many of his late period songs.

George had Lennon play organ on this one and then erased the track and put on his own organ work. Touche!

COME TOGETHER: Wonderful menacing nonsense from the King of Pain. Note the fact that John keeps saying, "shoot me" over and over on this track.

SOMETHING: No less a luminary than Frank Sinatra said this was his favorite Lennon/McCartney song.

MAXWELL'S SILVER HAMMER: Ironically, *HELTER SKELTER* rocks hard and heavy and is about kids enjoying a day in a playground while this light weight fluff is about a sociopath going on a mass murder spree.

OH! DARLING: Frank Zappa-like imitation of a 50's rocker.

OCTUPUS'S GARDEN: There is nothing like a remake of a novelty song.

I WANT YOU-SHE'S SO HEAVY: I don't have much to go on, but I think John is singing about a Japanese woman who he met at an art gallery. It's just a hunch.

HERE COMES THE SUN: Written in Eric Clapton's garden while keeping an eye on him.

BECAUSE: Beautiful three part harmonies.

YOU NEVER GIVE ME YOUR MONEY: A McCartney multi-part track. It helps the illusion that he's got a lot more songs in the medley than John does. For the record, side two of *ABBEY ROAD* has six numbers from Paul and four numbers from Lennon.

SUN KING: George usually stole songs from others, here Lennon steals from George.

MEAN Mr. MUSTARD: John borrowed an idea from another John. This was basically a rewrite of John Entwistle's *SILAS STINGY*.

POLYTHENE PAM: I think this is a song about perversion.

SHE CAME IN THROUGH THE BATHROOM WINDOW: Fan broke into Paul's house and he had to play detective to get back some prized possessions.

GOLDEN SLUMBERS: Another one about sleeping but this time from Macca.

CARRY THAT WEIGHT: The legend about them is on their shoulders.

THE END: You think this would be the end of their last album, but no...

HER MAJESTY: This was the end.

COLD TURKEY: A blistering one about heroin withdrawal that for some reason Paul didn't want to record as the follow up to *BALLAD OF J&Y*. What a wimp.

INSTANT KARMA: Amazing drumming from Alan White.

LET IT BE: This was the year L/M made a pact to put out songs about their mothers.

YOU KNOW MY NAME (LOOK UP THE NUMBER): Bad comedy. It sounds like an off day for the Bonzo Dog Band.

TWO OF US: A song about Paul and Linda that sounded more like a song about Paul and John.

DIG A PONY: It's hard to believe, but this was the only new song Lennon finished for *LET IT BE*.

ACROSS THE UNIVERSE: Spector did a good job of taking this out of the vault and making something out of it.

I ME MINE: A nice companion piece to *DON'T BOTHER ME*.

DIG IT: The longer version on bootlegs is a little better but over all a waste of time comparable to *WILD HONEY PIE*.

I'VE GOT A FEELING: When I was a kid I was walking around the house singing about wet dreams. My parents called me in for a little talk.

ONE AFTER 909: A song written in time for their first album release ends up on their last album release.

THE LONG AND WINDING ROAD: Did Spector ruin this, like McCartney claims? I like Phil's version.

FOR YOU BLUE: George at his most simple.   C+

ALL YOU NEEDED WAS LOVE: The Beatles After The Beatles by John Blake (1981 Parigee)

This is a book about the four solo careers of the 70's and very early 80's. I tried desperately to find something interesting in it. I couldn't. There is no humor, of course. There is a by-the-numbers recitation of the facts. There are no sentences that jump out at the reader with flair and panache. There is nothing except the fact that Lennon's death made any Beatles book in 1981 more likely to score with the public. There was so much mourning going on that anything put out might sell well. It reads like it was whipped out to cater to a market that exploded at Xmas time 1980 and has never abated to this day. When Lennon died there were suddenly many more Beatle books. When Harrison died suddenly he became very interesting. If McCartney ever dies there should be a landslide. As for Ringo I'm sure he'll make the cover of *Modern Drummer* when he croaks. D

ARTIFICIAL PARADISE: The Dark Side of The Beatles Utopian Dream by Kevin Courrier (2009 Praeger)

This is a book supposedly about the dark side of the Beatles' utopian dream. I wish it were. I wish that it spent all it's time on Charlie Manson, Mark David Chapman, Michael Abram, the Paul is dead conspiracy, John Lennon killing Stuart Sutcliffe, and a partridge in a pear tree. However, what we get is another biography with an epilogue about the solo years and the Threatles experience. Here are some of the problems:

1. *POLYTHENE PAM* "...is a punchy bit of rock and roll where each band member calls out to the other in a spirit of generosity as if feeling the indelible pull of what brought the Beatles together before they were so torn apart." Huh? What? I've heard of poetic license but this is ridiculous.

2."...the Beatles dream had died after 1966" Huh? What? Have you ever heard of *SGT PEPPER*?

3. I guess he has. "On the first cut of *SGT PEPPER* it was immediately clear that the Beatles had fashioned a mirage of Nowhere Land for themselves to live in." Huh? What?

4."It's not surprising that Charles Manson heard the beginnings of a race war on *THE BEATLES*." Huh? What?

5. "The music heard on *THE BEATLES*, in the wake of Martin Luther King Jr.'s assassination, does emulate black discontent." Huh? What?   B-

<u>AS I WRITE THIS LETTER: An American Generation Remembers The Beatles</u> by Marc A. Catone (1982 Greenfield)

As fans worldwide mourned throughout 1981 (this book is dedicated to the Dreamweaver), Marc Catone knew he had a way to bring Beatle land together. From June 1979 to June 1980 he had made a survey of Beatlemaniacs asking them to write their own stories of how the band had changed their lives, enriched their lives, and gave them philosophical guidance on how to live their lives. He shared the stories with the public as a way of aiding the healing process. The results were quite moving at times, though inevitably, sometimes the fans went a little overboard with reverence. After all, they were only four musicians. They weren't gurus no matter how much some of their disciples wanted to believe they were.

Surprisingly, Marc Catone thought Beatlemania was something that it was almost shameful to feel. Mr. Catone stated right out, "I am a Beatlemaniac. There are many others. Some of us 'hide in the closet', confining our preoccupation to the privacy of our homes, others proclaim themselves in the open, but we all acknowledge the same thing (at least to ourselves)...we are Beatlemaniacs. Beatlemania is a joyful affliction. Once it makes its way into your heart, there is no return; it blossoms and grows. It fills me with euphoria when I'm sad, hope when all I see about me is despair and an appreciation of the value of peace among all peoples of the world when I'm lost in the everyday cycle of the material. Beatlemania makes me high. There is one large insurmountable problem about Beatlemania...(there is) no cure." You see what I mean about fanatics going overboard. Though I myself lived through the dark days of the 60's, 70's, and 80's I had no idea there were so many hiding their feelings so as not to be ostracized by straight society. Thank Vishnu that in the 21st century we can all be out in the open, out in the bright sunshine singing *ALL TOGETHER NOW*. No more need for us to meet in church basements drinking coffee and eating donuts. ("My name is Greg and I'm a Beatlemaniac." "Hi, Greg!") Let me now share with you some of the most emotionally honest testimonials; words of love that I believe will touch your heart and your soul.

1. C.C. from New York, New York: "I'll never forget that first Ed Sullivan show. Tears running down my cheeks. I had no idea what was happening to me."
2. C. A. from Mishawaka, Indiana: "If it weren't for the Beatles, you and I could very well be fighting someone we don't know, in a rice paddy or worse."

3. C.H. from Wappinger Falls, New York: "My whole concept of love derives from the emotions I felt as I watched them sing."
4. B.C. from Louisville, Kentucky: "After 7 years of marriage, I contemplate divorce when my husband announces he has to go to the men's room in the middle of the (Wings) concert. And me!...25 feet from Paul...and he insists I accompany him. He cannot and will not ever understand my feelings."
5. A.L. also from Louisville, Kentucky (I wonder if B.C. and A.L. ever got together to comfort each other): "Their music is practically orgasmic to me....I've decided that I'll stay single, because if I can't have John, I don't want any man. Nobody except John could make me happy."
6. S.P. from Fennville, Michigan: "I lead a normal respectable life...I'm still single and live alone...there was a man in my life a few years ago, but I felt a great deal of intolerance in him, and believe it or not, his idea that I should rid myself of my Beatle collection and thus my past youth (he had to be kidding) was truly part of the reason our relationship fell apart...I have a whole secret life that most of my friends know nothing about and which I allow to surface once every summer in Chicago when I go to Beatlefest."
7. V.F. from New York, New York: "I saw the Beatles in 1966, in Chicago (the ticket stub is in my wallet to this day)...I was one of those fans who yelled 'Shut Up!' to everyone else. The other fans didn't and I never really heard anything except one verse of *YESTERDAY*."
8. T.A. from Denver, Colorado: "I was a miserable teenager...when I look back at those years, the few

moments of happiness came from listening to the Beatles."

9. D.L. from Tulsa, Oklahoma: "I was 15 years old when the Beatles broke up and I felt a deep personal loss....The teachers of millions of young people had decided to close down the school before everyone was ready for graduation."

10. G.C. from St. Louis, Missouri: "I think *Rolling Stone* has several bad reviews pre-written, awaiting the next new (solo) record from Ringo, John, Paul, or George...and that's irritating. How can you turn your back on those who have given you so much? How can you write off the most powerful force of a decade which the world has ever known?"

It's nice in a way to read these but it also scares me a little bit. I feel this is what John Lennon was thinking about when he sang about freaks not leaving him alone. B-

AT THE APPLE'S CORE: The Beatles from the Inside by Dennis O'Bell and Bob Neaverson (2002 Peter Owen)

The man who almost gets mentioned in *YOU KNOW MY NAME (LOOK UP THE NUMBER)* presents us with quite a good behind the scenes story. He pulls no punches. On *HELP!*: "Insipid performances, tiresome plotting, and directionless satire." On *Magical Mystery Tour*: "The decision to show it in black and white was monumentally stupid." On *Let it Be*: "They metamorphosed from greatest group of century to a washed up pub band that hadn't had a booking for months," and this guy was good friends with them! B+

P.S.: For people who like reviews of Beatle books appendix 1 features O'Bell's 20 favorite tomes.

BAND ON THE RUN: A History of Paul McCartney and Wings by Garry McGee (2003 Taylor Trade)

You think that people would have had enough of Paul McCartney. I look around me and I see it isn't so. There's another book about Wings called *Man on the Run*, which I find to be a more honest title. All you need to know about whether or not Wings was a legitimate band, as opposed to Paul's backing musicians, can be summed up thus:

1. The cover of this book has only two people. One is a master pop star who can sing well, write well, and play many instruments; and the other is Linda.
2. Denny Laine goes on tour and performs *BAND ON THE RUN* in its entirety. Denny realizes he has no fans of his own despite nine years in one of the most popular "bands" on earth. Denny knows where his bread is buttered. People don't want to hear his music. They want to hear Paul's music.
3. There is no Plastic Ono Band biography. I mean, wouldn't that be ludicrous?

Don't bother with this blandly written book, unless you're a Wings fanatic, in which case you should consider getting professional help. With a little luck we can make this whole damn thing work out. C-

THE BEATLES **by Hunter Davies (**1968 McGraw-Hill)

Some would say that this version of their story, by virtue of it being their only authorized biography, would be essential to any Beatle library. If you're going for historical importance then by all means put this in your shopping cart. Just make sure you do the right thing and also treat yourself to Nicholas Schaffner's superb *The Beatles Forever*.

It's not just that Hunter Davies' writing strikes me as pedestrian. It's not just that Lennon made sure this was a white washed account. It's not just that it's self-serving with many glaring omissions. Through no fault of Hunter's own this book came out prematurely in terms of their career. It only goes up to early 1968. The family portraits taken by ace photographer Richard Starkey were already out of date by the time the book was published. John is shown at home with Cynthia. Paul is shown at home with Jane. Within months of the publication of this John would marry Yoko and Paul would marry Linda. So reading this you get nothing of what happened with Apple Corps, nothing about the protracted break-up, and nothing about *THE BEATLES, LET IT BE,* and *ABBEY ROAD*.

To make matters worse Hunter was not big on analyzing the most important facet of the group, namely their music. He gives it a go in Chapter 30 but otherwise shies away. Davies is not up to serious study of the Beatles' songs. This is what Davies had to say about the best book about their recordings, (Ian MacDonald's *Revolution in the Head*) "...now and again you feel a bit lost." Funny, that's the way I feel whenever I read a Hunter Davies book. B

THE BEATLES by Geoffrey Stokes (1980 Rolling Stone)

This nothing special coffee table book was published just in time to be a stocking stuffer for the saddest Christmas ever. *Rolling Stone* has always been keen on beating a dead horse. Nary has an issue gone by in the last half century when there wasn't a mention of the boys, or Yoko, or Sean Lennon, or Julian Lennon, or Wings, or the Plastic Ono Band. In the late 1970's they realized there were millions of readers out there still suffering from Beatlemania. So why not a ridiculously expensive oversize hardback wrapped in a cover by Andy Warhol ("An exact reproduction of Mr. Warhol's art suitable for framing") and featuring a high brow fawn fest by the maestro himself Leonard Bernstein. If there was any one who understood rock and roll it was good old Lenny. Who do you think gave *West Side Story* its sweaty edge? It turns out Lenny not only dug their sound but he, "...fell in love with their four faces-cum-personae." According to the conductor, "...the very thought and memory of

SHE SAID SHE SAID recalls all the beauty of those Vietnamese Varicose Veins." Just in case you're wondering, there is nothing to explain this crazy quote. It comes out of nowhere and means nothing as far as I can tell. Somebody must have hit him in the head with his baton. As for the text by Geoffrey Stokes it seems aimed at first graders despite his claim that insights from Robert Christgau and Greil Marcus inform his writing throughout. Either one of them would have been a much better choice to handle this assignment; and don't get me started on the art direction by Bea Feitler. It's strictly high school yearbook level.

C-

THE BEATLES by Allan Kozinn (1995 Phaidon)

It turns out you can judge a book by its cover. Without even opening this one you can get an idea where author Allan Kozinn's head is at. On the front cover of the first edition of this book is the leader, the walrus, the dream weaver, the working class hero, the man of the decade, the martyred messiah, and the guru who can see through your eyes. On the back cover of the first edition is the hustler, the public relations man, the cute one, the one who could write melodies that would haunt you for the rest of your life, the bossy one, the bassist and guitarist and drummer and pianist (sometimes all on the same track), the one who got back, the one who let it be, and the man who would be king. Somehow there was no room on the cover for the Liverpool mystic, the quiet Beatle, the man who plays the sitar, the one who steals other people's songs, and the guy who turned the world on to transcendental meditation. There is also no place on the cover for the ringed one, the actor, the drummer, the lackluster songwriter ("oh, look! Ringo's written a song. We'll put it up on the fridge so everyone can see it"), the replacement for Pete Best, the one who always needed a little help from his friends.

I can see Kozinn's point in as much as this book is about 20th Century composers. Lennon himself said in 1980, "It only matters if Paul and I got back together because we're the ones who made the music" and "I think it's possible for John and Paul to have created the same thing with two other guys." This is a serious book about artists. Kozinn became aware of them during U.S. Beatlemania (i.e. 1964) but he had reservations. At the time he was devoting his "...musical energies to classical music." But quickly Kozinn "...stopped thinking of the Beatles' work as a lesser musical sub species." How enlightened of him. Cut to 1995 and as Allan looks back "The music of many of the Beatles' contemporaries seems quaint and time bound. The Beatles' music has worn well by comparison. I can still find twists and subtleties that have not been apparent before." For instance, on *ABBEY ROAD* "*HERE COMES THE SUN* is a relatively straightforward song, whereas *I WANT YOU (SHE'S SO HEAVY)* is full of novel and experimental touches." Here is some more analysis to blow your little mind... "But experimentation aside, the group's songs are so durable because they are good." I never thought of that before. Now that he mentions it, the Beatles did write good songs. Note to my readers: listen to their recordings and see if you agree.

This paperback is set up in the standard Beatles in the 60's mode which consists of Chapter 1: Paul meets John in 1957, Chapter 2: gigs in Liverpool and Hamburg, Chapter 3: English Beatlemania, Chapter 4: U.S. Beatlemania, Chapter 5-9: album three to album 12, and then the obligatory epilogue that reports on the first 25 solo years in a mere 12 pages. Plus, a handful of black and white photos, including one of the Rolling Stones and one of Zimmerman, just to let you know that they "...did not create their music in a vacuum." Yes, it can now be revealed fab listeners; they were not the only pop icons of that crazy hazy time.

Check out the astute LP reviews you'll be treated to when you peruse these pages:

1. *PLEASE PLEASE ME* (1963): "The real points of interest on PPM are the originals." This would be true if you didn't count the immensely popular last track *TWIST AND SHOUT*.
2. *WITH THE BEATLES* (1963): "Musically, the album is a decisive step forward." This was the case with every LP except for BEATLES FOR SALE and *LET IT BE* (erroneously marketed as a "new phase Beatles album").
3. *A HARD DAY'S NIGHT* (1964): They expanded the "...percussion battery...the main addition to this was the cowbell." Always ahead of their time. This was a dozen years before (*DON'T FEAR) THE REAPER*.
4. *BEATLES FOR SALE* (1964): "A collection that sounds dark and autumnal after the radiant energy of *A HARD DAY's NIGHT*." They should have used more cowbell.
5. *HELP!* (1965): The title track was "...a song Lennon later called one of the few honest songs he wrote for the Beatles." Other examples of honest John tunes in their repertoire include *YER BLUES*, *I'M A LOSER* ("part of me suspects I'm a loser and part of

me thinks I'm God Almighty"), and the Brian Epstein tribute number *BABY YOU'RE A RICH FAG JEW*.

6. *RUBBER SOUL* (1965): In the song *GIRL* "Harrison and McCartney sang tit-tit-tit-tit." That's four tits. Double your pleasure. Double your fun.

7. *REVOLVER* (1966): "After six albums, all packed with songs about love, Lennon and McCartney had discovered there were other things to sing about." This album has ditties about death (*ELEANOR RIGBY*), sleep, submarines, more death (*SHE SAID SHE SAID*), sunshine, birds (also known as chicks), drug taking (*DOCTOR ROBERT*), more drug taking (*GOT TO GET YOU INTO MY LIFE*), and a lot more drug taking (*TOMORROW NEVER KNOWS*).

8. *SGT. PEPPER'S LONELY HEARTS CLUB BAND* (1967): "*SGT. PEPPER* quickly became all things to all people." To me it was always the album sold at Woolworth's for $2.99 plus tax.

9. *THE BEATLES* (1968): "To all appearances, life was still fine in Beatle-land." Sure. If you don't count Prudence Farrow's self-imposed exile of existential pain and agony (*DEAR PRUDENCE*), transcendental meditator Bungalow Bill killing tigers in between spiritual awakenings (*THE CONTINUING STORY OF BUNGALOW BILL*), how shooting something to death can give you a nice, warm feeling in your guts (*HAPPINESS IS A WARM GUN*), realizing those damn piggies really need a beating (*PIGGIES*), John wanting to commit suicide (*YER BLUES*), and Paul commanding in no uncertain terms that the time is ripe for a bloody race war (*HELTER SKELTER*).

10. *YELLOW SUBMARINE* (1968): "...the full length cartoon for which the Beatles half-heartedly agreed to provide a few new songs." All four previously unreleased tracks were not new. All their new songs were put out on *THE BEATLES* a month before *SUBMARINE*.
11. *ABBEY ROAD* (1969): "Lennon thought the McCartney-Martin suite idea was nonsense." John "I only like old time rock and roll" Lennon couldn't have been more wrong. The suite takes up most of the last side of their last record together and it is magnificent. My favorite album side ever by anyone. Contrary to popular myth, the suite is not a McCartney only showcase. Lennon contributes four songs to side two.
12. *LET IT BE* (1970): "If every new song tried out at these sessions had gone through to completion, the group could easily have filled another double album." Giving the lie to the myth that they were out of originals after putting out 30 on *THE BEATLES* (released only weeks before the *GET BACK/LET IT BE* sessions). The truth is they were mostly out of good songs.
13. *DOUBLE FANTASY* (1980): "...had some of Lennon's best post-Beatles music on it." This quote makes me think Mr. Kozinn is not the musical expert he presents himself to be. Maybe, like a lot of fans, he was mistaking his own grief for poignant not banal Lennon songwriting. As far as I can remember everybody thought *DOUBLE FANTASY* was worthless schlock until you know what happened. This music has no balls. Except on Yoko's cuts, of course.   B+

THE BEATLES: A Celebration by Geoffrey Giuliano (1986 St. Martin's)

You've sure got to hand it to Geoffrey Giuliano. He realized earlier than most that there were people out there who would buy any Beatle book. It didn't have to be well written. It didn't have to give fans new insights. It didn't have to be about the music. The folks who would pay to see Ringo Starr and his All Starr band (but would never think of buying one of his terrible new albums) were the ones that would buy a slapped together coffee table book. It was all about filling a hole in the lives of baby boomers. The boomers had grown up with the boys from Liverpool and as time went by they got a little bit older and a little bit slower. But the Beatles remained eternally young. The fab foursome were all still in their 20's when they finished working together. With the death of John Lennon there was no way to put humpty dumpty back together again. The dream was over. But getting down to so called reality was not what Beatlemaniacs wanted to do. They didn't want to embrace change. They wanted nothing to change their world. They wanted it to be the 1960's forever. John Lennon noticed this, "Everybody is acting like it's the end of the world. It's just a rock band breaking up. You've got all the old records and films there if you want to reminisce." Post-1980 they began to reminisce in a way that was unhealthy. According to Lennon, they missed the whole point of the Beatles which was BE HERE NOW. That's why the band kept changing on every album and single. That's why live performances of the solo members in the 1970's hardly featured any Beatle songs. John, Paul, and George wanted to play their solo material. The stuff they were working on NOW.

With Lennon's death the trickle of Beatle records and books became an avalanche. Geoffrey Giuliano saw the writing on the wall and helped usher in this new era where anything Beatles related was fair game for a book. The band's ex-wives, former assistants, producer, director, and engineer put out their own tell-all-tomes. Ringo and Paul joined in with their lucrative nostalgia tours of the 80's, 90's, oughts, and teens. Paul went from his 1970's stance of only singing a handful of *Beatle* classics at his Wings gigs to playing every Beatles hit you can imagine! It was either sickening or delightful depending on the way you felt about endless wallowing in the past. *The Beatles: A Celebration* is a big book of random photos of the band and people of whom I've never heard. If you ever wanted images of Paddy Delaney, Tom McKenzie, Tony Mansfield, and Pete Maclaine this is the book for you. If you want to read useless interviews with these irrelevant people: Ronnie Hawkins, Makunda Das Gosmvami, Nellie Coutts, or Shambu Das this is a must have. But visually, it's fun city with lots of nice color photos of Beatles memorabilia. If you can just ignore the wooden text and focus on the visuals you'll be alright.   B

THE BEATLES A MUSICAL EVOLUTION by Terence J. O'Grady (1983 Twayne)

A book clearly influenced by Wilfrid Meller's 1973 classic *Twilight of the Gods*. Unfortunately it doesn't have the same poetic feel of Meller's work. O'Grady does not have a way with words. DAY TRIPPER is a "hard driving up tempo pop rock song dominated by a blues influenced riff." WITH A LITTLE HELP FROM MY FRIENDS is "...typical mature Beatle music." LOVELY RITA is a "...novelty song about a parking meter maid." On the MAGICAL MYSTERY TOUR double EP "None of the five new songs recorded for the soundtrack is particularly innovative." FOOL ON THE HILL is "...a model of lyrical simplicity." HAPPINESS IS A WARM GUN is one of "Lennon's most fragmented and discontinuous songs." Tell me something I don't know; and Mr. O'Grady does. THE BEATLES thirty track double album "...contains a total of 31 songs." I wonder what the extra song sounds like. He might mean Paul's CAN YOU TAKE ME BACK? but he doesn't make this explicit. Get this one... Ringo's piece of garbage DON'T PASS ME BY is an "...attractive rockabilly song." No and no. I never met anybody who thought this ugly country and western number was attractive and it sure as hell isn't rockabilly. It might be a good idea for the classical music academics to learn about rock and roll before coming down from the sky to pass judgment on the people's music. They know something's happening but they don't know what it is.

D+

THE BEATLES: An Illustrated Record by Roy Carr and Tony Tyler (1975 Harmony)

This is the most important book to have in your Beatle library. It beats out *Revolution in the Head* because as the title suggests this masterpiece is illustrated. That is to say it is lavishly illustrated in the size of a 12 inch long player. Every album sleeve from *PLEASE PLEASE ME* through *LET IT BE* is reproduced on a full page except for HELP! (I guess they realized what a shoddy cover it was*)*, *A COLLECTION OF BEATLES OLDIES…BUT GOLDIES* (I guess they realized what a shoddy cover it was… not to mention its unimaginative song selection. Oddly enough, this compilation was not released by Capitol stateside to rip off the public like they habitually did), *THE BEATLES* (Not reproduced at all. I guess they thought a white page with numbers on it would look bad.), and *YELLOW SUBMARINE* (probably mad that it wasn't released as an Extended Play like the soundtrack before it). Speaking of *MAGICAL MYSTERY TOUR*, this British centric book gives us a photo of the U.S. MMT LP rather than the U.K. double EP just for variety's sake.

But it's not just the album covers that make this book pop visually. There are splashy layouts announcing each of the four main sections (The Early Years, Beatlemania!, At Shea Stadium, and The Studio Years). Plus a fine selection of pics from the post-war years through Lennon at the Beacon Theatre to promote the Sgt. Pepper stage show.

There's also a diary of landmark events from January 1st 1962 (the day they failed the Decca audition. Decca signed the legendary Brian Poole and the Tremoloes instead. Decca A&R man Dick Rowe, "Groups of guitars are on the way out, Mr. Epstein-you should really stick to selling records in Liverpool.") through Lennon with Reginald (when two great Johns meet it is a humbling experience) at Madison Square Garden in November 1974 (erroneously listed as taking place in December 1974. I guess Brits don't know what month we celebrate Thanksgiving).

Plus, there is a nice section on the "immoral" practice of bootlegging. It's a handy guide to the treasure trove of illegal recordings available in the mid-70's. Do you remember *YELLOW MATTER CUSTARD, KUM BACK*, and *SPICY BEATLES SONGS*? This chapter was deleted in the two subsequent editions of this book with the nonsense explanation that the release of *HOLLYWOOD BOWL* had made all bootlegs irrelevant. I'm sure Carr and Tyler had just gotten pressured not to advertise illegal records in their book. There are way better live recordings out there than *HOLLYWOOD BOWL*. For example: Apple should finally release full versions of Shea Stadium (1965) and the rooftop show…and what about all the studio outtakes that exist on Beatlegs? Fans want easy access to them. The three mediocre *ANTHOLOGY* double CD sets did not do full justice to what's still out there waiting to be heard.

What makes this book number one on the hit parade is its comprehensive and fascinating reviewing of every band and solo official release between *LOVE ME DO* and *DARK HORSE*. Roy and Tony share their eloquent, intelligent, hilarious, and thought provoking take on the canon. Be prepared to be dazzled. John's "*SOMETIME IN NEW YORK CITY* was undoubtedly Lennon's worst mistake." Paul "has always excelled on straight rock 'n' roll songs-and, curiously, their antitheses: dreamy weepies." George "possesses that peculiar quality of stubbornness which interprets (as a reflex) all criticisms of his work as Godless Mouthings, mainly to be pitied." Ringo "is no judge of his own best material."

Check out some of my favorite Carr and Tyler moments:

1. *PLEASE PLEASE ME* 45: "The vitality of the music was complemented by the sexual leer inherent in the lyric."

2. *WITH THE BEATLES*: "It was a simply staggering achievement from every point of view, a landmark par excellence."

3. *A HARD DAY'S NIGHT* LP: "...unlike similar music from other artists, it utterly failed to embarrass: the effect is wholly positive."

4. *RUBBER SOUL*: "It was obvious the group were no longer concerned with their public image as 'lovable mop tops' etc. They were Artists and, like artists, they wanted things done their way (for the sake of the art). 'Rubber Soul' was."

5. *REVOLVER*: "This almost flawless album can be seen as the peak of the Beatles' creative career. Revolver is the kind of achievement which any artist would be more than satisfied to regard as some kind of culmination to his career." I believe side two of *ABBEY ROAD* was the perfect culmination of their time together.

6. *PENNY LANE* b/w *STRAWBERRY FIELDS FOREVER* : "Both these tracks represent definite English acid-rock (as opposed to its American cousin) full of arpeggio trumpets, ever-faithful backward tapes, surging strings, surreal lyrics, fade-outs, fade-ins, false endings, mysterious mutterings,

hypnotic, insistent drumming, jokes galore and almost endless ambiguities."

7. *SGT PEPPER*: "Speculation was rife as to the message intended by the enigmatic sleeve photo (for the next three years all Beatle albums were similarly searched for hidden meaning)."

8. *MAGICAL MYSTERY TOUR* double EP: "Nobody liked the film either."

9. *LADY MADONNA*: "It was not unknown for people to be caught playing the labels (or even the sleeves) of Beatle records in order to find Revelation. They believed in gurus in those days."

10. THE BEATLES: "The brilliance was certainly there but the Beatle Dream was almost over and, try (sic) as they might, they couldn't prevent an uncomfortable amount of the sordid world outside from creeping in. They were no longer invulnerable."

11. *TWO VIRGINS*: "What was it all trying to prove?"

12. *DON'T LET ME DOWN*: "A superb sobber from misery-expert J.W.O. Lennon MBE."

13. *LIFE WITH THE LIONS*: "Only pain aficionados need bother."

14. *ABBEY ROAD*: "The album dissatisfies because it is not perhaps their most honest record-but Beatle honesty veered perilously close to masochism on occasion and *ABBBEY ROAD*'s slickness is also its salvation."

15. *LET IT BE*: "It was will power they lacked on *LET IT BE*- both to create a worthwhile album and to display the necessary toughmindedness (sic) to follow it through to a reasonable conclusion."

16. *PLASTIC ONO BAND*: "In the word of a review of the time, he placed his balls defiantly on the line; out of sheer respect, the train ground to a halt."

17. *DARK HORSE*: "It is a boring album. One wishes that it had not come from an ex-Beatle."

Of course, even the best pop critics make a mistake now and then:

A. On discussing *THE BEATLES'* final song "Nobody but McCartney could get away with the closing track, *GOODNIGHT*." This is actually a song Lennon wrote for his number one son the same way he wrote *BEAUTIFUL BOY* for his second child. I guess Carr and Tyler thought only Paul was able to write sentimental, saccharine, and schlocky tripe but John was equally adept at doing so.

B. In their review of *ABBEY ROAD* they mention Lennon's "unmistakable voice." Then they credit Paul with the vocal on John's *MEAN Mr. MUSTARD*. I guess his voice wasn't as unmistakable as they thought.

C. According to the book, John sings along with Paul on *WHY DON'T WE DO IT IN THE ROAD?* but the only other Beatle who appears on the track is Ringo. In 1980 Lennon said he still resented not having been asked to participate. That makes sense because even Paul described it as, "a very John song." Paul started recording it on John's birthday in 1968 and Ringo added drums the following day. So my guess is that Lennon was busy at a surprise birthday party that Yoko had thrown for him. It was probably a two day blow out. Apparently, Paul was not invited. It sounds like Ringo was hung over when he laid down the drums on October 10th.

Note to all readers: This book was updated twice; once in 1978 and again in 1981 after Lennon's death.

Note to U.K. readers: Back in 1975 many Americans, including myself, were under the impression that the band had made albums such as *MEET THE BEATLES, SECOND ALBUM*, and *YESTERDAY AND TODAY*. We didn't know they were product put together by evil Capitol records to squeeze more dollars out of us. This book woke us up to the facts though we wouldn't have the "real" albums released domestically until 1987 (albeit in somewhat bad sounding CDs). Many Beatle fans growing up in the 1960's in the U.S. A. thought *REVOLVER* contained 11 songs and only two of them were sung by Lennon. Many did not realize how the executives in California were mistreating the art of our heroes. All we want is the truth, just give us some truth.

A+

THE BEATLES ANTHOLOGY by The Beatles (2000 Chronicle)

First there was *Anthology* the mini-series. It's a version of two earlier documentaries that never reached our television screens. *The History of the Beatles* went out to some repertory screens in the 1970's but it was done without the blessing of Apple Corp so it soon disappeared from view. *The Long and Winding Road* was the late Neil Aspinall's baby and being that he had become the head of Apple it should have made it out to the fans. Instead, it lay dormant for close to a quarter century until George Harrison became strapped for cash and then decided it was an okay project to pursue. George did have one stipulation; it could not be named after a McCartney song so it became known as *Anthology*. To be precise they should have called it *Documentary* but all's fair in love and war. It's quite worthwhile despite (because?) of no input from their wives. The five DVD set fairly explodes with footage by which to be hypnotized. There they are opening a Cavern set with a blistering *SOME OTHER GUY*, leaving for America as John does all the talking, having to keep moving Ringo's drum set around at their first U.S. gig, making some of the earliest music videos in a style much like MTV would popularize in the 80's, playing a little show at the New York Metropolitan's baseball park, hanging with Mike Nesmith during the *PEPPER* sessions, wearing animal costumes during *WALRUS*, taking their last trip together to India, being changed by a new woman in their lives who never seemed to leave Lennon's side even when he went to the use the bathroom, bickering with bossy McCartney, playing a big show on a rooftop, and taking their last photo together.

Then came *ANTHOLOGY* the three double compact disc sets. After being relentlessly bootlegged for decades, the remaining trio decided to get in on the action with these bloated collections of flotsam and jetsam. In between the inferior, the trivial, and the worthless tracks are a smattering of minor gems and the two weird playing along with John from the grave songs. If you didn't already know this was the best pop and roll band of all time you would be hard pressed to find evidence of it here.

Finally, there is this massive coffee table paper weight which should be one of the first items on your list when building your Beatle book collection. Its 300 plus pages capture the Beatles experience better than anything on the market that isn't a record, a CD, a VHS tape, or a DVD.

Amidst the cavalcade of wondrous pictures are the words of the four horsemen themselves. You can really learn a lot here, such as:

1. How Lennon wanted to go even further than the dead baby motif on the butcher sleeve, "My original idea for the cover was better-decapitate Paul-but he wouldn't go along with it." Coincidentally, the McCartney is dead rumors were based on the quaint notion that Paul had lost his head, ala Jayne Mansfield, in a horrible car crash.
2. Being more popular than Jesus can wear you out. Lennon in 1966, "I don't mind writing or reading or watching or speaking, but sex is the only physical thing I can be bothered with anymore."
3. They would never be able to top *REVOLVER*. McCartney in 1966, "We couldn't do any better than we've done already, could we?"
4. Before they were famous it was hard to get the world to take them seriously. Brian Epstein, "One shouted from the rooftops about the group when there was no enthusiasm for groups. People thought you were mad, but you went on shouting."

5. The group always knew not to get involved in the dog eat dog record industry because business just wasn't their thing. John in 1965, "We'd never start our own label, it's too much trouble."
6. George didn't enjoy their trip to the Philippines. Paul remembers Harrison saying, "If I had an atomic bomb I'd go over there and drop it on them."
7. Yoko let John know who was boss. Lennon on posing with his thing showing, "She forced me to become avant-garde and take my clothes off, when all I wanted was to become Tom Jones."
8. How Allen Klein won over John, George, and Ringo. McCartney, "I think Allen had a very good way of persuading people. Basically, he used to say 'What do you want?' and you'd say 'Well, a lot of money…'-'You got it!'"
9. Why Paul wouldn't just let the others relax and enjoy a lovely day. Ringo, "That's how he is."
10. Why the love scene faded in San Francisco. John, "It couldn't make it with a name like Haight-Ashbury."
11. Why we didn't have to mourn when our loved ones kicked the bucket. George, "There is no such thing as death." Very comforting. Thank you.
12. What people tended to notice when they met Phil "six gun killer" Spector. Ringo, "He's as mad as a hatter."
13. Why Lennon quit the band. George, "John wanted to go off and do his avant-garde or whatever it was." Actually he did his three non-musical albums while the band was still together. George was never too good at Beatles trivia. On Shea Stadium, "We played there twice?"   A+

THE BEATLES ARE COMING!: The Birth of Beatlemania in America By Bruce Spizer (2003 498 Productions)

This one is really something to behold. It is 250 big splashy pages of fun. Bruce Spizer concentrates on the period starting with their first U.S. release (the *PLEASE PLEASE ME* single on Vee-Jay in shops on February 7, 1963) and continuing with their arrival in America (at Kennedy airport in New York on February 7, 1964) and ending with their flight back to London on February 21, 1964.

Out of all the books that cover the initial burst of Beatlemania in the greatest country on earth this is the ultimate. Dig out your mono copy of *INTRODUCING* or *MEET* and sit back and let the evening go.

It all begins with an introduction by the most trusted man in news, Brian Williams. I'm just kidding. It's actually an intro by highly acclaimed Beatle expert Walter Cronkite. I was hoping for Dan Rather but you can't have everything. Walter is very honest, "I did not care for the appearance of the Beatles very much. I was offended by the long hair. Their music did not appeal to me either. I was not a Beatlemaniac by any means." And that's the way it is. He did score big points with his daughters by introducing them to the band backstage at The Ed Sullivan Show. "Even now (40 years later), they still mention that they met the Beatles in person."

In November 2000 Bruce Spizer, wearing his Beatles wig, visited the site of the first U.S. fab gig in Washington, D.C. and found that the Washington Coliseum was now a garbage dump. That's like finding out Ford theatre is a crack house. Then he began to put this book together, a book that would highlight tons of fun stuff.

On their first plane flight over Phil Spector hung out with John and Cynthia. In a perfect bookending way six years later John would bring Phil in to reproduce the last Beatles album release. Phil would go on to work with Lennon and Harrison solo, produce the first sub-par Ramones LP, and shoot a woman to death while on a date.

The first magazine coverage in the states is shown here in all its glory. The week before JFK was blown away they were covered in *Time* and *Newsweek*. In mid-December *Life* had a photo of them in an issue graced on the cover by new president LBJ.

The same day their second album *WITH THE BEATLES* came out in Britain, JFK was killed and LSD user Aldous Huxley passed away. It was the *real* beginning of the 60's. It was the start of a brave new world.

Mister Spizer makes a good point that it's a myth that the Kennedy murder played a key role in the band's U.S. takeover, "The Beatles were extremely popular in England, Japan, Germany, France, etc." and "None of these nations was suffering the trauma of having its head of state assassinated."

Spizer also points out *INTRODUCING THE BEATLES* was not the first North American album release. I always thought it was. Nope. It was *BEATLEMANIA! WITH THE BEATLES* issued by Capitol Records of Canada. It looks like *WITH THE BEATLES* except it has quotes from periodicals about the phenomenon on the front cover such as, "A new disease is sweeping through

Britain…and doctors are powerless to stop it." and "…they stamp around and shake…prance…skip." I don't know if this is a reference to the screaming fans or the band onstage.

According to TV Guide for 2/9/64 after the first Ed Sullivan appearance at 8:00 p.m. the country relaxed at 9:00 with Bonanza (in color!) or a Judy Garland concert special (in black and white).

The Carnegie Hall shows were very expensive. Tickets topped out at five dollars. What are we, made of money?

According to *TV Guide* for 2/16/64, "The Beatles are back and so is Mitzi Gaynor; each gets an extended portion of the show." Thank God Ed was giving Mitzi her due. At 9:00 Judy had *Wizard of Oz* co-star Ray Bolger on to sing *WE'RE OFF TO SEE THE WIZARD* and *IF I ONLY HAD A BRAIN* to celebrate the 25th anniversary of the premiere of that beloved film.

To top off all that entertaining stuff we get lots of great things to look at. There are record covers, advertisements, invoices, telegrams, letters, magazine covers, press releases, memos, and ticket stubs. Plus… a photo of a transistor radio that looks like a Pepsi machine, two color pages that show the best Beatles books to buy, and eight pages of groovy ads for mop top merchandise. I feel like I've died and gone to Pepperland.   A-

THE BEATLES A REFERENCE & VALUE GUIDE 2nd Edition by Barbara Crawford, Hollis Lamon, and Michael Stern(1998 Collector)

One of the most fun things about being a Beatles fanatic is collecting all the merchandise that has been pouring down on us since the 1960's. Brian Epstein probably thought; what harm can be done by letting people sell Beatle product of all kinds to those crazy kids out there? You never know how soon the bubble will burst. So in the meantime let's keep laughing all the way to the bank. Unfortunately for the band they got little of the cash as the makers of the items decided to pocket it themselves. Fortunately, for the fans we got an overload of gear stuff like plastic cups, bubble bath, booty bags, handkerchiefs, napkins, megaphones, pennants, matches, puzzles, *Yellow Submarine* candy cigarettes, bubble gum cards, guitar pins, TV trays, bongs, and pinball machines. Come back with me now to those thrilling days of yesteryear. Flip through 200 pages of lovely color photographs of assorted treats, the likes of which we'll never see again. Of course, this book is over 15 years old so the practical value is all but gone but we can still have fun by imagining we own all these wonderful trinkets. Also, check out *National Lampoon's* October 1977 Beatle issue where you'll learn about fab items such as Norwegian Wood polish, I am the egg man eggcups, the Sgt. peppermill, and Magic Alex's electronic penis enlarger.   B

THE BEATLES ARE HERE!: 50 Years After the Band Arrived in America, Writers, Musicians, and Other Fans Remember edited by Penelope Rowlands (2014 Algonquin)

Ever sit around the fireplace with your family talking about how the Beatles arrival in America changed your life forever and made you a better person? Me neither. However, I get the feeling that some of the people in this book did just that. Such as Billy "I married a girl the same age as my daughter" Joel, "This young, vigorous, vital man…was snatched from us. And the country really had the blues. Then all of a sudden there was this band with hair like girls. John Lennon had this look when he was on Ed Sullivan like: Fuck all of you. This is such total bullshit to me. And I said at that moment I want to be like those guys." Or Joe Queenan, whose book Queenan Country has an *ABBEY ROAD* parody cover, "My sisters and I grew up despising Lawrence Welk and all those of his ilk, so when the Beatles showed up , we felt the way the French must have felt when the GIs swarmed into Paris in August 1944." Or Greil Marcus, "I was reading that this British rock 'n' roll group was going to be on Ed Sullivan. I thought that sounded funny. I didn't know they had rock 'n' roll in England."

My favorite recollection is by Fran "non-fan" Lebowitz, "At some point in my adult life I was at a party and Paul McCartney came and sat down and started to play the piano. I turned around and said to him, 'Hey, I'm trying to talk here.' He was quite stunned. It did not stop him from playing the piano. Everyone else, of course, wanted him to play the piano. That's the level of Beatles fan I am." I wish this book had more memories from non-fans. I like to read a fair and balanced account of history not just a bunch of biased worshippers who haven't got over the shock a half a century later of four guys in suits playing cute little pop songs.   C+

THE BEATLES: A HARD DAY'S WRITE: The Stories Behind Every Beatles Song by Steve Turner (1994 Carlton)

Big time pop star Bono found this book inspiring but I still haven't found what I'm looking for. Despite the fact that the copy I read was the 4th printing of this average examination of the canon there didn't seem to be any one checking for errors.

1. A photo of the band climbing on top of a sled during the shooting of HELP! is identified as a still from *A Hard Day's Night*. HELP! is the only movie where they frolic in the snow.
2. Next to the famous *Life* magazine cover of August 1964 is a caption identifying it as a *Time* magazine cover.
3. A photo of the MAGICAL MYSTERY TOUR LP features a caption that identifies it as the MAGICAL MYSTERY TOUR double EP.
4. Charles Manson is credited with writing 'pig' on the wall in blood after the Manson family murders. Charlie wasn't at the Polanski/Tate love house massacre and he left the LaBianca house to get an ice cream cone at Denny's before the bloodletting began. They also credit

him with killing eight people in 1971. The so-called Helter Skelter murders took place in 1969 and Manson didn't kill any of those victims. He ordered his family to kill them, which they did.

5. John was influenced by the 1960's Fleetwood Mac hit *ALBATROSS* when he was writing the music for *SUN KING*. Somehow, I'm not surprised that the photo used to illustrate this point is a pic of the mid-1970's Fleetwood Mac featuring new at the time members Lindsey Buckingham and Stevie Nicks.

My favorite one! In the chapter on *Let it Be* Steve Turner lets us know that when making their last major motion picture they had, "...no inclination of emulating *HELP (sic)* or *A Hard Day's Write (sic)*." To clarify for you, Mister Turner: your book is subtitled *A Hard Day's Write*. The Beatles first movie was entitled *A Hard Day's Night*. You can look it up.   B

THE BEATLES ALBUM: 30 Years of Music and Memorabilia by Geoffrey Giuliano (1991 Viking Studio)

Giuliano's masterpiece is the one to get if you are partial to masterpieces. Forget about his biographies of Townshend, Harrison ("This guy knows more about my life than I do"), and McCartney. Skip his lost Beatle interviews. This is the one. Even when it came out a quarter of a century ago, it was a bargain at $29.95. Peter Max designed the cover but Giuliano brings it all back home. It's over 250 pages of intoxicating delight. You'll be punch drunk by the time you get through it all. It is as if you went over to a friend's house and they wanted to show you their Beatle collection. It is a collection that they spent decades building and you go to their home twice for five hours at a time, yet you still don't see everything. This is despite the fact you were going fast, checking all the items out at lightning speed. Of course, the great thing about this book is you can go at your own pace. Light up some monk berry moon delight and get this into your life.

It's a smorgasbord of 45 rpm picture sleeves, maxi-singles, colored vinyl, acetates, bootlegs, and test pressings. Feast your eyes on:

1. The Apple cassette boxes for *ALL THINGS MUST PASS* and *SOME TIME IN NEW YORK CITY*.
2. Keith Moon's ass hanging out of his limo window.
3. The LIE album by Beatle disciple and singer/songwriter Chuck M.
4. The extremely tacky back cover for IT'S ALRIGHT where a ghostly figure of John is superimposed over Mother and Sean. You can do things like this forever Ms. Ono but it won't make things alright.
5. *JOHN LENNON by 101 Strings*. Just the kind of tribute that would have meant a lot to him.
6. *HELP!* by George Martin and his orchestra. If you dig this, you might want to check out side two of the fabs' theatrical cartoon soundtrack.
7. Apple's 1972 re-release of Phil Spector's *XMAS ALBUM* which was put out over Paul's dead body.
8. Ugly little cassette singles of *WOMAN* and *WATCHING THE WHEELS*.

9. The seldom appreciated, for very good reason, back covers of U.S. junk vinyl records *SECOND ALBUM, A HARD DAY'S NIGHT,* and *BEATLES VI* (which needless to say was not the sixth album released by Capitol).
10. *THE BLACK ALBUM* which comes complete with its own version of the collage poster.
11. Wings 1979 Xmas card which features Denny Laine giving us the finger.
12. *LIVE PEACE IN TORONTO's* giveaway calendar insert for the year of our lord 1970 or is it really year one?
13. The legendary *THRILLINGTON* album cover art featuring a ram playing a violin.
14. The *U.K. THE BEATLES* where the records come out at the top.
15. The *U.K. LET IT BE* which comes in a box sans title and includes a wonderful Ethan Russell picture book. Why America was deprived of this I'll never know. We are suckers for box sets that cost a lot. For proof check out the U.S. sales of George's two triple record sets that were also released in the early 70's.
16. Chapter titles that reference obscure and unreleased songs such as *SHIRLEY'S WILD ACCORDION* from *MAGICAL MYSTERY TOUR.*
17. The naked women from the *RED ROSE SPEEDWAY* booklet. Paul treats objects like women, man.
18. The classy gatefold for McCartney with its poignant photo of Paul picking his nose. This is some of Linda's best photographic work.
19. The bootleg No. 3 *ABBEY ROAD* which uses Linda's best photo ever for its cover and is reputed to have a McCartney/Donovan track.
20. One photo of James Nicol, the 85th Beatle.

21. *LISTEN TO THIS PICTURE RECORD.*
22. Gerald Scarfe's *Time* cover from September 22, 1967 in which the Time/Life Company discovered three months later than the rest of the world that the Beatles were going in a new direction. Gerald would go on to collaborate with Roger Waters on a little known musical called *THE WALL*. Gerald would also go on to marry Jane Asher because Layla, Linda, and Maureen were taken.

Despite the unqualified excellence of this book at least two people went overboard in their praise of Geoffrey Giuliano.

Anthony "*Miracle in Buffalo*" Violanti opines, "...nothing less than the memoir of a generation."

Roy Orbison of the country pop band the Traveling Wilburys states, "He's that one in a million who can whittle down the dreams of an entire generation into something tangible."

Only the lonely know how I feel about that quote.   A+

THE BEATLES: Beatlemania for fans of the Fab Four by Mike Evans (2014 Igloo)

Igloo books know who purchases snazzy little impulse buys at the register. It is Beatlemaniacs like myself who are fading into the sunset but can still remember how alive they felt back in those wonderful 60's and 70's. This one came out just last year but I still was able to pick it up for $6.98. There is nothing more beautiful than when supply meets demand.

I hear tell that some kids in the 21st Century discover the Beatles and want to know more about them. For those whippersnappers this would be a useful primer. For older fans there is nothing new, but most of us don't want anything new. If we did we'd be buying a Lorde lunch box or a Kendrick Lamar bobble head.

This book follows the traditional fab format of Chapter 1 covering the early years, Chapter 20 covering *LET IT BE*, and bonus Chapter 21 summing up 1971-2009. It looks nice and it feels fine. That's good enough for me.　　　　　　　　　　B

THE BEATLES BOOK edited by Edward E. Davis (1968 Cowles)

As one of the earliest books on our heroes this would have some historical significance even if it wasn't very good but it's fabulous. Great cover featuring the psychedelic portraits by Richard Avedon. It's a fine collection of writings by some of the most important music critics and social observers of that crazy time we call the 1960's. You can pretty much tell the liberals from the right wingers without a scorecard.

1. Timothy Leary - LSD guru, "I declare that the Beatles are mutants. They are Divine Messiahs. Evolutionary agents

sent by God, endowed with mysterious power to create a new human species."
2. William F. Buckley, Jr. – Political talk show host, " The Beatles are not merely awful, I would consider it sacrilegious to say anything less than godawful. In my defense I wish to say that I am tolerant beyond recognition where modern music is concerned."
3. Nat Hentoff – Jazz and folk aficionado, "The Beatles are increasingly for the comfortable and afraid."
4. Ralph J. Gleason - Pipe smoking seer, "The new electronic music by the Beatles exists somewhere else from and independent of the Negro."

Suffice it to say, this book is a mind blowing trip. It's fascinating from my 21st century perspective to read intelligent politically incorrect musings from some of the best minds of that golden era. So much of Beatle writing has been post-1970 and therefore colored by nostalgic backward glances. This book came out in early 1968 before the band completely soured on each other, before there was the backlash from the public over John and Yoko's nude album cover, before they busted John and George for marijuana possession, before Ringo started his atrocious solo acting career, and before the Apple Corp debacle. It was released at a time when the group was making its last trip together to India to meditate with sexy Sadie. This is the closest thing in print to being there as the summer of love fades and the long slow death of the Beatles begins.   A

THE BEATLES COME TO AMERICA by Martin Goldsmith (2004 John Wiley & Sons)

Martin Goldsmith is a classical music expert and he knows his singer/songwriters. He wrote a book before this that was a true story of music and love in Nazi Germany and for all I know he loves his wife and never had a cavity. But I'm not sure he's the one I want to turn to when I'm looking to go back to those wonderful days of yesteryear. He's a little too hyperbolic for me. The first Sullivan show brought "…the reassurance of life-affirming art." It was "…an event both timely and timeless." It was, "…the latest plateau achieved in their ever-ascending journey. Forty years later it remains the greatest musical story ever told." Roll over Beethoven and tell Tchaikovsky the news.

Mister Goldsmith wonders if post-Lee Harvey Oswald "Is it giving the Beatles too much credit to imagine them coming to our wounded country…and restoring our emotional health and happiness?" Yes it is. Oh, yes it is. Yeah.

Martin further lets us know the band "…were supreme artists who contributed a singular voice to an eloquent generation." Even Ringo?

Plus, their "…accomplishment provided an artistic parallel to the greatest scientific venture of the era…the journey to the moon," and they "…brought us joy, a feeling comparable, as John Updike told me 'to the sun coming up on Easter morning'- endlessly renewable and life-affirming."

To be fair, Goldsmith points out some obvious things in an eloquent manner. For instance "Paul was fundamentally a happy, contented soul, and John was forever haunted by sadness and anger stemming from his earlier days."

But then it's back to poetic hyperbole (to be truthful I'm tearing up a little bit) "The holiday season of 1963 seemed dreary, colder, and gloomier than usual. And then, as the country and the hemisphere lurched toward the darkest days of the year, a song was released on the day after Christmas. A hand was outstretched to us all." When that hand touched us we felt happy inside.

Also, just in case you didn't know "The Beatles invited us to join them on a magical journey of music, of ideas, and of the deepest emotions. They were...explorers who led their followers to new artistic and spiritual places. If they wouldn't restrict themselves...why should we lower our sights or rein in our ambitions and dreams? The Beatles started out great and only got better; what a magnificent example to emulate!"

Goldsmith has won me over. Maybe I do want to take a trip with him back to a time when submarines were yellow, carnations were black, and albums were white.   B+

THE BEATLES DAY BY DAY by Mark Lewisohn (1990 Harmony)

The only book by Mister Lewisohn I can't quite recommend. Mark stumbles badly with this small trade paperback of what the group was doing from 1962-1989. He was apparently drunk on the acclaim for *THE BEATLES LIVE!* and *RECORDING SESSIONS*.

If you're like me you don't care about non-Beatle Yoko Ono flying to London "...for business discussions at Apple," on 5 December 1978. Or, that Wings played at the Kupittaan Urheiluhalli in Turku, Finland on 5 August 1972. Or, that Paul and Linda flew "...from London Airport to New York," on 17 March 1969. Or, that John and Yoko returned "...to England" on 21 January 1971. Or, that Ringo went to the ballet on 22 July 1986. Or, that George went to the women's bathroom by accident on 14 September 1963. Or, that John had some candy that didn't agree with him on 19 November 1965. Or, that Ringo learned how to knit on 24 February 1974. Or, that Paul ate his last piece of meat on 12 June 1973.

You'd have to be a Beatle-lunatic to want this book. All others can disregard without another thought.   D-

THE BEATLES FOREVER by Nicholas Schaffner (1977 Cameron House)

The title of this masterpiece says it all. It seems certain that barring the apocalypse, the rapture, the second coming, nuclear destruction, Armageddon, mass hypnosis, or the end of the world as we know it, the four little children from World War II England will continue on forever. The band will remain a cultural icon in the same vein as Shakespeare, Mozart, Socrates, Lincoln, and that guy from the bible who did all the miracles. It's very likely because unlike the aforementioned luminaries there is plenty of audio and video of the fabulous ones. We know how they talked, sang, and moved. It's almost like they are our buddies.

It was the 1970's, a time when the counterculture had lost hope. The revolution had not been televised. In fact, there had been no revolution. There were a lot of kids walking around London with long hair but that was about it. Nicholas Schaffner looked around in despair and wondered where had all the good times gone? Schaffner had been born in the 50's and was therefore the perfect age to catch the *Ed Sullivan Show* on Sunday, February 9, 1964. He had been saddened by the shattering of the president's skull (when you talk about destruction don't you know that you could count him out) but now just weeks later the decade was really beginning, changing from black and white to color. Nicholas was an Anglophile (his mother was from London so it came naturally) and rode the British Invasion train for the rest of his short, but sweet, life. He even christened himself the first American fan of another well-known quartet because his mom just happened to come home in 1967 with a fresh U.K. monaural copy of THE PIPER AT THE GATES OF DAWN. Schaffner not only wrote one of the best Beatle books but he wrote the very best work about Roger, Roger, David, Richard, and Nicholas. It's called *Saucerful of Secrets*. I'll wait here patiently while you go to Amazon and snag a copy.

Now back to our story. Nicholas changed as the Beatles changed. When they started smoking grass he started smoking grass. When they turned on to LSD he turned on to LSD. When Lennon spoke out against the war in Vietnam Nicholas spoke out against the war in Vietnam. When Lennon declared the dream over Schaffner said no way it's the Beatles forever. There had been an authorized biography (*The Beatles* by Hunter Davies); a highfalutin examination of their music (*Twilight of the Gods* by Wilfred Mellers); a *New Musical Express* analysis of their rock and roll (*The Beatles: An Illustrated Record* by Roy Carr and Tony Tyler); but now *Beatles Forever* would be a book from the U.S. male fan's perspective. This meant less lusting after cute McCartney and more emulating of cool Lennon. This was pre-Chapman so there was still light at the end of the tunnel. The band members were all still in their 30's and you never knew what the future might have in store. Now we know, so the poignant nostalgia of this book becomes even more acute.

On the front cover we get the iconic RUBBER SOUL photo. On the back cover we get pictures of memorabilia because this book is also about the collecting of artifacts. That always went hand in hand with record collecting.

Then the introduction "Imagine what our world would be like today, were it not for the Beatles." As well as "One of their attributes was the ability to live their colorful lives in a virtual fishbowl and yet never for a moment bore or disappoint their millions of riveted voyeurs and eavesdroppers." Plus, "...many...emerged quite different people from those they might otherwise have been." On one of Schaffner's personal notes "The Beatles ultimately helped me 'find myself' as an individual."

Schaffner explains that "This book is an attempt to chronicle the phenomenon of which the Beatles were the focus point...and to recapture the experience of growing up with the Fab Four."

Chapter 1: The world is at your command. Covering December 1962 through November 1964

Jumping right into it by ignoring all that David Copperfield crap we get right to White Friday when the Beatles landed in New York. It was February 7, 1964 and "They could scarcely have stirred more hysteria and fascination had they just arrived from another planet." One reporter asked, "What's your message for American teenagers?" Paul answered, "Our message is...buy some more Beatle records." Next, came the question, "What about the movement in Detroit to stamp out the Beatles?" Paul responded, "We're starting a movement to stamp out Detroit." Now we know why the Paul is dead thing started in Michigan.

Check out the big time media response:

1. Chet Huntley, NBC evening news 2/7/64, "Like a good little news organization, we sent three cameramen to Kennedy airport today to cover the arrival of... the Beatles. However, after surveying the...subject of that

film, I feel there is absolutely no need to show any of that film."

2. *New York World Telegram* editorial 2/8/64, "These lads cultivate a vague illusion to being musicians, in a gurgling sort of way. They tote instruments, but blandly assure their fans they know not a note. (All their notes are in the bank.) Their production seems to be a haunting combination of rock and roll, the shimmy, a hungry cat riot, and Fidel Castro on a harangue."

3. *Newsweek* 2/24/64, "Visually they are a nightmare…musically they are a near disaster…their lyrics (punctuated by nutty shouts of yeah, yeah, yeah!) are a catastrophe, a preposterous farrago of valentine-card romantic sentiments."

And did you know, "Back in 1964 a good majority of Beatlemaniacs were female. In the U.S., teen-age girls seemed to be particularly turned on by an alternative to the all-American male, whose notions of 'masculinity' evidently ruled out appearance as a means of self-expression."

Chapter 2: Getting better all the time. Covering December 1964 through February 1966

Things get interesting as the band discovers there's more to life than just holding hands "Lennon-an uncompromisingly honest, somewhat bitter man who felt uncomfortable with the notion that pop stars should radiate non-stop mindless good cheer-was beginning to explore his own emotions and imagination in his new lyrics."

But not everybody liked their new direction in 1965. *Melody Maker* called RUBBER SOUL "monotonous." "Fans wrote to The

Beatles Monthly, complaining that the L.P. cover made their heroes look like corpses."

Chapter 3: Listen to the color of your dreams. Covering March 1966 through May 1967

Then things got really trippy, "Most Beatle people were caught quite unawares by the strange new terrain their heroes would explore in 1966, a year when the Beatles really did begin to tear away so many of the conventions into which the pop song had been straight-jacketed, to inaugurate what has been called their 'psychedelic' period." Additionally, "1966 certainly marked the end of, as one irate *Beatles Monthly* correspondent put it 'the Beatles we used to know before they went stark, raving mad."

This chapter also covers the banned L.P. jacket. Rich Friedland, editor of *The Inner Light* "offers...advice on how to tell whether your copy of YESTERDAY AND TODAY conceals a 'butcher cover'- and if so, how to go about extricating it."

In 1966 there was a quote of Lennon's that made bible thumpers a little angry. It was something about the group being more popular than the messiah. According to Schaffner, some band member also had this to say, "Show business belongs to the Jews, it's a part of the Jewish religion." John admitted to this at the Capitol Records press conference on August 28, 1966.

Chapter 4: I'd love to turn you on. Covering June 1967 through August 1968

"With mind-bending drugs, thousands of people began to snap the bonds of empirical logic, to overwhelm their senses with heightened perceptions, and bring to their waking hours many of the sensations and images of dream sleep." That doesn't sound sensible.

A handy guide to who is on the cover of *PEPPER*: Aleister Crowley (the Beast 666-black magician), Mae West (floozy icon), Lenny Bruce (filthy drug user), Karleinz Stockhausen (pro World Trade Center disaster of 9/11), W.C. Fields (child hater), Edgar Allan Poe (sicko from Baltimore), Aldous Huxley (LSD promoter), James McCartney (busted for drug possession), Marilyn Monroe (floozy icon, druggie), William Burroughs (heroin abusing murderer), Karl Marx (communist), Richard Starkey (alcoholic wife beater), Lewis Carroll (pedophile), John Lennon (degenerate), Dylan Thomas (drunken sod), Sonny Liston (vicious boxer), T. E . Lawrence (sadomasochist), Shirley Temple (child star), George Harrison (meditator), and Fred Astaire (male dancer). Albert Einstein (virtual freak of human nature) and Adolph Hilter (vegetarian) would have made the cut but Lennon blocks our view. Are these the kind of role models we want for our children?

Chapter 5: Shine on till tomorrow. Covering September 1968 through April 1970

On the rise and fall of the Apple Empire "The Beatles eventually realized that a hip corporation was something of a contradiction in terms."

On *TWO VIRGINS* in your face underneath brown paper wrapping album cover "...there were John and Yoko, stark raving naked, not so much as a fig-leaf in sight."

On *OBLADI-OBLADA* "McCartney was getting tired of having to weather Lennon's disdain whenever he tried to record one of his more mawkish ditties-although this situation did keep Paul's facile sentimentality within tolerable limits."

On *ABBEY ROAD* side two "The...sequence resembles a dream not so much in the subject matter of the individual segments but in the almost hallucinatory way one musical/lyrical setting unfolds into another."

With the Beatles' split still not official the *Beatles Monthly* decided to put out its last issue in December 1969. Its "...swan song consisted primarily of an editorial harangue against the boys...a harsh coda to the gushy tone the publication had sustained through the previous six-and-a-half years. The Beatles were denounced for having grown uncooperative about posing for photographs, for having failed to come out against drugs, for having lost their sense of humor, and even for their appearance ('The Beatles are certainly photogenic, or at least they were in the days when you could see all of their faces')."

Chapter 6: All things must pass away. Covering May 1970 through November 1971

Now we come to the weepy part of the story o my brothers, "For *ALL THINGS MUST PASS*, Harrison and Phil Spector assembled a rock orchestra of almost symphonic proportion." Meanwhile Spector co-produced *PLASTIC ONO BAND* at the same time using only three musicians with a couple of keyboard parts added by Phil and Billy. "*PLASTIC ONO BAND* shows John striving to demolish every icon in sight-be it Krishna, Jesus, or the Beatles." John dismisses, "mysticism as 'pie in the sky', another drug to dull the pain of reality. Lennon's music is as raw and claustrophobic as George's was lush, expansive, and uplifting."

"Minus the inhibitions formerly imposed by his fellow Beatles, each was free to indulge his most maudlin obsessions." This didn't work out too well with the home made *McCARTNEY* or the ill-advised *SENTIMENTAL JOURNEY*. There would not be a more horrible singer doing an album of crooning until Robert Zimmerman in 2015. On the other hand *ALL THINGS MUST PASS* was George's most popular ever and *PLASTIC ONO BAND* was John's best ever. The problem with those two is they never went back to full-on-lush or full-on-raw. That was their downfall...if you don't count being shot, or stabbed, or getting cancer.

Chapter 7: Take a sad song and make it better. Covering December 1971 through August 1974

Shaffner tells us, "1972 was a bleak year for the Beatles." I don't agree.

- John's *SOMETIME IN NEW YORK CITY* (the studio record) is awesome despite people often putting the lyrics down. "(John) began to mouth the...banal clichés of a clique of New York 'revolutionaries.'"
- The U.K. punters finally got the excellent *HAPPY XMAS (WAR IS OVER)*.
- John did his only full length solo gigs at Madison Square Garden.
- *CONCERT FOR BANGLADESH* was released on vinyl and as a major motion picture.
- Wings toured (the first solo Beatle tour) and got revved up on record for the first time with three interesting singles. Two of them had lyrics so controversial that they were banned by the BBC. First up *GIVE IRELAND BACK TO THE IRISH*

(politically controversial) then to punk off the censors *MARY HAD A LITTLE LAMB* then *HI HI HI* (sex and drugs controversial) with a much loved B side *C MOON* (though I never understood what people saw in it).
- Ringo's fascinating *Blindman* film came out.
- Ringo's directing debut *Born to Boogie*, the flick that captured T Rexmania.
- Ringo surprisingly joined in the *HOW DO YOU SLEEP?* sweepstakes with his anti-McCartney anthem *BACK OFF BOOGALOO.* Funny story; Paul on Jimmy Fallon is asked what his favorite Starr song is and he tells Jimmy Fallon *BACK OFF BOOGALOO.* Great! Only took him 42 years to subtly fight back.
- BBC Radio One commences *The Beatles Story* audio special.

Chapter 8: The act you've known for all these years. Covering September 1974 through April 1977

1977 was the only year of the 70's to feature more Beatle recordings released than solo recordings. There were two live albums (one a double) *HOLLYWOOD BOWL* and *STAR CLUB*. Meanwhile solo wise only Ringo's two horrible singles *WINGS* (seemingly not another swipe at Paul) and *DROWNING IN THE SEA OF LOVE* and his horrible long player *RINGO THE 4th* that practically no one ever heard (it peaked at #162 on the charts even worse than *TWO VIRGINS*). Plus, the, up to that point, greatest selling 45 in U.K. History *MULL OF KINTYRE* from *Wings*. I bought RINGO THE 4TH as a promo copy at Play It Again, Sam's used record store/head shop (all your bootleg and bong needs on sale here). Put side A on once and I never listened to it again. I bought *MULL OF KINTYRE* b/w *GIRL SCHOOL* at the Sample record store. I didn't like *MULL* but I kind of liked *GIRL*. That was the same store I bought the *MAGIC CHRISTIAN* soundtrack after seeing the movie on the late, late show in 1975. I got it for 99 cents plus tax. I still have it. It's a great album featuring Badfinger's *COME AND GET IT,* Thunderclap Newman's *SOMETHING IN THE AIR and* Peter Sellers. I bought *WINGS OVER AMERICA* and *SHAVED FISH* there in 1977. Peace out.

Back to Schaffner, 1977 made him a little wistful. "...for vintage Beatle people, it seems hard to believe that more time has lapsed since the Beatles went their separate ways than during the whole period spanning *"I WANT TO HOLD YOUR HAND"* and *"LET IT BE."* As Bobby D. once sang, time passes slowly when you're lost in a dream."

The Beatles Forever ends with an informative review of all the Beatle books published between 1964 and 1977. I knew I stole this idea somewhere.   A+

BEATLES GEAR by Andy Babiuk (2001 Backbeat)

This is gear in every way. It's perfect for that hard to shop for classic rock loving musician on your list. The kind of guy who plays Beatle covers at acoustic open mike night or the kind that gigs in a tribute band. You know; one of those bands who start out wearing black leather, then switches to collarless suits, then puts on colorful Sgt. Pepper type costumes, and ends their set wearing fake beards and moustaches. They have names like Beatle Magic, Rain, the BBC band, the Day Trippers, the Yellow

Submarines, or the Apples in Stereo (surprisingly the Apples in Stereo are not a Beatle cover band and I actually find their original music to be more Kinks like than fab like). The kind of band that makes sure the bassist plays left handed, the drummer is short, the rhythm guitarist has a pointy nose, and the lead guitarist is an Indian. For these kinds of pop rockers it's not enough to love the music so much that they put on concerts that recreate *ABBEY ROAD* note for note. They have to know what equipment the group used to get all their groovy sounds. Many fans know that Ringo played a Ludwig kit but I hear musicians like to be knowledgeable about John's first Rickenbacker, John's second Rickenbacker, John's Vox metal clad python strap, John's Mellotron, Paul's Hofner bass, George's sitar, the Leslie speaker cabinet used for *TOMORROW NEVER KNOWS*, George's rosewood Telecaster, George's Gibson ES-345, and how they utilized the famous Tone Bender fuzz-box. For the lay man who might not care as much as the axe men do, there are lots of pretty pictures and a few interesting quotes. There's the one where Paul admits he was wrong to tell George what to do on guitar during the session for "Hey Jude". McCartney said, "It was a bit of a number for me to dare to tell George-one of the greatest, I think-to not play. It was like an insult." Actually, it was an insult. This was the beginning of the decades long ranting by George about what a pain in the ass McCartney was. He said he would be in a band with Ringo and John again but not Paul (see the recording session for *I'M THE GREATEST*), he would choose Willie Weeks over Paul if he needed a bassist, and he'd be damned if Paul was going to boss him around again during the *ANTHOLOGY* recordings. George insisted on Electric Light Orchestra's front man Jeff Lynne to be the producer of the Threatles.

The writing in this book passes my patented test. I was strongly interested even though I wouldn't know a major chord from a minor chord, a black key from a white key, a snare drum from a hi-hat, a tuner from a harmonica, or a moog from a mouth organ. B+

THE BEATLES ILLUSTRATED LYRICS edited by Alan Aldridge (1990 Black Dog & Leventhal)

This is a hardcover compilation of Alan Aldridge's essential *The Beatles Illustrated Lyrics* and *The Beatles Illustrated Lyrics 2*. To say no to this book is to say no to life. As we all know their lyrics are just as important as their music and their voices. Thankfully they enunciate fairly clearly but isn't it still nice to be able to sing along with assuredness. I mean, *ABBEY ROAD* and *LET IT BE* not having lyric sheets always pissed me off. Problem solved.

The first book covered up to 1969. The second book covered those last two albums plus a few obscure leftovers like *NOBODY I KNOW, WOMAN, TIP OF MY TONGUE, LOVE OF THE LOVED, I'M IN LOVE, STEP INSIDE LOVE, IT'S FOR YOU, HELLO LITTLE GIRL, LIKE DREAMERS DO, I DON'T WANT TO SEE YOU AGAIN, THAT MEANS A LOT, I'LL KEEP YOU SATISFIED, FROM A WINDOW, BAD TO ME, GOODBYE,* and *ONE AND ONE IS TWO.* It's tough to be comprehensive when it comes to 1960's Lennon/McCartney words but you can't say they didn't try. Unfortunately, George is only partially represented. These classics don't make the cut: *SOMETHING, HERE COMES THE*

SUN, WHILE MY GUITAR GENTLY WEEPS, and OLD BROWN SHOE. It's probably because they weren't giving him enough of a cut. Richard Starkey is not represented at all. I guess they left his two compositions up on the fridge.

Dozens and dozens of groovy hippie artists are represented here. While perusing this book it'll be easy for you to lay down all thought and surrender to the void. There's eroticism aplenty, psychedelic images in droves, cigarettes stubbed out in fried eggs, wonderful dreams, spiritual longing, old men on acid, David Bailey photos, Peter Max to the max, partial Popeye, Ralph Steadman pre-gonzo, clowns to the left of us, jokers to the right, and Alan Aldridge's amazing paintings. It's a cornucopia of delight. A splendid time is guaranteed for all.   A

THE BEATLES IN THE BEGINNING by Harry Benson (1993 Universe)

This is my favorite photo book of the Beatlemania era. There are a lot of classics here. You've got pillow fights; Ringo attempting to play piano, Paul and George shopping for post cards in Paris; two great photos of John in front of a Napoleon Bonaparte bust; one terrific shot of the whole band in front of the same bust (maybe now we have proof who the fifth Beatle is); all four drinking Pepsi at a bar (wholesome lads these); reading the fan mail; Paul shaving; John shaving; fans going ballistic in New York; Ed Sullivan goofing around in a Beatle wig; George checking out the ladies; Cassius Clay holding Ringo in his arms and then pretending to punch George in the face; the first ever photo of George, John, Paul, and Jimmy Nichol in yoga like poses (foreshadowing beautifully the Maharishi years); Layla nuzzling George's ear; and a press conference in Memphis that looks like Super Bowl media day. It's almost too much to take in. But I did it because I'm a man.   A-

THE BEATLES' LONDON: *A Guide to 467 Beatles Sites in and Around London* by Piet Schreuders, Mark Lewisohn, and Adam Smith (2009 Interlink)

My wife went to London and all I got was this book. Fortunately, it's a good one. If I ever go to England I will use this book to complete my full blown Beatle dementia. What could be more fun than standing where they stood, eating where they ate, drinking where they drank? Don't even get me started on Abbey Road. I will definitely walk barefoot in a suit with a cigarette in my right hand. Maybe I'll ring up Sir James McCartney and commoner Richard Starkey when I get there and they can tag along with me.   A-

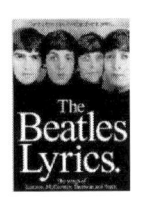

THE BEATLES LYRICS: *The Songs of Lennon, McCartney, Harrison and Starr* (1996 Hal Leonard)

Not to be confused with official biographer Hunter Davies' *THE BEATLES LYRICS* from 2014.

"For the first time ever together in print." says the front cover of this functional but unnecessary piece of product. Of course, this is a lie. Alan Aldridge had already put out his two volume *Illustrated Lyrics* all those years ago. Aldridge's books have all the words and illustrations to go along with them. Each lyric is represented by fine art designed exclusively for the books.

On the other hand, *The Beatle Lyrics* is just that. Lyrics plus a handful of nondescript apropos of nothing photos. Skip this and spring for the out of print Aldridge gems. Or at least get the Hunter Davies' version of *The Beatles Lyrics* because bland thoughts on their songs from a man who knew them personally and reproductions of the words in the band's own handwriting are highly preferable to this. C+

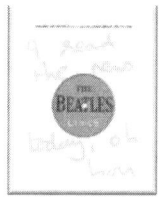

THE BEATLES LYRICS: *The Stories Behind the Music, Including the Handwritten Drafts of More Than 100 Classic Beatles Songs* edited by Hunter Davies (2014 Little, Brown and Company)

According to their official biographer Hunter Davies, by his reckoning in 2014, "There must by now be well over 2,000 different books about the Beatles." I've decided not to review them all. I don't want to have a nervous breakdown. However, any time Hunter Davies puts out a new work on the old boys you can bet it will be included. This is more fun than his straight bio *THE BEATLES* (1968) but it's not as enchanting as that time he went through John Lennon's garbage can to create *THE JOHN LENNON LETTERS* (2012). Now that he's on pace to put a new work out every two years I wonder what 2016 will bring. I'm hoping he covers their houses next. It would be great to see their bedrooms, kitchens, and sofas through the years. It would be like a deluxe edition of *Architectural Digest*.

Check out his scintillating comments about their classic songs:

1. I WANT TO HOLD YOUR HAND: "The song has several internal crescendos, and descendos." Look for *Words I Made Up* by Hunter Davies.
2. I FEEL FINE: "The big attraction is the music…" As it is on many musical recordings.
3. THE WORD: "The word in question is love-but John is not actually singing a love song."

4. I'M ONLY SLEEPING: "I believe it really is about sleeping." By god, Holmes, you've done it again.
5. TOMORROW NEVER KNOWS: "This is their most psychedelic song, their most Indian." Mr. Davies must have been sleeping when the Beatles issued George's trilogy featuring Indian musicians. Remember "Love Me To" (1966), "Within You, Without You" (1967), and "The Inner Light" (1968)?
6. A DAY IN THE LIFE: "...probably the most cataclysmic, orgasmic, crashing, vibrating, shuddering, juddering, shattering, echoing end in the whole of popular music." I couldn't have said it better myself.
7. ALL YOU NEED IS LOVE: "The basic message is clear: you can do anything you want, if you want to." A very dangerous philosophy.
8. I AM THE WALRUS: "Some words are made up, such as crabalocker."
9. COME TOGETHER: "The BBC banned the record for a while. It was that reference to Coca-Cola that upset them. Commercial endorsements were not allowed."

I recommend this strongly to fans who would like to see the original scribbled lyrics to many of the classics. That's right! This book contains two dozen (or more!) of the lyrical masterworks in the fabs' own handwriting, complete with coffee stains, ink blotches, and blood, sweat, and tears. This is not for the faint of heart. Plus, at no additional cost, Hunter Davies shares his mostly bland ideas about their whole damn song book. For a more fun lyrical time may I suggest you instead track down the beautiful two volume set of *THE BEATLES ILLUSTRATED LYRICS* edited by Alan Aldridge, then turn off your mind, relax, and float downstream. B+

BEATLES MEMORABILIA: The Julian Lennon Collection by Brian Southall with Julian Lennon (2010 Goodman)

Even Julian Lennon wants to get in on the hangers-on thing. It's the old, I knew the Beatles so give me a book deal so I can make some money, thing. Julian says, "This collection represents something of great importance to me, as it is part of my history." That's wrong, old buddy. It's part of *their* history. It's sad when parents treat their son badly and then the son turns around and does the same thing to his kid. John had Julian but Julian didn't have him. Julian wanted John but John didn't want him. John was left to live with his Aunt Mimi. Julian was left to live with his mother Cynthia. When John became a teenager he started to have something of a relationship with his mother Julia. Then she was killed violently by a hit and run. When Julian became a teenager he started to have something of a relationship with his father John. Then he was killed violently by a madman; which brings us to this book. John Lennon collected Beatles memorabilia because he was proud of his past. Julian Lennon collects memorabilia because he is proud of his father. There aren't a lot of snazzy items in this book. These are the highlights: the four track recorder from John's attic, an Apple Corps watch, and John's pinstripe trousers he wore during the shooting of *MAGICAL MYSTERY TOUR*. This is strictly a scraping the bottom of the Apple barrel book. Take the 30 dollars you would have spent on this and buy something nice for your son.

C-

THE BEATLE MYTH: The British Invasion of American Popular Music, 1956-1969 by Michael Bryan Kelly (1991 McFarland & Company)

Disaffected Yank Michael Kelly wants all of us full-blinders-on Liverpool lovers to face the truth. American tunes were popular in the 60's too. Being a student of English rock and roll only I had never heard of these artists that Doc Rock (Kelly's self-given nickname) claims made U.S. top 40 in that zany decade. Who are these Beach Boys he speaks of? Could there really have been a combo called the Nashville Teens? And I sure as hell don't remember Elvis having hits in the 60's. Didn't he die when he was in the army? (John Lennon, "Elvis died when he went in the army") Ah ha! I thought so.

This is much ado about nothing. We get charts and graphs to make us understand. We get refutations of myths to wake us up. You know how people made up all those ridiculous stories about the father of our country? Such as the one about chopping down a cherry tree or the one where he skips a silver dollar across the Potomac? Same thing happened with you know who.

Just in case you're interested:

1. They did not invent the phrase "yeah yeah yeah."

2. So called "Beatle boots" had been available for some time before they started wearing them.

3. *YESTERDAY* was not the first rock record to use strings.

4. George Harrison's contention that the group made the first music videos was a joke. There were many videos before them such as the one for Ricky Nelson's *TRAVELIN' MAN* (1961).

5. They were not the first stars to regularly write their own songs. Buddy Holly, Chuck Berry, Brian Wilson, etc. all beat them to the punch.

This is a well written and well thought out term paper. But please lock me away and throw away the key. I don't care what you say I can't live in a world without myth.   B+

THE BEATLES NOW AND THEN by Harry Benson (1998 Universe)

I got faked out by this one. I thought for sure it was another overpriced little Beatlemania photo journal. I should have paid attention to the title. It covers the mid-60's (then) and the solo years (now).

There is a problem, though. Five years earlier Universe publishing put out most of these same Harry Benson classic 60's pics in a big, beautiful book entitled *The Beatles in the Beginning*. It is well worth owning. Why shrink them down five years later? Is smaller better?

Case closed, right? Buy *In the Beginning* and skip *Now and Then*. Except the handful of solo years shots are pretty cool. The series featuring Linda and Paul on their farm with her on a horse and him smoking pot should be put up in an art gallery. The photo of these same two backstage at a Wings show getting stoned is sublime. The black and white one of them dancing on the Queen Elizabeth II is funny. It looks like Paul is dragging Linda around against her will. Good buddies Harrison and Zimmerman are also caught on film at the QE II party and George is captured with his new girlfriend Olivia looking like he's thinking *I hope she's not another Layla*.

But the best is saved for last. Harry got together with Sean and Yoko in 1985 and they took a little journey across the street to Central Park. He shows them sitting on the ground at Strawberry Fields all alone on top of the Imagine circle. You'd have to have a heart of stone not to find it poignant.

So what you should do is have somebody buy you both books.

B+

THE BEATLES: ON CAMERA, OFF GUARD 1963-69 by Mark Hayward (2009 Pavillion)

Just when I thought there were no more photos I had yet to see along comes this nifty item for the coffee table set. It felt nice in my hands. It lit up my eyes. I began to tear up with a sadness that can only come from joy. From the *MYSTERY TOUR* front cover to gaunt John two days before the assassination it takes you there and plummets you right into the action. There are terrific Mad Day Outtakes; shots of Paul in Kenya; John, George, and Ringo running for the train sans Paul in a *HARD DAY'S NIGHT;* and chaos like you can't imagine. Plus, it includes a DVD that I could never get to play. The lord must have wanted it that way. He has a plan for us all.   B+

THE BEATLES ON RECORD by Mark Wallgren (1982 Fireside)

You might be a Beatlemaniac if you enjoy this book. Many small black and white photographs of records released solo and as a band including half a dozen Wings 45's without picture sleeves. There is nothing like black and white images of singles with plain black sleeves to get your heart racing. Just in case that's not enough for you, you'll receive at no extra cost cogent analysis under these photos to give you context about what you're looking at. You'll learn that *HELEN WHEELS* was a "...solid rocker", George's *ALL THINGS MUST PASS* was "...an almost unbelievably ambitious and impressive collection of his own songs", *DOUBLE FANTASY* "...not surprisingly rose to the top of the charts following the untimely events of December 8th", and Ringo's *STOP AND SMELL THE ROSES* was "...strongly disliked by the critics and airplay was virtually nil."

The obvious thing to do here is to ignore this and go and buy *The Beatles: an Illustrated Record* by Roy Carr and Tony Tyler. Buy the first edition plus the two updated versions. They cover the same time period but with many large color photos, not to mention irreverent and insightful writing. C+

THE BEATLES, POPULAR MUSIC AND SOCIETY: A Thousand Voices edited by Ian Inglis (2000 St. Martin's)

A dozen learned men (no women allowed) come from universities around the world to enlighten us commoners about the band we've known for all these years. We get enthralling chapters on anti-intellectualism, the spectacle of youth, austerity to profligacy in the language of the Beatles, artistic freedom and censorship, and the relationship between postmodern art and kitsch. I thought I understood the band's music and their place in the pop culture firmament but I was wrong. This book opened my eyes to things I never thought before. I was blind but now can see. You've come to the right place for:

1. Graphs that explain the fractional incidence of 'I' in lyrics of albums, the fractional incidence of 'you' in lyrics of albums, and the fractional incidence of 'love' in lyrics of albums.
2. A collocation analysis that enables us to see how target words gain meanings from the company of other words. For example: the word she is used four times on the *HARD DAY'S NIGHT* album and 18 times on the *SGT. PEPPER* album while the word girl is used nine times on *HARD DAY'S NIGHT* but only three times on *SGT.*

PEPPER. Please see table 5.2 on page 102 and table 5.3 on page 103 for further details.
3. Finding out about the rhythms Lennon/McCartney employed. They employed a wide variety of tempos overall but make no use of very slow tempos. Please see table 4.9 on page 64 for a comparison of tempos, beats, and riffs as used by the Beatles, Stones, Kinks, and Dave Clark Five.
4. An explanation of rock and roll dance as metaphor.
5. A computer based text analysis of the changing quality of Beatle songs from the early to the later period.
6. The formation of affect and connection as it pertains to their celebrity legacy.

Suffice it to say this book is not for the casual fan. It is a serious work of sociological impact. It is a devastating commentary on the conventions and cultural constructions of pop music.   B+

THE BEATLES "QUOTE UNQUOTE" by Arthur Davis (1994 Crescent Books)

This is one of those throwaways that prove the rule that any book on the boys will sell. Despite the title and despite the dust jacket that reads "In their own words…the stars reveal their innermost thoughts," all we get is a few dozen lifeless quotes and a few dozen nothing photos. Plus, as a bonus, if you order right now, 80 whopping pages covering their whole time together, their first quarter century apart, and of course John's untimely death. This book is for extreme fanatics only. You know who you are, Bobb.   D-

THE BEATLES RECORDING SESSIONS: The Official Abbey Road Studio Session Notes 1962-1970 by Mark Lewisohn (1988 Harmony)

Mark Lewisohn has come up with many a good Beatle book but this is his best. Mark dives into the EMI vaults and comes out with a treasure trove of day by day recording information about the canon. It starts with the Peter Best version of the quartet in the spring of 1962 and ends in the spring of 1970 with Phil Spector's version of the *GET BACK* sessions. In between we get all the facts including:

1. Mark's rave review of Ringo's playing on *PLEASE PLEASE ME* "…very competent indeed."
2. The first album had a working title of *OFF THE BEATLE TRACK*. George Martin later used it for his orchestral LP of fab tracks.
3. On *I CALL YOUR NAME* "The writer of the song was capable of giving the only true interpretation." May I recommend the version by the Mamas and Papas?
4. On *EVERY LITTLE THING* "Take six was aborted when Paul burped a vocal instead of singing it."
5. June 14, 1965 McCartney and friends recorded all three of these Paul numbers: *I'VE JUST SEEN A FACE*, *I'M DOWN*, and *YESTERDAY*.

6. According to George Martin John wanted his singing on *TOMORROW NEVER KNOWS* to sound like he was the Dalai Lama singing from a mountain top with 4,000 monks chanting in the background. Now we know how many monks it takes to fill the Albert Hall.
7. On the final tour in 1966 they performed nothing from their new album *REVOLVER*. I wonder if anyone noticed at the time.
8. The gibberish at the end of the U.K. *PEPPER* played backwards says, "We'll fuck you like Superman."
9. George Martin helped Lennon/McCartney with *PEPPER* by cheerleading, "Come up with more of these great ideas!" Very helpful, George.
10. On Yoko, "Disputes still rage as to whether or not her presence disturbed the other three Beatles." I can only imagine Lewisohn is sugar coating the obvious truth here because this was an authorized project he worked on at the behest of those three Beatles and Ms. Ono. George told her she gave off bad vibes and Paul requested her to get back to where she once belonged.
11. The *GET BACK* recordings were saddled with Yoko's constant presence and even John called them, "The most miserable sessions on earth." Lennon also said some nonsense about how even the biggest Beatles fan in the world wouldn't have been able to sit through them. Yeah, right and I am the Crimson King.

The book also includes an interview with Paul where he makes the amazing claim that the Bonzo Dog Band homage *YOU KNOW MY NAME* (*LOOK UP THE NUMBER*) is, "...probably my favourite Beatles track…just because it's so insane." That's insane!

This book might be all too much for casual Beatle fans but as a card carrying maniac I have to give it an A+

THE BEATLES' SECOND ALBUM by Dave Marsh (2007 Rodale)

I like Dave Marsh. I really do. It's just that I hardly ever agree with him. Dave's opinions never seem to make sense to me. I've been reading him since the 70's and I believe I only agreed with him twice. Just when I thought it couldn't get any worse, Mr. Nostalgia writes a whole damn book about an album neither the band nor rabid Beatlemaniacs consider to be part of the canon. For chrissakes, it's a bastardized Capitol records release in 1964 created to rip off as many U.S. fans as possible before the Beatles fad ended and Dave knows all this. So he spends the whole first chapter rationalizing his bullshit decision to write a love letter to an LP that "…wasn't even the Beatles' second album-not in America or anywhere else." Dave also admits "The record does not at all reflect the Beatles intention." Better pay close attention to it then. Just because he heard this music in this configuration when he was 15 is no reason to lovingly praise it when he's 58. Dave says the record is a happy accident like *Casablanca*. That's right. He is comparing this "…ungainly, fraudulent mess" to a best picture winner at the Oscars. Dave hasn't shown this much gall since he wrote in *Glory Days* that

"African Americans can't get into Springsteen because his rhythms are too flat." So how can anybody like this ungainly, fraudulent mess of a book? Beats me.   D+

THE BEATLES: SIX DAYS THAT CHANGED THE WORLD February 1964 photos by Bill Eppridge (2014 Rizzoli)

When the Beatles landed in America for their first Ed Sullivan appearance, it did indeed change the world slightly, especially for female teenagers in the U.S. who seemed to get positively orgasmic over the whole thing. Any of them running into the band at this point could have been talked into more than just holding hands. Alas, this book comes 50 years too late. In 1964 a book of great photos like this would have been awesome to own. Unlike 1964, we now have all the Sullivan shows of that magical February on DVD and, though a picture is worth a thousand words, a video leaves nothing to the imagination. Still, there is something to be said for nostalgia presented as nicely as this black and white artifact of a time before life turned to color and we found out the band was a bunch of pill popping, orgy sharing, and alcohol swilling young men who wanted to do much more than just meet you.   A-

THE BEATLES STORY ON CAPITOL RECORDS PART ONE: Beatlemania and the Singles by Bruce Spizer (2000 498)

Bruce Spizer is the Beatlemaniac's Beatlemaniac. He sure knows his obscurities. This is a narrative and pictorial discography so comprehensive that 200 giant pages are not enough to contain it. This is only part one, Beatle lovers!

Bruce's earlier book covered those amazing Vee-Jay releases. This one covers the more famous rip off of the American public; Capitol vinyl. Despite the fact that the Beatles' themselves had disavowed interest in the distorted U.S.A. 1960's record catalog, Bruce lovingly goes over every detail from his well spent youth. Just because the band had this stuff deleted when they took control of the canon in 1987 doesn't mean it was deleted from our hearts.

You get the rundown on Beatlemania in the states, an overview and under view of the hit singles up to *LADY MADONNA*, and a look inside Capitol itself. If you were ever interested in the history of this great company (also responsible for bringing us the Beach Boys, Klaatu, and the Steve Miller Band) you've come to the right place. Find out pertinent details relating to their record club, their merchandising department, their press kits, and their press releases. Take a walk down memory lane; you will never be the same. A-

THE BEATLES: Ten Years that Shook the World by Mojo (2004 Dorling Kindersley)

After the release of *Anthology* in 2000 I thought that giant size masterpieces about the boys had peaked. I didn't expect to see another book match the visual impact and story-telling insight any time soon. Leave it to the folks at retro mag *Mojo* to prove me wrong. *Ten Years that Shook the World* shook my world. I was browsing at the World's Biggest Bookstore in the consumer paradise of Toronto, Ontario when what did I see but this gem nestled in a corner. I didn't buy it that day because I'm not made of money but it did become my favorite book to take out of the library. Recently, I finally purchased a copy off the internet and already I think of it as my bible. I have it on a stand in front of my Beatle shrine where every day I meditate for 20 minutes before my morning joint. It's a ritual that should last for years.

This is a staggeringly great collection packed with scintillating writing and knock off your socks photography. It starts with a foreword by acid casualty Brian Wilson in which he tells us his, "...favorite John song was *ACROSS THE UNIVERSE*." No surprise, there. If anyone can relate to Lennon's drug inspired stream of consciousness you figure it would be cosmic surfer Brian "playing in the sandbox" Wilson.

It continues with musical analysis from pop greats Robyn Hitchcock, Lemmy, Trevor Horn, Jack White, Tjinder Singh, Neil "I was in *Magical Mystery Tour*" Innes, and Captain Sensible.

Then it makes sense of the Beatles universe with sections on:

- Brian Poole and the Tremeloes, Stuart Sutcliffe, and Pete Best
- John's marriage to Cynthia
- Paul's girlfriend Jane Asher ("they all tried to pull her")
- Lennon and Epstein's "intense relationship"
- Their Christmas Shows
- Meeting with Cassius Clay ("So who were those little faggots?")
- Astrid Kirchherr's bravery
- Freddie Lennon's scum bag personality
- Jimmy Nicol's winning of the lottery
- The "Nuremburg-style proportions" of their one tour down under
- The time they met the king
- Zimmerman struggling not to vomit on John in the back seat of a limo
- The meat is murder cover of *YESTERDAY AND TODAY*
- Imelda Marcos locking them in her shoe closet
- The holy war waged against them in 1966 by bible thumping rednecks ("Lennon saves")
- George's trip to Bombay that would influence the future of western culture
- John's solo movie debut in a satirical war flick
- John at the 14-hour Technicolor Dream watching the Move
- The Greek island idea
- Singing background on *WE LOVE YOU*
- Taking leave of the Maharishi (John, "If you're so cosmic, you'll know why")
- The genesis of *REVOLUTION 9*

- Being busted by the man
- The fat control of Allen Klein
- The legendary Beatles coat hangers

If you act now you'll also receive:

1. Ian MacDonald's riveting report on their psychedelic experiences ("...a magical, all-beautiful, all-loving vision").
2. A wondrous selection of Tom Murray's Mad Day Out snaps next to the Thames, at the Old Street Station roof, on Saint Katherine's dock, and at Paul's Saint John's Wood home. The best one is the one where John lies on the dock pretending to have drowned and George is wearing Lennon's glasses.
3. An album by album guide complete with track listings, notes on the sleeve designs, and quotes from reviews at the time of issue.
4. Sharp looks at the four post-split solo albums of 1970. Mat Snow's *PLASTIC ONO BAND* critique is particularly well written. Snow points out the "studied rawness" of Lennon saying "good riddance" to the 1960's dream......Paul Trynka's *BEAUCOUPS OF BLUES* review points out "Many of Ringo Starr's supporters concede that he wasn't the best musician in the Beatles. Some of his detractors contend Ringo wasn't even the best drummer in the Beatles." According to Joe Donnelly in *Rock and Roll Cage Match* when Lennon was "asked if Ringo was the best drummer in the world" John replied, "he isn't even the best drummer in the Beatles."

5. A photo from the *PEPPER* cover shoot featuring Lennon and noted author Adolf Hitler.
6. Jim Irvin's startling and probably apocryphal 'lost weekend' story about a fan asking John if HEY JUDE was about Julian. Lennon replied, "Actually, that one's about Brian Epstein. Originally it was called GAY JEW."   A+

THE BEATLES THE BIBLE AND BODEGA BAY by Ken Mansfield (2000 Broadman & Holman)

Ken Mansfield, the U.S. manager of Apple records during the 60's (he was at the rooftop gig) gives us the first of two books about his experiences with those four men from England. In this memoir he conflates the kings of rock and roll and the King of Kings. Mansfield points out how the Beatles and the Bible both touched so many lives. The band "...traveled a musical bridge across the Atlantic Ocean into the hearts of their fans." The Bible "...shaped the character of mankind." Knowing full well that some readers will "...insist that this is two different books..." Ken says "Simply treat it like a hamburger-take the meat out and just eat the lettuce." I found that the meat and lettuce worked well together. I savored both the rock and the religion. It reminded me of the Warren Beatty biography by David Thomson that was half the story of Hollywood and half a new novel from Thomson. It's well designed and features great scripture quotes like, "He gives power to the tired and worn out, and strength to the weak," and great Lennon quotes like, "If the Beatles or the sixties had a message, it was to learn to swim."

For a band whose leader said they were more popular than Jesus, thought the Apostles were thick and ordinary, called a meeting to tell the others he was the son of God, and compared the bad press he and Yoko were getting to being crucified it's surprising how well these disparate subjects meld together. I guess it's because the boys from Liverpool stressed peace, love, and understanding and so did a well-known child from Bethlehem. B

THE BEATLES: The Biography by Bob Spitz (2005 Little, Brown and Company)

First of all, great title. Simple but thought provoking. Second of all, great job of research especially because one of the drawbacks in preparing a definite biography of the Beatles is the stunning lack of reliable source material.

I always dreamed that someday there would be a biography that captured the spirit and the energy of the world's greatest rock and roll band. It would be written by an author who had a lot of flair. It would vividly bring the story to life. It would get all the facts right. I'm still waiting.

Bob Spitz falls into the trap of making the story melodramatic. Every little thing becomes magnified out of all proportion. For instance, getting a new song together for the *Our World* broadcast in 1967 didn't mean much to the band. John just whipped out a little number as the deadline approached. Spitz reports that writing a new song "…seemed like a crushing task." Thank God Lennon was strong enough to come up with ALL YOU NEED IS LOVE.

Spitz does an adequate job here just like his adequate job on *Dylan: A Biography* but he didn't grab me and pull me in. I didn't feel fine while reading this. I felt empty. I guess I'm always looking for the rush provided by Nicholas Schaffner's vibrant *The Beatles Forever* which is a dedicated fan's look at the group. Straight biographies, whether they be Hunter Davies' official one (1968) or Philip Norman's *Shout!* (1981) or Jonathan Gould's *Can't Buy Me Love* (2007) leave me cold.

There are a few mistakes in the photo sections that I feel compelled to point out:

1. John met Paul at a Quarry Men gig on July 6, 1957. This was the beginning of the greatest partnership in pop music history. It is a date as important as April 10, 1962; February 9, 1964; June 1, 1967; April 10, 1970; December 8, 1980; and November 29, 2001. Below a picture of John singing that fateful day it says this show took place on July 8, 1957. I'm nitpicking, of course. But when the book jacket informs readers "Bob Spitz's *The Beatles* is the biography fans have been waiting for" and "Bob Spitz's masterpiece is, at long last, the biography the Beatles deserve" I expect there to be a fact checker involved.

2. The Cavern had a very distinctive look. You can't mistake it for any other venue. At least, I thought you

couldn't. Until Bob Spitz and his crack team did. There's a photo captioned "One of the Beatles' last performances at the Cavern." I don't know where the band is playing but it sure isn't the Cavern. To make matters worse, on the same page is a snap shot of them performing on stage at the Cavern with a caption reading "The classic Cavern stage shot, under the club's distinct brick archway."

3. There is a famous photo of the group standing next to a brick wall outside EMI studios in 1963. It makes a great bookend to that even more famous photo of them crossing the street outside EMI studios in 1969. In what almost seems like a joke the caption reads, "The Beatles, posing in the backyard of one of their houses, 1964." The year being wrong would be no big deal but somehow deciding they were in one of their backyards is ridiculous. Were they in the backyard of John, Paul, or George? Maybe it was the backyard of little Ringo.   B-

THE BEATLES THE DAYS OF THEIR LIFE foreword by Bruce Johnston (2010 Chartwell)

This photo extravaganza is so good it doesn't need an author. But we do get a little introduction from Bruce "I write the songs that make the whole world sing" Johnston. Bruce seems to think the fab four were heavily influenced by the Beach Boys. You can tell he's getting a little ridiculous because he changes his tune real fast, "Now don't get me wrong. I'm not saying the Beatles copied the Beach Boys but it was a time of great musical creativity." Thanks for that clarification, Bruce. I never knew that 60's pop was creative.

There are over 300 pages of classic pictures here suitable for framing. So get your frames out and get to work. We only have a little time left on this planet, folks.

Amongst the gems are three glam girls sitting on their laps (mascot Ringo doesn't get one), George in black leather and a tie, Harrison eating corn flakes from a box that reads, "Win the woman a dream house", all four with a giant snowman, crowd sitting on stage with them at Carnegie Hall, John and Ringo feeding future Traveling Wilbury Roy Orbison cake, all four in a cockpit, black and white Beatles in front of a color American flag, Ringo in a towel waving a gun, fan fainting at *HELP!* premiere, Paul wondering why he's sitting next to Mickey Dolenz, all four wearing fake moustaches on their chin and three wearing real moustaches under their nose at *SGT PEPPER* launch party, Linda kneeling on floor at the same party to get a good shot, George looking up at the sky after being told Brian is dead, blissing out with the Maharishi, watching Zimmerman at the Isle of Wight, and John screaming into a microphone at his last concert of the 60's.

This book makes a great gift. It says so right on the cover, "GREAT GIFT IDEA!" My friend Bad Ronald gave this to me for my birthday, which was really a nice gesture because he thinks the Beatles are overrated.   A-

THE BEATLES: THE TRUE BEGINNINGS by Roag Best with Pete and Rory Best (2003 Thomas Dunne)

Pete Best keeps his hand in with this visually appealing early years coffee table stocking stuffer. BBC news called it, "Popular Culture's Sistine Chapel." It's more like a kid remembering his years at camp. *The Standard* called it, "The best-looking Beatles book published yet. Literally." That's a ridiculous assessment unless they're just making a pun on Pete's last name. It has been known to happen. Remember his album *BEST OF THE BEATLES* that was designed to separate teenagers from their money?

The text does not illuminate. However, the design of this book did kind of fill with me a longing to time travel to the early 60's to see Pete playing with those other guys at his mother's Casbah Coffee Club. Then again, my whole life I've dreamed of doing just that.

A man named Matthew Best (no relation) gave me a free ticket to see the Pete Best band live in concert after this book came out and I didn't go. So you can see that Pete means nothing to me. If you're the kind of fanatic that goes to see Pete Best play drums because he once was the beat man for John, Paul, and George then this book is for you. I'm content with my complete collection of the paintings and poetry of Stuart Sutcliffe.   B-

BEATLES VS. STONES by John McMillian (2013 Simon & Schuster)

This is a great concept for a book. Too bad author John McMillian drops the ball. He takes the Beatles versus the Stones and turns it into a cure for insomnia. I'll fill you in on all you need to know about how the two groups intermingled:

The Beatles were managed by Allan Klein. The Rolling Stones were managed by Allan Klein. *YESTERDAY* (a ballad with strings) went out as a single in the U.S. but not in the U.K. *AS TEARS GO BY* (a ballad with strings) went out as a single in the U.S. but not in the U.K. *THE BEATLES* was released in late 1968 with a white album cover. *BEGGARS BANQUET* was released in late 1968 with a white album cover. *ALL YOU NEED IS LOVE* was put out as a 45 in 1967 with Mick and Keith among the background singers. *WE LOVE YOU* was put out as a 45 in 1967 with Paul and John among the background singers. Lennon and McCartney gave vocal giant Richard Starkey *I WANNA BE YOUR MAN* to sing. Lennon and McCartney gave performing dynamo Michael Phillip Jagger *I WANNA BE YOUR MAN* to sing (Lennon, "We weren't going to give them anything great, were we?"). LET IT BE was reproduced by Phil Spector and issued as the last fab album. LITTLE BY LITTLE was produced by Phil Spector and issued on the first Stones album. *SGT. PEPPER's* front cover from 1967 mentions the Rolling Stones. *THEIR SATANIC MAJESTIES REQUESTS'* front cover from 1967 features photos of the Beatles. *LET IT BE* released in 1970 had live tracks on it. *GET YOUR YA YAS OUT* released in 1970 had live tracks on it. Don

McLean sings in *AMERICAN PIE* of the sergeants trying to take the field and Jack Flash being the devil. John Lennon said Mick's, "...fag dancing is a joke." Mick appeared in *All You Need is Cash* so he could mock out the Beatles. The Beatles had a bassist named Stuart Sutcliffe who left the band and no one cared. The Stones had a bassist named William Wyman who left the band and no one cared. John Lennon believed his song *BLESS YOU* was sped up to become Mick Jagger and Keith Richard's song *MISS YOU*. Mick Jagger hung out with John and his wife Yoko. Mick Jagger hung out with John and his girlfriend May while they had their affair that thoughtful wife Yoko had set up. The Beatles started their own record label called Apple. The Stones started their own record label called Rolling Stones. John put out a single with David Jones called *FAME*. Mick put out a single with David Jones called *DANCING IN THE STREETS.* The Beatles enjoyed prostitutes in Germany. The Stones enjoyed prostitutes in Germany, France, England, etc. John Lennon felt the Stones copied everything the Beatles did, "...just look at what we did and what they did six months later." He was right, except for Allan Klein becoming the fab four's manager. The Klein debacle was them copying the Stones. D+

THE BEATLES WAY by Larry Lange (2001 Beyond Words)

Browsing one day in the Personal Growth section of my favorite locally owned bookstore, I came upon this remarkable work. As the front cover says it is "Fab wisdom for everyday life."

Couldn't we all use some of that? I hurriedly stuffed it into my shoplifting satchel and scurried out the door, shuffled off to my favorite locally owned coffee house, and sat down to glean its pearls of wisdom. What pearls they were! I learned how to:

1. Not take my dreams too seriously. After all, as George Harrison admitted, "The Beatles were very funny."
2. Be myself or as Ringo once sang, *ACT NATURALLY*.
3. Overcome fear of the unknown, for as Ringo once blurted out, "tomorrow never knows."
4. Search my subconscious by listening to the color of my dreams.
5. Do whatever it takes by working like a dog.
6. Find my Significant Other, *SHE'S A WOMAN* (I should hope so).
7. Publicize myself, Dear Sir or Madam: Will you read my book? It took me months to write. Will you take a look?

Without looking out of my window I can see all things on earth. Neat trick, huh?   D-

BEOWOLF TO BEATLES AND BEYOND by David R. Pichaske (1981 Macmillan)

It is David Pichaske's contention that the Beatles lyrics were poetry. Yet no less an expert on the band than the late great Ian MacDonald felt that, "If you asked an average listener what the

Beatles lyrics mean they would likely say very little." As we all know, poetry says everything about our culture and our world. I don't know which way to vote on this. I think I'll go with yes, their lyrics are poetry. In fact, I bet the Beatles are probably some of the best poets ever (not counting Ringo, of course). Please compare and contrast them with e.e. cummings, Yeats, Frost, Tennyson, Ginsberg, T.S. Eliot, Wordsworth, Emerson, Dickinson, Plath, and Whitman. Then get back to me. I'd like to know if I'm right.

No grade on this one. It turns out it's not really about the Beatles. It's a poetry anthology. I got faked out by the title.

BLACKBIRD SINGING: Poems and Lyrics, 1965-1999 by Paul McCartney (2001 W.W. Norton)

Paul lovingly selects for the fans what he thinks are the best poems and lyrics he's ever written. I'm surprised such gems as *THINGS WE SAID TODAY, FOR NO ONE,* and *I'VE JUST SEEN A FACE* didn't make the cut but that still leaves a lot of classics in this book. Unfortunately, Paul has never been a good editor of his own work. If not for Lennon's withering sarcasm we would have been in real trouble from the start. Somehow in a book of his masterpieces we find *ALL TOGETHER NOW*. I'm pretty sure he wrote that while asleep. Somehow, in a book he thinks "…convey(s) great depth of feeling…" we get his all-time low hit single *LET 'EM IN*. I think it's pretty obvious he was yelling this to his butler from the toilet. However, he redeems himself by viciously putting Mark David Chapman in his place. Mark will think twice before he shoots another Beatle. Check out what McCartney can do when pulling no punches with no holds barred. It's a blood bath. Paul labels Mark a big jerk then puts himself in Mark's head. "I'm the guy with the pistol/Who kills your best friend/You can't really blame me/'Cos I'm round the bend." Not quite at the level of *HOW DO YOU SLEEP* or *POSITIVELY FOURTH STREET* but you can feel the "It's a drag," emotion of December 1980. Buy his records.   C+

BLACK MARKET BEATLE: The Story Behind the Lost Recordings by Jim Berkenstadt and Belmo (1995 Collector's Guide)

Part of being a super duper Beatlemaniac is being a Bootleg maniac. You don't want to just own every official Beatle LP, EP, 45, CD, and video in every different permutation from every country on the planet. No, you want to own all the unofficial releases too. The fact that they're illegal only makes it more exciting. You never know what you'll find with bootlegs. It could be *THE BEATLES vs. DON HO* ("Each delivering their greatest vocal punches. You be the judge and jury!") or *GET BACK JOURNALS* (an 11 LP box set featuring unstructured rehearsals and trivial discussions) or *SPICY BEATLES SONGS* ("that's a spicy meatball!"). This book only covers Beatlegs up to the mid 90's and there's been an avalanche of illicit material since then. So you're on your own for the last 20 years. Still, this functions as a nice overview of the first quarter century of under the counter recordings. It's a nostalgic walk down memory lane to the early days of head shops, the counterculture, and the innocence you'll never get back. B

A BOOK OF BEETLES by Dr. Josef R. Winkler (1964 Spring)

This sold so many copies to teenage girls in America in 1964 that there was a second impression edition rush released in 1965. The second printing did less in the way of sales because most teenage girls already had a copy and because everyone had wised up to the fact that this book was not about the boys from Liverpool but was in fact a tome about entomology.

Still, if you like these beetles and want to learn more you could do a lot worse than this. Prosaic scientific treatises cannot do justice to the colour and form of these living jewels. But this is no run of the mill entomology book. It is an illustrated record complete with artistic portraits that "reproduce the metallic shimmer seen in some of the tropical chafers." Without a doubt, Vladimir Bohac's stunning paintings expand our horizons as Dr. Josef R. Winkler's text blows our little minds. B+

THE BRITISH INVASION: From the First Wave to the New Wave by Nicholas Schaffner (1982 McGraw-Hill)

For you anglophiles on a budget you get seven biographies here in one volume. In part one of this three hundred page opus you get the Beatles and five of the other towering superstar acts England gave us in the 1960's. There's the Rolling Stones, the Who, the Kinks, the Pink Floyd, and Jones. Plus, if you care, a long chapter on Marc Bolan who had a documentary about him directed by Richard Starkey, MBE.

Part two covers the remaining British hot one hundred from the early 60's through the early 80's. It's Adam and the Ants to the Zombies. It's a very fun read and it's fairly comprehensive. The only drawback is the late great Nicholas Schaffner farms out most of the hot hundred entries to other writers. Schaffner gives away Led Zeppelin, the Police, and Be Bop Deluxe to other scribes while wasting his talent on the Dave Clark Five, Herman's Hermits, and Freddie and the Dreamers. On the plus side Schaffner does indulge us with his thoughts on Roxy Music, Psychedelic Furs, and Mott the Hoople. So it's a mixed bag but very nourishing. A-

THE BRITISH INVASION**: How the Beatles and Other UK Bands Conquered America** by Bill Harry (2004 Chrome Dreams)

No! Please! Not Bill Harry! He strikes again. Say you want to slap together a bunch of junk about English pop bands of the 60's. Throw you-know what-band on the front cover and all of sudden you're in Barnes and Noble. Throw you-know-what band on the back cover and all of a sudden strangers are perusing you. In between, feature some crap about Peter Noone, Marilyn Monroe (why?), the Bee Gees, and Suzi Quatro (huh?) and you've got yourself a piece of nothing.

And if I see one more picture of Bill Harry with them I'm going to roll up in a big ball and die. F

THE CAMBRIDGE COMPANION TO THE BEATLES edited by Kenneth Womack (2009 Cambridge University)

When you think of the Beatles you don't think of Cambridge. At least I don't. Unlike Pink Floyd, the fabs never lived there or went to school there. Still, there is a certain highbrow, "It vaguely bothers me if someone knows something I don't know" attitude that emanates from the band (with the exception of Ringo). These guys were searchers. Just look at the seekers on the *SGT. PEPPER* cover. There's Aleister Crowley, Edgar Allan Poe, Robert Zimmerman, Lenny Bruce, T.E. Lawrence, and Oscar Wilde. This book encapsulates all the inner and outer exploration the band would undertake as they strolled down the long and winding road.

It is divided into three sections: Background, Works, and History/Influence. All three make a point of trying to impart facts and wisdom. Even the foreword by Anthony DeCurtis sheds some interesting light on things. It's much better than his somewhat similar introduction to Peter Brown's *The Love You Make*. Kind of like the difference between the U.K. *REVOLVER* and the U.S. *REVOLVER*. Mr. DeCurtis writes, "The Beatles are like a young artist who died tragically before his time." Right! When last seen together on *ABBEY ROAD* they were all still in their 20's and operating at peak efficiency with high level artistry. Much like James Dean, Jimi Hendrix, Janis Joplin, Kurt Cobain, Basquiat, Gram Parsons, Eddie Cochran, Buddy Holly, and Paul McCartney were. That last one just might be a rumor. Mr. DeCurtis, "The band never were (sic) tempted to hang on past their expiration date, cashing in on their audience's longing for days gone by and creating lucrative, mediocre music." That's where Wings come in. One of the eye openers in this book comes in the chapter on their works. My favorite album by them has always been *THE BEATLES*. It has been enriching my life since I've been a child (except for *WILD HONEY PIE*). Turns out there were good reasons I liked it the most. I never knew this before but it was the first post-modern album. The strategies utilized by the Beatles on *THE BEATLES* include, but are not limited to, bricolage, fragmentation, pastiche, reflexivity, plurality, irony, exaggeration, anti-representation, and meta art. No wonder it got past my defenses and touched my heart. I used the same tactics in the writing of this review. A-

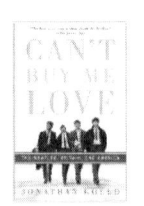

CAN'T BUY ME LOVE: The Beatles Britain and America by Jonathan Gould (Harmony 2007)

Only two years after Bob Spitz's *The Beatles: The Biography* here is another full length look at their lives from humble beginnings until the 1970 break-up. It is complete with obligatory epilogue that superficially covers the 70's solo years, John dying, and Paul writing *HERE TODAY* as a tribute to his slain comrade. It's a little better than Hunter Davies' *The Beatles* and Philip Norman's *Shout!* but that's not saying much. Jonathan Gould tries to go beyond their lives and their music. Gould wants to show the role they played in the history of their times and he succeeds to some degree. He is definitely a sharp thinker though he doesn't reach the level of intellectual criticism of an Ian MacDonald or a Wilfrid Meller. B+

THE CATCHER IN THE RYE by Jerome David Salinger (1951 Little, Brown)

Despite the fact that Lennon wrote three books himself, despite the fact his ex-wife and his mistress put out two memoirs each about their time with him, despite the fact that Yoko keeps authorizing new titles about him like there is no tomorrow, and despite the fact that many of his closest associates have written tell-all tomes about what he was really like *The Catcher in the Rye* is the work most associated with him. Whenever a crazed psychotic utilizes an old novel about a dysfunctional teenager as the impetus to shooting a world famous stranger to death in front of his apartment building that novel is always remembered as the reason for the tragedy. This is especially true when said psychotic believes he has literally become a character in a fictional story and that the next thing on Holden Caufield's mind after he left the carousel in Central Park would be taking a short walk over to the Dakota to kill a man who would not become famous in the U.S. until 13 years after the publication of Salinger's masterpiece. It's crazy!

I have some questions:

1. Holden Caufield tells dorm mate Robert Ackley that his red hunting cap is a "people shooting hat." Caufield shows his murderous intent by stating "I shoot people in this hat." Is there any other moment in *Catcher* that would lead anybody to believe it is an assassination manual or are two sentences all it takes for a sick mind?
2. Was Salinger a Beatles fan? He seemed more like a sing along with Mitch type to me.
3. Had Lennon ever read Salinger? If he had, did he ever imagine Holden Caufield would come not to save him but to send him on his way to the next life?
4. What did Salinger think of his classic story being used as an excuse for killing (or attempting to kill) the leader of rock's biggest band and the president of the United States? Hinkley utilized *Catcher* and Jodie Foster's prostitute in *Taxi Driver* as reasons to try and take out Reagan. In fact, he was in the huge crowd that gathered

at the Dakota shortly after midnight on Tuesday December 9th, 1980.
5. Would I ever have read *Catcher in the Rye* in 1981, if Lennon had not been shot? I'm guessing yes, because it was one of those books they wanted you to read in high school. However, I'm sure there would have been no *Catcher in the Rye* speeches in major motion pictures delivered by Hollywood icons Will Smith (*Six Degrees of Separation*) and Mel Gibson (*Conspiracy*) to Hollywood icons Donald Sutherland and Julia Roberts.
6. How can I go forward when I don't know which way I'm facing?   A+

A CELLARFUL OF NOISE by Brian Epstein and Derek Taylor (1964 Doubleday)

A gay man walks into a bar. He sees four attractive young men with long hair shaking their asses on a stage while wearing tight fitting leather trousers. He thinks they may have something. He doesn't like the racket they're making but he does like the trousers. So off they go together on a magical mystery tour. He puts them in suits. He gets them to stop cussing. He makes them perform *TILL THERE WAS YOU* from the Broadway hit *The Music Man*. He takes them all over the world. He goes on vacation with the leader of the band. He points out to the leader what men he finds attractive and why. He helps them, and helps them, and helps them until he can't help anymore.

Then the man takes a handful of pills and dies. And now you know the rest of the story. Good day!   C+

CHANGIN' TIMES: 101 Days That Shaped A Generation by Al Sussman (2013 Parading)

I always kind of thought the assassination of John Kennedy was tied psychologically to the arrival of the Beatles in America and I'm happy to report I was right. Al Sussman makes the connection explicit as he covers one of the most exciting and turbulent periods in recent U.S. history. As our friend Bob so eloquently put it, the times they were a changing. This book is a time machine. From that Friday in Dallas through the suddenly-out-of-place Arthur Godfrey Thanksgiving TV special through a New York New Years' Eve Sussman takes us back to the end of 1963. The catastrophe the country had gone through set the stage for the British invasion and leading the charge were our four new friends. Things would never be the same. But this book is about more than the terror unleashed by Lee Harvey Oswald and the most talked about *Ed Sullivan Show* ever. In between these world-shaking moments Sussman fills in the details about the shape of our country at this precarious time.

We witness the end of Vaughn Meader's career (as Lenny Bruce said, "What's Vaughn going to do now?"). We visit the war in Vietnam. We see the struggle for civil rights. We find the Surgeon General's Report spilling the beans on the danger inherent in smoking. ...and let us not forget sports (the toy department of life). The Jets played their last game at the Polo grounds (losing to the Buffalo Bills) before moving on to Shea Stadium. Joe Namath and O.J. Simpson (in Simpson's case setting the record for running yards in one season) would have very special moments at Shea but the most wonderful night at that famous stadium would be in 1965 when our lads played there after being introduced by, you guessed it, Ed Sullivan. The point is November 1963 - March 1964 was the period that set the tone for the 1960's and we the people were never the same. B+

COME TOGETHER: The Business Wisdom of the Beatles by Richard Courtney and George Cassidy (2011 Turner)

Richard Courtney is the founder of the Fab Four Festival. My dream is to one day be a guest speaker at the Fab Four Festival. So it is with great sadness that I must report that this book on the business wisdom of the Beatles is a piece of junk. If any rock band was known for its lack of business wisdom it was these guys. See Brian Epstein, Apple Records, the Apple Boutique, Apple Electronics, Zapple Records, Allen Klein, Harrison's A&M Records debacle, George's Handmade Films, the Hindenburg disaster, and the Great Depression. This is a self-help book on running your own business, based on advice gleaned from rock stars that ran their own business so badly they had to fire most of their friends. Genius! It's simply written and simply dreadful. I have the bad feeling they wrote this book just because they found a cute photo of the band looking at *The Financial Times* to use on the cover. The first sentence in the introduction is "Why another book on the Beatles?" Good question.   D-

THE COMPLETE IDIOT'S GUIDE TO THE BEATLES
by Richard Buskin (1998 Alpha)

Never has a book title rung so true. What market is this idiotic primer aimed at? If it's old people, it doesn't make any sense. What senior decides to embrace the world's most popular band decades after they broke up? As for young people, why would they want to find out about something from before their time? That seems like a history lesson and you know most kids today don't care about history. Of course, there are always exceptions to any rule and so there might be some young Americans interested. However, they would turn to the internet to find information. That leaves middle aged people, but the Beatle fans amongst them are already buying every DVD, album, and book thrown their way. Oh, now I get it. I'd like to thank all you middle agers for buying my book. Your support will allow me to sock some dough away for my golden years. Don't let me hear you say life's taking you nowhere. Good things about Richard Buskin's *Complete Idiot's Guide*:

1. It's more rock and roll than his first book, *Princess Diana: Her Life Story*. It turns out she also blew her mind out in a car.
2. It taught me that John's grammar school Quarry Bank has a similar architectural design as the

Dakota. That's kind of creepy. The past is never over. In fact, it's never past.
3. It has eight pages of color photos.
4. It is divided into chapters.

Any fools out there who want to start scratching the surface of the Beatles should follow my advice. Buy the two best overview albums available (*1962-1966* and *1967-1970*). Buy the books *Anthology*, *Ten Years That Shook the World* and *An Illustrated Record*. Buy the DVDs *Anthology* and *A Hard Day's Night*. Buy a VCR so you can play the VHS copy of *Let It Be* you found on eBay. I'd also recommend the documentary *The History of the Beatles* but it would have to be a bootleg copy and that's illegal. I hope you pass the audition. C-

CORN FLAKES WITH JOHN LENNON: And Other Tales from a Rock and Roll Life by Robert Hilburn (2009 Rodale)

This is the first of a series of books in which Robert Hilburn spends the morning with famous people. It's way better than *Pepto Bismol with Paul McCartney*. The introduction is by the greatest rock star to hit the planet since the 1970's, good old Bono. Bono's finally spills the beans on why he hated his first name (Paul) so much he changed it to Bono. It turns out he despised Wings with a passion when he was growing up and he wanted to get as far away from Paul as possible. Oddly enough, McCartney hated his first name (James) and decided to go with his middle name Paul. The only time Paul ever used his first name for show biz purposes was for his pathetic 1973 TV special entitled *James Paul McCartney*.

Robert Hilburn got together one morning in the fall of 1980 and had breakfast with John Lennon. He found John to be "down to earth." He and John had the same "favorite rock hero, Elvis." He thought John was doing drugs in the lounge next to the recording studio but "Lennon's private stash turned out to be a giant-size Hershey bar." Lennon felt, "The split up in 1970 was probably the best thing that ever happened to the Beatles myth." Lennon said about his five year retirement from the rock scene, "It was the hardest thing I've ever had to do in my life - not make music. Not because I had this love for music or because I was so creative and I couldn't bear not to be creative, but because I felt that I didn't exist unless my name was in the gossip columns of *Rolling Stone* or the *Daily News* or whatever. Then it dawned on me that I do still exist."

I didn't find the rest of Hilburn's interview with Lennon to be insightful or interesting. So I was hoping that I would dig the conversations he has in this book with other rock stars. But, alas... C-

<u>THE CYNICAL IDEALIST: A Spiritual Biography of John Lennon</u> by Gary Tillery (2009 Quest)

This is a Very Serious Work about John. I believe this tome will be studied for thousands of years. It must be treasured. I'm writing a rebuttal volume entitled *The Drunken Drugged-out Violent Sarcastic Obnoxious Callous Hypocritical Cynical Idealist*.

This is a spiritual biography so get ready for some piercing revelations about the old boy. According to Gary Tillery, Lennon "crashed" in 1965 (whatever that means) and then began "...an honest search for meaning." If you mean this was the year his dentist spiked his coffee with acid at a dinner party giving John his first inadvertent trip to be followed by countless trips taken on purpose, then yeah, 1965 was the beginning of his honest search for meaning. It was also the beginning of several crazy years of navel gazing, bad trips, bad judgment, dissolution of ego, and great songwriting that culminated with an insane love for an East Village gold digger and a 1968 official Beatle meeting in which John "maybe a bit too spiritual" Lennon announced to the holy trinity that he was Jesus Christ, back and ready for action.

Now get this, fab fans! Gary Tillery takes the cake by putting John Lennon in the same category with one of the greatest philosophers ever to grace the planet. You guessed it, "With Socrates, Lennon encourages us to view experts with cynicism and think for ourselves." Don't worry. That is exactly what I'm doing.

Lennon's "...legacy endures as a beacon of truth that urges us to be the change we want to see." Every day I kneel at my John Lennon altar and look inside myself. Too bad there's nothing there.

But thank the lord and lady, Mister Tillery is not all about genuflecting "Lennon had his share of faults, as anyone who has read about him knows very well. He tended to be abusive both verbally and physically, and existed in a self-centered fog that left him inconsiderate of the feelings of those around him." Now that's the house husband I know! 　　　　　　　　　　B

DAKOTA DAYS by John Green (1983 St. Martin's)

If you're looking for a down to earth account of Lennon's last half decade what better source could there be than Yoko's professional tarot card reader. Ono hired John Green in 1974 and he was there with the power couple as they got back together and lived a Greta Garbo/Howard Hughes type existence. It turns out John was "only human" (who knew?) and "the last six years of his life were his darkest" (say it isn't so).

John Green tells us that tarot readers "are by both preference and necessity a discreet lot." Right! There is nothing more discreet than doing a tell-all book that exploits the private moments of your clients. Lucky for us, Mr. Green remembers every last detail and every word of every important conversation he ever had with J&Y. His recall is amazing! "You may well ask how this card reader remembered all this information." I was kind of wondering about that. "I have a fine memory." Well, that explains it then.

Just in case you're beginning to get the feeling that Green is one of those horrible authors out for a quick buck earned off a terrible tragedy he sets your mind at ease: "There are certain elements of the story that I have left out because they do not belong in print. After all, even public figures deserve their share of privacy." Discretion is the better part of valor.

You'll learn the truth here. John was interested in Celtic mythology, "vast quantities of cheap booze", and searching for the Spear of Destiny. One time Lennon asked Green to get drunk with him, "We'll get disgusting and abuse the wife a bit." John was always a romantic.

Despite the fact that Green was able to divine the future and communicated with the spirit world ("I'm psychic") his fortune telling was a little off in the fall of 1980. On December 9th Yoko abruptly fired him. You can't win them all. C-

A DAY IN THE LIFE: The Music and Artistry of the Beatles by Mark Hertsgaard (1995 Delacorte)

This is an examination of the music and artistry of the Beatles. Unfortunately the analysis couldn't be more rote. Mark lets us know *I FEEL FINE* was a "first rate piece of work", *DAY TRIPPER* is "one of their best pure rock 'n' roll songs", and *ABBEY ROAD* was a "masterpiece." Thanks for the insight. Now when I listen to the music it's like I'm hearing it for the first time. My favorite part of this book comes when Hertsgaard shares his opinion that "John regarded Yoko as his artistic equal, if not superior, but it was clear that he was a minority of one in this respect." Exactly! This book is further hurt by the release in the same period of the greatest Beatles book ever, Ian MacDonald's *Revolution in the Head*. If you're looking for analysis of the music and artistry of the Beatles that's what you should read. Accept no substitute. D

DAYS THAT I'LL REMEMBER: Spending Time with John Lennon and Yoko Ono by Jonathan Cott (2013 Doubleday)

The man who conducted the first and last _Rolling Stone_ interviews with John (both far inferior to Jann Wenner's _Lennon Remembers_ sessions) takes a trip down memory lane. There we find warm and gracious John and Yoko who help Jonathan understand that nothing is real. It's an illusion. John says, "…the Christians or the Jews were doing something to me. I don't think that anymore 'cause I found out that it doesn't fucking work! All you're doing is jacking off, screaming what your mommy and daddy did." Speak for yourself, John. Lennon also says, "Most assholes just accept what is and get on with it, right?" I'll try John. I'll really try. B

DECEMBER 8, 1980: The Day John Lennon Died by Keith Elliot Greenberg (2010 Backbeat)

To commemorate the 30th anniversary of the worst night in Beatles history Backbeat books presents a publication fit for masochists, lovers of the macabre, pop culture historians, and true crime addicts. All the gruesome bloody details are here. All the craziness of Lennon's assassin is captured. John Lennon was having a good day, beginning with a _Rolling Stone_ photo session, and a little later, before returning to the studio to work on his new record, giving an enthusiastic interview, declaring, "I consider that my work won't be finished until I'm dead and buried, and I hope that's a long, long time."

John's killer was a Todd Rundgren fan and he interpreted Todd's song ROCK AND ROLL PUSSY to be about the Beatle and felt Todd's song AN ELPEE'S WORTH OF TOONS captured where he was at as he got ready to kill Lennon. Beyond insane, he later recalled to CNN's Larry King, "He was living inside a paperback novel, J.D. Salinger's *The Catcher in the Rye*. He was vacillating between catching the first taxi home, back to Hawaii, (and) killing...an icon." Unfortunately, he went with the latter. "If he didn't kill John he had other ideas-like going to the crown of the Statue of Liberty with the other tourists, then jumping off. People would remember him for that."

Just like JFK fans keep going back to November 22, 1963 over and over as they remember where they were when they heard the news, I am one of those Beatle nuts who keep on thinking about 12/08/1980. How I skipped my usual *Monday Night Football* ritual because I was so tired. How my brother Mark woke me up to tell me Howard Cosell had just announced that John Lennon was dead (John Lennon's dead/I can't get it through my head/though it's been so many years/John Lennon's dead). I was mad at being woken up so I said to my brother, "What do you want me to do about it?" The next morning as I watched the *Today* show I assumed it was a drug overdose. It wasn't until later in the day that I found out he was shot by a demented "fan." I went to school but didn't go to any classes. Instead my friend Craig and I headed downtown to hang out. I was sad. Craig didn't care about Lennon. He just wanted to play hooky. That week a local movie theatre played *Magical Mystery*

Tour (the TV movie that had a British soundtrack double EP that featured a booklet with a photo of Lennon standing before a sign that read "The best way to go is by MDC" and was released on Dec. 8, 1967). I couldn't enjoy it. I was grieving too much for a man I never met.

If you're like me and you're a Beatlemaniac who remembers Christmas 1980 as one of the most horrible times in your life then this book will bring it all home vividly. If you're a youngster who missed this moment it won't have as much impact but I guess you can still get a little something out of it. Like most of the JFK assassination books it's not a great read but the subject matter draws you in. Happiness is definitely not a warm gun. B+

'EVERY SOUND THERE IS': The Beatles' Revolver and the Transformation of Rock and Roll edited by Russell Reising (2002 Ashgate)

A whole bunch of musically inclined intellectuals are gathered here to pay tribute to what many find to be the greatest long player ever made. Forget about Klaus Voorman's gauche cover and listen to the colour of your dreams. Here you'll find sections on the band's vocal harmonization, how they fugued the postmodern, how they birthed the psychedelic sound, how they explored female identity via *ELEANOR RIGBY*, and these obvious ideas about *TOMORROW NEVER KNOWS*:

1. It is a deeply introspective self-portrait.

2. It transcends the subjective and embraces the holistic of metaphysical experience.
3. It places an overall emphasis on timbral colour.
4. It utilizes an upward movement in pitch which can be compared with an hallucinogenic high.
5. It's shifting textual relationships are collages and soundscapes that suggest a disorientation of more conventionalized musical structures that stimulate a sense of absorption with/within the sound itself.

I couldn't have put it better myself. Though, I always thought of it as John's tripping his head off on acid while reading the *Tibetan Book of the Dead* song. This is the place to turn to for chapters on the tonal family resemblance in REVOLVER, the use of accidentals on the album, and how REVOLVER influenced Roger Waters and Roger Barrett as they set their controls for the heart of the sun. A lot of this is over my head but I like to laugh and when I read this I've got something I can laugh about, my complete lack of musical knowledge.   A-

FAB: An Intimate Life of Paul McCartney by Howard Sounes (2010 Da Capo)

I'm one of those ghoulish people glad about November 9, 1966. I think it was probably for the best. Some people call it the day the music died. I call it dying young and leaving a good looking corpse. Did we really want to see Paul McCartney grow old? To go bald, to get fat, to stop being cute. For every James Dean who left the scene early and remains eternally young in our mind's eye there is the bloated corpse of a Marlon Brando. For every Bob Zimmerman, who checks out in his 20's thanks to a motorcycle accident, we've got a nine lives cat like David Crosby stumbling and bumbling through the new millennium. Don't we want our heroes to remain forever vibrant? Can you imagine Zimmerman in his 70's doing Victoria Secret commercials, recording Christmas albums (the guy is Jewish for chrissake), and doing one of those horrible American Songbook collection of standards that Stewart and Ronstandt keep foisting on the public on their way to their graves. It's alright for excellent singers like Rod and Linda to pull this shit (they were always interpreters) but can you imagine Bob "I've got a dead frog in my throat" Zimmerman doing it? It is to cringe.

The cover of this book says it all. James Paul McCartney is all alone. He's staring at the camera, so adorable in his little black suit, with his whole life ahead of him. He lived faster and harder in the four years between *LOVE ME DO* and his journey to the undiscovered country than most of us will if we make it to 100. He was racing at the speed of sound. He traveled the world being worshipped by fans. There were women throwing themselves at him. There were men throwing themselves at him. There were drugs and drink and parties. There were stadiums filled with people screaming so loudly he and the others couldn't be heard as they played their music.

Paul was angry that night. He wanted to stay on the magical mystery tour. The others wanted to get off. They weren't as outgoing as he was. They weren't as adventurous as he was. Ringo liked playing cards, John liked sitting around getting high, and George liked meditating and practicing the sitar. They had enough of being Beatles but Paul wanted to keep rocking. If the crowds were too much, if traveling was too hard, then how about playing little clubs in London on the spur of the moment under different crazy names? But the others just wanted to make music in the tiny little studio at Abbey Road. Why face the public anymore? Why not relax for once?

Paul stormed out of the studio after yet another horrible argument where he tried to get them to see it his way. Paul believed that only time would tell if he was right or he was wrong. He got into his Aston Martin and he sped away through London town. He crashed. Paul didn't notice that a light had changed.

We were spared the inevitable decline of his music. None of these rock guys are ever really too good after they hit thirty. It's usually all downhill. Look at the Stones, if you can stand to. Would you really want to see senior citizen Paul out there playing the oldies circuit trading on the memories of George and John? Think how unseemly it would be.

Plus, don't forget the great songs it inspired grieving John Lennon to write. We wouldn't have some of those masterpieces if McCartney hadn't blown his mind out in a car. There would be no *A DAY IN THE LIFE, WHY DID HE DO IT IN THE ROAD, DON'T LET ME DOWN,* and *REMEMBER* ("the ninth of November").

It's well known that some of the fans could never believe that Paul had shaken off the mortal coil. They write books and articles about how he's still alive. But he's deceased, folks. Get used to it. Andy Kaufman is gone, Jim Morrison is no more, and the king of rock and roll is dead. Keep in mind what John Lennon said, "Everybody's acting like it's the end of the world. But you've got all the old records there if you want to reminisce." Boy, that's cold. B+

FAB FOUR FAQ: Everything Left to Know About the Beatles...and More! by Stuart Shea and Robert Rodriguez (2007 Hal Leonard)

WARNING: This is only partially a book of frequently asked questions about the Beatles. There are lots of infrequently asked questions as well elucidating crucial facts about:

1. Beatle connections to Davy Jones, Trini Lopez, Phil Collins, Bertrand Russell and Andy Williams (chapter 40).

2. Rogues in their life like Bruno Koschmider, Nicky Byrne, and David A. Noebel (chapter 45).

3. Songs about the band from the 1960's like *A LETTER TO THE BEATLES* by The Four Preps, *TREAT HIM TENDER MAUREEN (NOW THAT RINGO BELONGS TO YOU)* by Angie and the Chicklettes, and *POP HATES THE BEATLES* by Allan Sherman (chapter 35).

4. Odd covers of Beatle compositions such as *DAY TRIPPER* by Mae West, *ROCKY RACCOON* by Lena Horne, and *HEY JUDE* by Bing Crosby (chapter 34).

5. Unexplained Beatle trivia such as why George yells to Paul, "John smells like shit!" during the original version of the

Revolution video, who are "Kevin and all at Number 9" as credited on the poster included in *THE BEATLES* album, and why does the *LET IT BE* album feature a red, not a green, apple on the label (chapter 47).

By far the best chapters are 9 (about their most famous photo sessions), 11 (about their cinematic achievements including Paul's *The Family Way* score, John in Richard Lester's *How I Won the War*, George's soundtrack for *Wonderwall*, and Ringo with Raquel Welch in *The Magic Christian*), and 13 (about the essential Beatle books to buy for your home library).

Half of what this book says is meaningless but I guess to fill 500 pages there had to be a lot of filler. So if you're willing to be a good little Beatlemaniac and separate the wheat from the chaff you'll be okay. This is not a book for novices. It is a scraping of the bottom of the apple barrel for fanatics. Of course, I'm one of those so I give this piece of work a   B

P.S.: Robert Rodriguez was to do a much better job with his follow up book *Fab Four FAQ 2.0* which covers the first decade of the solo years.

FAB FOUR FAQ 2.0: The Beatles Solo Years, 1970 - 1980 by Robert Rodriguez (2010 Backbeat)

There are many classic books that focus on the group during the 1960's. This is the one classic to focus on them during the 1970's. It was a time of great production. As four solo artists they cranked out 30 studio albums between the breakup and Lennon's death. Not to mention enough material on their 45's to fill two more long players. Robert Rodriguez reminds us of the excitement generated by the avalanche of product. Each Beatle's solo career followed the same script. Each one hit their peak in the early 70's with an album that was commercially huge and critically acclaimed. John had *IMAGINE*, Paul had *BAND ON THE RUN*, George had *ALL THINGS MUST PASS*, and Ringo had *RINGO*. Then they struggled to match these works. This is the story of that struggle. We get chapters on their flop singles and their worst releases. I love John's *SOMETIME IN NEW YORK CITY* (sometimes I think I'm the only one who does) but Rodriguez hates it's lyrical content so much that he pans it despite allowing that "...musically, John is in top form: his vocals are powerful and impassioned." Mr. Rodriguez despises Paul's *WONDERFUL CHRISTMASTIME* as well and points out Retrocrush.com deemed it the "...worst Christmas song of all time." I like it as much as I like John's terrific *HAPPY XMAS*. The holiday song that should have been singled out for derision is George Harrison's dreadful *DING DONG, DING DONG*. Rodriguez also doesn't care for Paul's first solo album *McCARTNEY* but considering it features the wonderful *MAYBE I'M AMAZED* I am amazed that he feels this way. In 400 action packed pages we get all the details on their most memorable live solo performances, their cool guest appearances on other star's recordings (Paul with Rod Stewart, John with Mick Jagger, George with Cheech and Chong), and the movies they made as actors and producers. You've haven't lived till you see Ringo's spaghetti western *Blindman*. This is the kind of book you'll go back to over and over not just as a reference guide to those crazy years but to savor the enthusiasm and insight the author brings to these proceedings. A+

P.S.: On page 446 Rodriguez says that "…no photos taken after 1969 containing more than two ex-Beatles are known to exist prior to Paul, George, and Ringo reuniting for *ANTHOLOGY* during the 1990's." Actually, there are photos of Paul, George, and Ringo together at both Clapton's 1979 wedding and Ringo's 1981 wedding.

FIRE AND RAIN: The Beatles, Simon and Garfunkel, James Taylor, CSNY, and the Lost Story of 1970 by David Browne (2011 Da Capo)

What a zany concept! It's all about 1970 and how rock changed as the Beatles broke up, Simon and Garfunkel split, and CSN&Y disbanded. Of course, it wasn't that much of a change because 1973 saw all four of our heroes performing on the *RINGO* album, 1974 saw the CSN&Y reunion tour, and 1975 saw a new hit single from Tom and Jerry called *MY LITTLE TOWN*.

Allegedly this is the lost story of 1970 but I couldn't find anything of the sort as I waded through what could be a vintage *Crawdaddy* puff piece. Nice eight pages of black and white photos, though. They're suitable for extremely small frames. The one of David "I can't believe I made it this long" Crosby posing with pillow flag gun to his head and a joint in his mouth takes first prize.

As a bonus for soft rock lovers this story includes the adventures of James "flying machine" Taylor who also broke up in 1970....with heroin. C-

THE FIFTH BEATLE: The Brian Epstein Story by Vivek J. Tiwary (2013 M)

Just when I thought I'd seen it all, along comes this graphic novel about the Beatles' most well-known manager Brian Epstein. In the works are more comic books about such important figures in the fab legend as Allan Williams and Allen Klein (also known as the Als), Neil Aspinall, and George's gardener Ishvish Kersmunkel

Considering Stan Lee's Marvel comics had already covered Brian and the Beatles in comic book form in the 70's and *National Lampoon* had done likewise in their laugh out loud way (the Beatles would take Brian's help on the way to the top but they would not sleep with him) you'd think all bases would be covered. But, no! This is an imaginative look at the Brian

Epstein we never really knew despite the autobiography and the two biographies. It is handsomely illustrated by Andrew C. Robinson and Kyle Baker and nicely lettered by Steve Dutro. It is poignantly written by incomparable graphic novelist Vivek J. Tiwary. It is boldly surreal and bluntly honest. It is more suited for adults than impressionable children. It's not NC 17 like it could have been but it is PG 13. It has John saying, "fucking" which is his favorite word by all accounts. It shows the band with groupies. It presents Brian being beaten up by a sailor who didn't appreciate his lifestyle. It shows John and Brian on a beach, boy watching. It highlights Brian's drug taking. It represents Lee Oswald's deed as "BANG! BANG! BANG." It shows Brian having sex. It tells us that Brian died as Ganesh, the Hindu elephant God, removed all obstacles to visiting the undiscovered country. Better make that an R rating, children under 17 not allowed to look at this without parent or guardian present. B+

FROM YESTERDAY TO TODAY, LIFE: The Beatles by the editors of Life (1996 Time)

When this came out nearly twenty years ago today, I felt like it was a little flimsy for $24.95 (U.S.) and $33.95 (Canada). It's only 125 pages and it has photos I'd already seen a thousand times. You get one photo of them with Peter Best, a lot of photos with Ringo including the last session in August 1969, and then like so many books it jumps to John on December 8, 1980. So if you can find it dirt cheap at a garage sale or on Amazon or you're giving it to a teenager to turn them on to ancient history it might be worth picking up. Otherwise, I would stick with Harry Benson's *The Beatles in the Beginning* supplemented by *Anthology* for the best in pretty pictures. Plus, *Anthology* has countless wonderful quotes from the four principals about the golden years.   C+

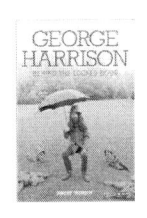

GEORGE HARRISON: Behind the Locked Door by Graeme Thomson (2015 Omnibus)

I'm not sure there is a need for a new biography of Georgie boy. After all, he hasn't been up to much the last fifteen years. He's been keeping a low profile. He wasn't at the opening of *Love* in Las Vegas. He didn't bother to take part when Larry King interviewed Ringo and Paul. At the Grammys in 2014 when they celebrated the 50th anniversary of the first Ed Sullivan show he was conspicuous in his absence. But I have an open mind. So here goes and good luck.

According to the hype this is a "rich, insightful account of (his) extraordinary life and career." They must mean the Beatle part because I don't remember anything too spectacular after the breakup. Though, I did kind of enjoy the *TRAVELING WILBURYS VOL. 1*, *Withnail and I*, and his cameo in *All You Need Is Cash*.

Graeme Thomson tells us that "The life of Harrison seemed to magnify the essential paradoxes of human nature." I'll go along with this one. He was famous but wanted to be left alone. He expected superstar treatment but just make sure to treat him like a normal person. He was intensely spiritual but also money grubbing.

In a surprising move Thomson starts off in his prologue by skewering George post-1971. I did not see that coming. I figure the people who'd want a new look at G.H. in 2015 would be the kind of true believers who'd get some fawning praise from the author. But instead we get "the promise of his first year as a solo artist was quickly spent" and his much derided 1974 tour "provided final confirmation that Harrison was no longer a genuine contender." Wow. Less than a half decade since the split and it's already "final confirmation" of his mediocre solo career. But there's more "A graph denoting the progress of his career in the ten years post-Bangladesh...would look like a very swift descent down a very steep Alp: lawsuits, increasingly lackluster albums, gloom, illness, drink and hard drugs, domestic discord, spiritual conflict, retreat. By the end of the decade he was, creatively and culturally, an irrelevance. An old fogey by his mid-thirties….." This sounds like how I would write about him, complete with litany.

Chapter 1: George musing on how he went from Arnold Grove to Friar Park, "There was no way I wasn't going to be in the Beatles...it was a set-up." It was all fated to be, I guess.

Chapter 2: You're not going to believe this but George dug playing guitar. He had a "love affair with the instrument."

Chapter 3: He felt a "slight superiority complex" from Paul and "particularly Lennon." It was obvious even before they were famous that some Beatles were more equal than other Beatles.

Chapter 4: As a young pop star "he was still largely without airs and graces." But he still seemed "both annoyed and pleased" when being stopped for an autograph.

Chapter 5: George said, "I felt ignored and undervalued for years." How weird! The world is worshipping you but Lennon and McCartney treat you like an unimportant junior partner.

Chapter 6: On *SGT. PEPPER*, "I didn't really like making that album much." How weird! The LP that was acclaimed by the world as their masterpiece was the one that George cared least about. He only got one song on the set (*ONLY A NORTHERN SONG* was thrown on the scrap heap) and the rest of the band didn't even play on it.

Chapter 7: "The other Beatles had taken to calling him His Holiness behind his back." Yet it was Ringo who played the pope in a movie (*Litzomania* directed by Ken Russell).

Chapter 8: Ringo, "He had the love-personality, and the bag of anger." I believe that about sums George up. He was a little sweet and very sour.

Chapter 9: Bobby Whitlock, "I know his meditation got in the way of he and Pattie's relationship." Not to mention his best friend.

Chapter 10: Bangladesh is a triumph before everything starts going downhill. "It shines like a beacon of practical, clear-headed, emphatic activism" compared to John and Yoko's "bed-ins, bagism, and myriad wooly gestures."

Chapter 11: George took a road trip in 1972. His wife wasn't invited. "The passenger seat was reserved for Krishna." He drove for "...23 hours and chanted all the way." Then he came back to planet earth.

Chapter 12: The mostly dismal '74 jaunt. "The pall of disappointment hung over the tour as it progressed."

Chapter 13: The last half of the 70's was so bad new music wise that " Martin Scorsese's 210 minute documentary makes no mention whatsoever of the records he made between 1975 and 1979" and "few people were terribly interested in his music anymore, regardless of its quality." I personally like *CRACKERBOX PALACE* and *BLOW AWAY* which are both catchy singles.

Chapter 14: In 1981 George received a "death threat from an American who phoned to say he had a gun and an air ticket and was on his way to kill him...later arrested in Baltimore." This would be chilling even if John wasn't shot outside his home and George wasn't stabbed nearly to death in his living room.

Chapter 15: The second and last tour. Japan this time, not America. "For a long time Harrison had seemed detached from the real world, but in recent years he appeared more out of touch than ever."

In between chapter 15 and 16 George states, "I have a son who needs a father, so I have to stick around for him...other than that, I can't think of much reason to be here." His wife Olivia must have loved this quote (preserved on video). Georgie was a romantic till the end.

Chapter 16: He shoves his producer of choice into the chair for the reunion with James and Richard. "His final-perhaps only-

victory in the Beatles was to get Jeff Lynne to produce the 'new' songs."

Epilogue: At the Royal Albert Hall Concert for George only three Harrison compositions come from later than 1973. No surprise there.

Not a bad try at making George seem interesting. I didn't find it rich and insightful but it was mildly enjoyable, kind of like a good Harrison solo album. B+

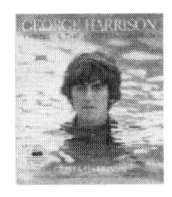

GEORGE HARRISON: Living in the Material World
by Olivia Harrison (2011 Abrams)

I like this a little better than the HBO documentary by Marty Scorsese that it was marketed in tandem with. Mainly because I don't have to listen to dreadfully boring talking head interviews with Eric "I stole George's wife away from him" Clapton, Jackie "Scottish race car driver" Stewart and Terry "couldn't make a watchable movie if he tried" Gilliam. Not to mention having to see Olivia Harrison and Paul McCartney talk about George cheating on her is so sad. McCartney points out that it was because George was a regular red blooded male who liked the things men do. Great rationale, Paul!

Oddly enough, Olivia chose a publishing firm called Abrams. That's like Yoko putting out her annual look back at Lennon book with a publishing house called Chapmans.

Marty Scorsese starts the book off with his memories of hearing guess what three record solo album. The Academy Award winning director clues us into G. H.'s life of, "...harmony, balance, and serenity." If anybody didn't have a life like that (despite trying to cultivate that type of existence) it was Harrison, who felt pestered by the fans and the media for nearly 40 years. His strong interest in meditation was all about getting away from the stress of great fame and great expectations.

Then we get acclaimed novelist Paul Theroux who clues us in that the guitarist was, "...at odds with himself, but who isn't?" Olivia chimes in with knowledge of how much her curmudgeon husband despised the material world and all that it requires.

The rest of this jumbo sized treasure trove is lovingly selected photos of George. The highlights are:

1. Shopping for guitars with Lennon.
2. On a rooftop with L/M looking like the Clash.
3. The quartet holding hands with Little Richard.
4. Visiting the Statue of Liberty on his trip alone to Manhattan in 1963. Just another tourist who hardly anyone in America had heard of. The women walk right by him without noticing anything special.
5. On top of the Empire State Building where no one pays him any mind. I know sometimes he wished he could have gone back to those anonymous days.
6. On David Frost discussing TM.
7. With Brian jones next to a pool.
8. Posing yoga style in front of a fireplace painted by The Fool.
9. Hanging with Bob and Sara in Woodstock.

10. Hanging out the window with Bob where they both look peaceful and contented away from the spotlight.
11. Playing tennis with Bob at the Isle of Wight.
12. In the yard with the gnomes.
13. On stage for Bangladesh.
14. Petting a cat with Ravi.
15. With Eric Idle in Tunisia.
16. Hugging Peter Sellers.
17. Sitting in a tree with Olivia.
18. Enjoying the sunshine in India 1994.

A bit pricey at $40 unless you're a dedicated fan but if you don't care about your karma you can pick up one a lot cheaper by skipping the register at Barnes and Noble and heading straight for the exit.   B

GET BACK: The Unauthorized Chronicle of the Beatles' "Let It Be" Disaster by Doug Sulpy and Ray Schweighardt (1997 St. Martin's)

This is all too much for me to take. Sure, I enjoy the 24 compact disc bootleg series that gives us every second of the fabs during January 1969. Sure, I love dragging myself through the grainy 80 minutes of *Let It Be* on VHS over and over. Sure, I wore out my vinyl copy of *RENAISSANCE MINSTRELS VOLUME II* by playing it backwards, forewords, and sideways. But this is ridiculous!

Gigantic Beatlemaniacs Doug and Ray give us a very dry rundown of every fart, cough, and hiccup that occurred during the fabled Glyn Johns' sessions and yet I must admit I'm so cracked that I kind of enjoyed it. To give credit where credit is due, in the introduction they refer to the 1968 double record set *THE BEATLES* as *THE BEATLES*.   B

<u>GLASS ONION: The Beatles in Their Own Words</u> <u>by Geoffrey Giuliano & Vrnda Devi (1999 Da Capo)</u>

Geoffrey Giuliano is one of the most prolific Beatle authors. He's great when he sticks to assembling memorabilia for coffee table books. He's poor when he writes about the band. He's decent when he collates obscure interviews together to form a trade paperback like this one. To get an idea of where Geoffrey's head is at check out how many pages he allots to each Beatle being interviewed. John gets 30 plus pages. Paul gets 50 plus pages. George gets 50 plus pages. Pete Best gets 10 pages. Ringo gets two pages. I gather from this that Mr. Giuliano believes Ringo is the fifth Beatle.

Mr. Giuliano is a very spiritual person who remembers when the world was a better place. Let me turn you on to his feelings:

1. "Today (1999), the world in which we live is so incredibly boring, bland, and unexciting that one can hardly be blamed for looking back over one's shoulder at the unequaled artistry, affable lunacy, and spiritual

poke in the ribs that was the Beatles and company in their time."
2. "I...wonder where all the good sex, hip talk, and utopian pipe dreams we shared in the sixties have gone."
3. "Gone are Lenny Bruce, George Carlin, and Dick Gregory, replaced not nearly as effectively by the questionable wit of Beavis and Butthead, Daisy Fuentes, and Kathie Lee Gifford. It's no accident that Jerry Seinfeld's famous sitcom about 'nothing' became the biggest thing on toast."
4. "These days Rosemary Clooney is Celine Dion is Tipper Gore is Geraldo Rivera is Katie Couric and so many squares and pompous airheads too numerous to mention."
5. "I came up in a time when there was an honest chance of finding a prophet on nearly every street corner. New ideas were everywhere and people were happy to at least listen. Nowadays nobody's really talking, so I walk the streets without expectation, chanting my mantra, looking past the golden arches, burned out buildings, and seamy technology dives that litter the landscape, remembering a time long before. The sixties are dead, long live the Fab Four! Hare Krishna Hare Krishna Rama Rama Rama Hare."

Now, here's how I feel about how Mr. Geoffrey Giuliano's thought provoking and eye opening look at where the world is at nowadays:

It's too bad that the last 45 years have been so horrible, so close minded. I wish that my life hadn't been boring, bland, and unexciting. But I had the bad luck of being born in the greatest decade the world has ever known but being too young to appreciate it. What a cruel trick fate has played on me. I missed the good sex and the hip talk. All I ever experienced was bad sex and square talk in burned out buildings next to McDonalds. Oh, how I wish I could get away from seamy technology and hear some new ideas. But I'm stuck with culture the way it is. There have been no truly funny and insightful comedians after 1970. There have been no great television programs, movies, concerts, paintings, books, or music since the end of the sixties. It's a vast wasteland. Ever check out the internet? It's just a bunch of advertising, grotesque pornography, and email. We don't talk to each other anymore. We type at each other and don't even get me started about Facebook. I try to have real friends who I see in person. But it doesn't work out. Nowadays nobody's really talking. I want people to hear me, to be happy to at least listen. But no one will. So I sit at my computer and type words day after day about the divine messiahs, the laughing freemen, the only band that ever really mattered, the group that changed the world and spread hope throughout the universe, the quartet that opened up our hearts and our minds to new possibilities, the only people that are really truly real to me, the men who I have taken into my heart, the men you should take into your heart. All hail the boys from Liverpool from whom all good things come. I would give them everything I have just to sit at their table. Just a smile from them would lighten everything, lighten my burden, and give me hope, help me cope with this heavy load while I try to reach them with all my heart and soul. Have you heard the word? The word is love, love, love. All you need is love! Give Peace a Chance!   B-

THE GOSPEL ACCORDING TO THE BEATLES by Steve Turner (2006 Westminster John Knox)

When four great saints meet it is a humbling experience. Steve "I actually interviewed John Lennon" Turner affirms what we all instinctively knew. What Mr. Lennon told the noted theological journal *Playboy*, "I'm a most religious fellow." This explains his blasphemous statement, "Christianity will go. It will vanish and shrink. We're more popular than Jesus." On the other hand, to be fair, George "I will not shave my head and wear robes" Harrison was a religious fanatic. He's so fine, his sweet lord. This is well written and quite engaging. A-

A HARD DAY'S NIGHT: A Complete Pictorial Record of the Movie edited by J. Philip Di Franco (1978 Penguin)

In the 19th century there was an exciting scientific breakthrough. It was called photography. It gave people the ability to capture images of their loved ones without having to bring in a portrait painter. You could have somebody stand in front of a photographic camera for a few days and eventually there would be a blinding flash and presto, you had a black and white keepsake to treasure for eternity. But wait. Things got even more exciting. Motion pictures were invented. That's right. These pictures moved. To make it even better they added sound to the equation so you could hear beautiful music over the images. This is where the Beatles came in. When they were growing up in the 1940's and 1950's they would go to movie houses in Liverpool, England and watch films. They saw Elvis Presley up on the screen singing his heart out. The girls around them in the theatre would shriek, moan, and cry. John Lennon remembered thinking, "That's a good job." So when Beatlemania capsized the world it was inevitable that the band would follow in the footsteps of the king. They would star in their own black and white visual extravaganza, a jukebox musical if you will. It was named after some offhand Yogi Berra type Ringo quote (or maybe not, it's also mentioned in John Lennon's book *In His Own Write*). Thus was released *A Hard Day's Night*. It perfectly captured Beatlemania it all its glory. Every time the band went out in public they were trampled by hordes of teenage girls who wanted to tear their clothes off and cut off their hair for souvenirs. Jolly good fun. When the movie played in the theatres fans went to see it over and over. It was the *Star Wars* of its day. Unfortunately, for over a decade after that the only time fans in the U.S. could see the damn thing was rare repertory theatre screenings or occasionally on television. To make matters worse the TV showings featured scratchy and extensively edited prints interrupted by a million damn commercials. But the fans had to take it. What else could they do?

Then, one glorious day in the late 1970's, the Chelsea House book publication outfit noticed that there was a best-selling book about the Marx brothers called *Why a Duck*. With video cassettes in their infancy, some genius realized they could take Marx brothers movies and turn them into books. Show the images from the flicks and add in word balloons featuring the dialogue and finally you could study these movies from the comfort of your rocking chair any time you wanted.

So Chelsea House decided to do the same for the Beatles first effort. Throw in Andrew Sarris' famous review in the leftist radical commie weekly Village Voice, "The trouble with sociological analysis is that it is unconcerned with aesthetic values", "I speak affectionately of their depravity", "They may not be worth a paragraph in six months", and "Their entertaining message seems to be that everyone is a person and that includes Beatles and squealing sub-adolescents as much as Negroes and women and so-called senior citizens." Add in a lengthy interview with director Richard Lester, "I know in my own mind what surrealism means to me-but it very rarely is what it means to most people," and "John Lennon's interest in beards was developed in *Help!* in that scene where they disguise themselves." Thanks for clearing up that mystery.

 Nowadays you can get the deluxe Criterion Blu-ray edition with gobs of extras and remastered crystal clear audio and video. But back then, in the waning days of the 1970's, this is all we had. Sad isn't it?   C+

HAVING READ THE BOOK by Greg Sterlace (2015 LuLu)

Just what the world needs, a Beatle book about Beatle books. In these fast paced times it's hard for a Beatlemaniac to keep up with the endless onslaught of fab picture books, biographies, cook books, graphic novels, discographys, tell-alls, memoirs, as told tos, books of Beatle postcards, books of John Lennon's letters, books by Time, books by Life, books by Rolling Stone, books by Mojo, books about Pete Best, books about Jimmy Nicol, books of McCartney poetry, histories of Wings, and Ringo's instruction manuals for people who want to be mildly proficient on drums.

In official Beatles biographer Hunter Davies' 2014 best seller *The Beatle Lyrics* he estimates there are now over 2,000 books about the band. It's a cottage industry that's spinning out of control. It's gotten to the point where there is actually a $26 book that lists all the books available up to 2008 (*Beatle Books: From Genesis to Revolution* by Fraser Sandercombe) so you can check them off as you buy them. Sandercombe only gives you the books' titles, authors, and publishers. Mr. Sterlace goes further than that. Sterlace reviews the best and the worst of the most famous works out there. He makes it easy for you to purchase the great ones and ignore the dreck.

The problem is that this is Sterlace's first book and he does try a little too hard at times to be clever. I think he fancies himself a comedian. Sometimes I chuckled at his jokes but other times I wondered what the hell he was trying to say. A little less irreverence and a little more serious analysis would have made a world of difference. A-

HELTER SKELTER: The True Story of the Manson Murders by Vincent Bugliosi with Curt Gentry (1994 W.W. Norton & Company) 20th Anniversary edition

My wife told me this was not a Beatles book. I beg to disagree. It is the ultimate Beatles book. Okay, I'm getting carried away. This is not the ultimate Beatles book but it is the second best-selling tome in history that is associated with the fab four. Number one with a bullet would of course be Jerome David Salinger's *The Catcher in the Rye* which is also linked to true crime. These are the reasons this book fairly screams Beatles:

1. Check out the title. When you pick this book up you might have a picture of fifth Beatle Charlie "J.C." Manson in your mind but what you're hearing are the dulcet tones of Sir James Paul McCartney M.B.E. screeching out the lyric. In 2010 my wife and I saw Paul in concert in Glendale, Arizona. He did *YESTERDAY* then followed it with *HELTER SKELTER* for sharp contrast. To make the point of what the song is really about he had a video of a roller coaster playing behind him (despite the fact that the song is about a playground slide, close enough I guess). But all I kept seeing in my head was swastika boy glaring into the void. There is no way for any old fan to disassociate this lovely little ballad from the crimes of the other quartet at Sharon Tate's love house.

2. Every Beatle lyric quoted in this book makes you want to sing along. Or should I say every Lennon/McCartney

lyric quoted within makes you want to sing along. To show his displeasure for random, gruesome, bloody mass murder George declined to let the words to his songs be used by Bugliosi. Spoilsport. I guess Harrison didn't think the LaBiancas needed a damn good whacking.

3. This shows more than any other fan obsessed article, book, website, or blog how terribly out of hand things can get for lovers of J, P, G, and R . I mean if you and I are Beatlemaniacs what does that make Manson? I guess he's a Beatlepsychotic/sociopath/misanthrope/messiah/madman and that's being kind.

4. One of the reasons I fell so hard for the group when I was kid in the mid-1970's was this book. I listened to the first two double album compilations over and over but the double album I was really into was *THE BEATLES*. Why? It was because I had picked up *Helter Skelter* at my local Walden Books and discovered how these two long playing records had influenced some ex-convict cult leader to attempt to start a race war by killing rich white people in their homes. It didn't make sense but as Manson was wont to say, "No sense makes sense."

5. The made for TV movie is bad but being a kid I didn't realize how poor its quality was. To me it was something I watched whenever it was on the tube. I liked it as much as *HELP!* and I liked it more than *A Hard Day's Night* and *Yellow Submarine*. For the record, I never ever saw *Let It Be, Magical Mystery Tour* or *Shea Stadium* on TV. I ended up catching them at repertory screenings. In summer 1980 I saw *Shea* and in early fall 1980 I saw *Let It Be*. Thankfully I got to both before

Lennon's death. I first saw *Mystery Tour* Dec. 15th, 1980 and I could not enjoy it at all.

6. We'll never know for sure how many copies of *THE BEATLES* were sold as the soundtrack to this book but it had to be a lot. I wonder if it made it back on the charts in the 1970's.

7. Eerie coincidence: Manson nicknamed bloodthirsty killer Susan Denise Atkins ("The more you do it, the better you like it") Sadie before Lennon nicknamed the Maharashi Sexy Sadie.

8. One of the main reasons this book became the bestselling true crime book of all time was the Beatles' connection. Manson commanding others to murder strangers for him is compelling stuff. Manson being charismatic in an evil icon kind of way is fascinating. The Tate-LaBianca murders are certainly bizarre but what makes them the all-time most popular mass murders in world history is the fact that a crazy little runt thought the love and peace pop music advocates were sending him personal messages to kill. I believe that is called irony.

9. In this 20th anniversary edition of the book non-rock music fan Vince Bugliosi writes a new afterword in which he tries to figure out the reasons for the immense success of this work. Not once in 30 plus pages does he mention the Beatles. This is akin to not mentioning Mark David Chapman when trying to figure out why *Catcher in the Rye* was having a huge spike in sales in the early 80's. A+

HERE COMES THE SUN: The Spiritual and Musical Journey of George Harrison by Joshua M. Greene (2006 John Wiley &Sons)

This is the *Bhagavad Gita* of Beatle books. For those who have always wanted more info on George's religious life this is no doubt edifying. For somebody like me who knows the guy was a money grubbing, materialistic, alcoholic, womanizing, egomaniacal drug abuser this book has to be taken with a grain of salt. Author Josh Greene makes many an invalid point:

1. "God had to be real. How could anyone have so much love for God if he were only a myth?" I feel the same way about the Easter Bunny.
2. "Washing is like chanting. They're both a cleansing process." I feel the same way about pissing.
3. "Here is the story of a man who gave up one of the most spectacular careers in entertainment history for that goal of seeing God face to face." No. George had a 30 year solo career in which he put out many a record, toured twice, played several charity/tribute concerts, formed a band with Bob Zimmerman, reunited with Paul and Ringo to record with dead Lennon, produced many movies including one with Madonna(the singer), and wrote a book.

George himself also comes up with several howlers:

1. "Everybody is looking for Krishna. Some don't realize that they are, but they are." No. Not everybody digs

fairy tales. Some folks are agnostics and some folks are atheists.
2. "By chanting Hare Krishna, Hare Hare, Rama Rama over and over one inevitably arrives at Krishna-Consciousness." No. It gave me a headache.
3. "The best thing anyone can give to humanity is God-consciousness." Or a nice shrubbery.

Oddly enough, the only Beatle who ever shaved his head was Ringo. Maybe he was the real Hare Krishna. Though I don't think he ever danced around the airport or Central Park.   C-

HERE, THERE AND EVERYWHERE: My Life Recording the Music of the Beatles by Geoff Emerick and Howard Massey (2006 Gotham)

This is an entertaining behind the scenes look at the legendary recording sessions of the 1960's. This is quite a page turner. I learned a lot, such as:

I used to think the Beatles and George Martin were the masterminds behind the amazing new pop music sounds of *STRAWBERRY FIELDS FOREVER* and the *SGT. PEPPER* album. Wrong. It was Geoff Emerick, engineer par excellence. Geoff lets us in on this well-kept secret on page 132...and I quote "It was down to me-not George Martin, not anyone else-to turn the Beatles new vision into a reality." There was no with a little help from his friends for the Geoffster. Strictly on his own he changed the course of music history. This despite the fact that "working very late nights ...did make things a bit more tedious...put a strain on all of us" and "by the time we finished the long, grueling *SGT. PEPPER* sessions, it was almost as if we were working in a bloody factory." Poor baby. He even had to put up with the band showing up "much later than the scheduled starting time and no one ever phoned to let us know they were running behind." How rude those damn mop tops were! No wonder Geoff quit in 1968 during the recording of *THE BEATLES* (appropriately during the sessions for CRY BABY CRY). I have the feeling that recording engineers everywhere would have been very happy to be working with the best band in the world but what do I know? Emerick thought it over and came back and finished up with them on *ABBEY ROAD* and then continued to work with Paul on and off for years to come. So it's kind of a happy ending.

I guess when you write a book about your place in history you tend to put yourself up on a pedestal. We all like to think we're important. But to quote John Lennon, "When you're working with genius for 10-15 years you think it's you. It's not. Show me George Martin's music. Show me Dick James' music. I would like to hear it." I say play me Geoff Emerick's music. I would like to hear it. A-

HOW THE BEATLES DESTROYED ROCK AND ROLL: An Alternative History of American Popular Music by Elijah Wald (2009 Oxford University)

That's right. The Liverpool lads destroyed rock and roll. They didn't have enough respect to leave that beautiful music alone. They twisted it all out of shape. They made it more white English than black American. Those bastards! How dare they come over to our shores and screw up the purity of our children. These were kids who up to that point only paid attention to good old American pop. The Beatles were instrumental in leading the way to a more self- conscious drug inspired pretension that was no good for anybody. How I long for the days of rhythm and blues played by real hard working shit kicking Americans. The kind of men who kept their hair short and saluted the flag every chance they got.

The right honorable Elijah Wald opened my eyes to this historical tragedy. The first record he ever owned was *MEET THE BEATLES*. It was the record that fired the first shot of a new cultural war. It was the beginning of the end. He liked them a lot but by the time of *SGT. PEPPER* he had lost the faith. "It simply wasn't as much fun. I played it occasionally, but nowhere near as often as the band's early records. Same with *ABBEY ROAD* and *MAGICAL MYSTERY TOUR*, both of which I vaguely remember hearing but neither of which I can ever recall playing again." This is obviously a very discerning listener.

The right honorable Elijah Wald became more of a folk and blues guy as he made his way through life. His enthusiasm dimmed for the Beatles but he always remembered them and he could name all four if asked to. There was Ringo, George, Paul, and John. He "was shocked to realize that there were young people who couldn't do that. I could understand not liking the Beatles-but not being able to name them?" That's correct, Eli. Some kids today don't give a damn about some band that broke up decades before they were born. Thank god for that. Just because a lot of middle agers and seniors are trapped in the 60's and 70's mindset is no reason for children, teen-agers, and young adults to care about a phenomenon that hit its peak half a century ago.

The right honorable Elijah Wald informs us of the sad fact that "The Beatles and their peers transformed teenage dance music into a mature art form...why are the Beatles to be applauded for doing (this)?" I think they should be applauded because they made rock more adult than it had been before though ironically there are a lot of very old adults hanging on to classic rock as if to ward off the grim reaper. It is their fountain of youth. *Rolling Stone* continues to thrive partly on this very premise. They put oldie acts on their cover while still giving you the lowdown on what 75 year old musician, manager, or disc jockey has croaked that week. We senior citizens love reading the obituaries.

Thankfully we do get this confession, "I am not claiming any clearer vision than previous writers." That's good because I don't see any. This so-called "alternative history of American popular music" is mostly the well written story of old musicians long dead. If that's your cup of tea then please enjoy.   B-

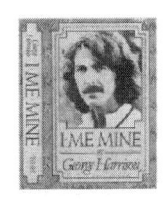

I ME MINE by George Harrison (1980 Simon and Schuster)

ONOTHIMAGEN - George was known for being self-deprecating. George was also known for his wicked sense of humor. He went on the *Smother Brothers Show* alone in 1968. He produced the drunken sods on holiday flick *Withnail and I*. He produced the extremely controversial side splitting madcap farce *Life of Brian*. He appeared in *All You Need Is Cash*.

However, if he really had a good sense of humor, he would have stolen a page from Gale Sayers' playbook and called this memoir *I Am Third*. Still, check out his foreword "I have suffered for this book and now it's your turn." Sure, he stole that line from Neil Innes who probably stole it from Mark Twain but his heart is in the right place.

This is not a comedy book nor is it a full memoir. It's a little bit of memories wrapped around a collection of his average at best lyrics. No wonder he calls the Lennon/McCartney Beatle classics "their wondrous hits" not our wondrous hits. Lennon was very angry because he thought George never mentioned him in this book. John said, "...not mentioned once! He mentions every two bit saxophonist or guitar player he met but my influence on his life is apparently zilch." Actually, John is mentioned several times ("John and I had taken LSD," "John and myself on David Frost show," and "John and Yoko were freaking out screaming") but Lennon gets no credit for helping with the lyrics of *TAXMAN*.

George doesn't spend much time on Lennon/McCartney but there are a lot of great anecdotes about his best friend in the group. My favorite concerns that time the Yankees held Richard Starkey Day on July 4, 1969. Ringo flew with Mal Evans to the States to be honored at the event. Ringo thought he was being honored at the NYC baseball stadium where they had filmed their TV special four years earlier. Mal had to point out to him that the Beatles had performed at the Mets home field in Queens. The event they were attending would be held in the Bronx. "What's the difference?" asked Ringo. Mal replied, "The Yankees are the kings of baseball. They have won the World Series more than any other team. The Mets are a joke. They will probably never win the World Series (little did he know what would happen that fateful October)." The Yankees beat the Red Sox on that hot Independence Day. There was much rejoicing. Then out strode the Yankee Clipper to the pitcher's mound. Dimaggio addressed the crowd, "Ever since Marilyn died I've been searching for somebody to love. Then I realized I do have someone to love. It's Lady Liberty. We took our freedom from those damn limeys nearly 200 years ago and we're never going to give it back. Still, there is one British invasion we can all get behind spearheaded by four young lads from Liverpool. One of those boys is here today to have his statue put up in Monument Park and I for one welcome him to the fold. We've honored Ruth, Gehrig, and Yogi. Now let's bring out the English Yogi, the drummer known for his way with words. It's been a hard day's night and tomorrow never knows but put your hands together for the one and only Bongo!" Out came Ringo wearing his day-glo pink Sgt. Pepper costume and little child's Yankee cap. Starr stared at the crowd for a moment, lit up a cigarette and told the crowd something they could all agree with him on. "I consider myself the luckiest man on the face of the earth...for obvious reasons. Thank you and bon voyage."

George says some interesting things about his songs. On *MY SWEET LORD* he says, "It saved many a heroin addict's life." Huh? On *THE ART OF DYING* Harrison says, "Everybody is worried about dying, but the cause of death is birth, so if you don't want to die you don't get born." What? More on *THE ART OF DYING*, "The whole trip we have gone through, has been like throwing boulders into the lake-because everything comes bouncing back and ties you up forever, or as long as it takes to untie it." Sure, I get it. Groovy, man. On *I ME MINE*, "I hated everything about my ego-it was a flash of everything false and impermanent that I disliked." I'm surprised that George first published this as a signed, limited edition of 2,000 copies, hand-bound in leather if he felt that way. If you end up buying this, try to get that version because it's a little snazzier.   B

<u>*I MET THE WALRUS* by Jerry Levitan (Harper Collins 2012)</u>

Jerry Levitan was lucky enough to meet Lennon/Ono in Toronto in 1969. Now we're lucky that he has shared his interview and photos from that day with us in book form and as an Oscar nominated animated short. What an amazing thing for a teenager to interview Lennon in the 60's. It brings up visions of the young Cameron Crowe.

Highlights from the interview:

1. Jerry: "What about Paul, Ringo, and what's his name?"

John (helpfully): "George."
2. Jerry: "Kids in school...don't like the Beatles...they say 'They're all hippies now and they've gone from us, they're dirty now."
   John: "Those kids, they sound like son-of-square and your job is to hip them up either to the Beatles or anything else. They've got to get from underneath their parents' wings.
3. John: "Piss for peace or smile for peace or go to school for peace or don't go to school for peace."
4. John: "You've got to work your own head out and get nonviolent. It's bloody hard because we're all violent inside. We're all Hitler inside and we're all Christ inside, and it's just to try and work on the good bit in you."
5. "To find a (movie) vehicle for four apes like us without making another *Help!* or *A Hard Day's Night* is pretty tough going."
6. Jerry with a strange opinion: "REVOLUTION 9, which I could go on about for ten years, that's the greatest thing you ever did."
   John: "Good.
7. Jerry: "Who's your all-time favorite singer or composer?"
   John: "Yoko."
   Jerry: "How about yourself?"
   John: "Yeah, me first then Yoko."   B+

THE IMPORTANCE OF PAUL McCARTNEY by Kate Boyes (2004 Lucent)

Not as droll as *The Importance of Being Earnest* but it is the best book aimed at turning your children into Beatle zombies. You've got to indoctrinate them when they're young. Give a boy a mix disc of *YELLOW SUBMARINE, ALL TOGETHER NOW, MAXWELL'S SILVER HAMMER,* and *HELLO GOODBYE* and I'll show you the man.

This is one from the *Importance Of* series. Paul and John both made the cut but George and Ringo aren't deemed important enough and of course they're not. Only the heavy hitters make it. You've got Hitler, Tolkien, Castro, Chaplin, Lenin, Sinatra, Gandhi, Lucille Ball, and Mother Teresa. It sounds like the cover of *SGT. PEPPER* or *SOME GIRLS*.

As I read this I kept shaking my head in agreement. This Sir James Paul McCartney MBE is a vital person in world history. He is the most successful popular music composer of all time and one hell of a charming guy. I'd marry him.

Nice Paul is dead quote from Macca, "I'm dead, am I? Why does nobody ever tell me anything?" Nice quote from Lennon, "Unless something happens, there's nothing to stop Paul and I writing hits when we're old." Nice photo of big George Martin sitting on a park bench in Cuba (!) with a statue of John Lennon. Is there no park bench with a statue of Paul way down south?

For a children's book this is tough stuff. It does not take a sad story and make it better. From beginning to end it breaks your heart. The McCartneys were poor when he was growing up in the 40's. They faced many hardships in postwar Liverpool. Paul, "We always felt like a pioneer family in a wagon train." When he was young he learned about religion. Paul, "I came to the conclusion that 'God' is just the word 'good' with the 'o' taken out, and 'Devil' is the word 'evil' with the 'D' added."

When he was a teenager his mother Mary died of breast cancer. When he was a young man former Beatle bassist Stu Sutcliffe was beaten up by a gang and subsequently passed away from head injuries. When he had become one of the most successful performers on earth he still had crosses to bear. His manager Brian Epstein died of a drug overdose. The band broke up and he "experienced many of the typical negative emotional effects of being unemployed." He started Wings and went to Africa to record *BAND ON THE RUN*. There he had "...an excruciating bronchial spasm" that was like "...a pillow being held over his face by some invisible hand. A terrible, searing pain ripped right through the right side of his chest and he could feel himself trembling. 'I'm going to die' he thought hazily….." Then having survived that he and Linda were mugged by five men at knifepoint. "Don't kill us," Linda screamed.

Wings guitarist Jimmy McCullough could not keep sticking his hand in the medicine jar and ended up out of the group and dead of a drug overdose. Paul also could not keep his hand out of the medicine jar and was busted in Japan for marijuana possession and put in jail. Later that year John was murdered. Looking around for a new collaborator he found Michael Jackson who promptly screwed Paul royally by buying the Lennon/McCartney song catalogue out from under him. In the

90's Linda died, like his mother, from breast cancer. At the beginning of the new century, George Harrison died of brain cancer. Then second wife Heather Mills turned out to be a ruthless gold digger.

Now that I think of it, maybe this isn't a book suitable for kids.

B

P.S. I noticed you can pick this up on Amazon for 19 cents.

IN HIS OWN WRITE by John Lennon (1964 Simon & Schuster)

A thin little volume put out to rip off the screaming teenage girls of 1964, getting their allowance money while the getting was good. This is the kind of stuff John would shoot out while doing the *Daily Howl* and later spill out on the pages of *Spaniard in the Works* and *Skywriting by Mouth*. If you enjoy the gobblygook lyrics of *I AM THE WALRUS* and *COME TOGETHER* you'll probably dig this.

Lennon makes up a bunch of wacky male figures and tells you their odd little stories. There's partly Dave, no flies on Frank, good dog Nigel, fat growth on Eric Hearble, Perry's wonder dog, Randolf's party, sad Michael, treasure Ivan, Alec speaking, nicely nicely (stolen from Damon Runyan) Clive Barrow and his friend Roger, the moldy moldy man who is such a humble Joe, Jumble Jim, the whide hunter, Jumping Gym who shall remain Norman, uncle Tom Cobra, Henry and Harry, deaf Ted, little Bobby, Victor, Arnold, and unhappy Frank. There are also vivid little illustrations from the drawing Beatle.   B

IN MY LIFE: Encounters with the Beatles edited by Robert Cording, Shelli Jankowski-Smith, and E.J. Miller Laino (1998 Fromm International)

 What I would call a potpourri of encounters with the Beatles. There's room for nuts of all kinds. Some who actually met J, P, G, and R and others who wish they had. Obviously you expect an eclectic collection like this to be hit and miss quality wise and so it is.

There is a crazy juxtaposition of comments from a wide variety of sources:

- The great poet Allen Ginsberg's poem *Portland Coliseum* finds "a line of police with folded arms stands Sentry to contain the red sweatered ectasy that rises upward to the wired roof" at a 1965 mop top concert
- Lesser poet Gary Soto's poem *Dizzy Girls in the Sixties* points out the fact that "The Beatles docked in the hearts of girls and young mothers."
- Stuart Sutcliffe remembers Liverpool as "…a huge organism, diseased in every part, the beautiful thoroughfares only a little less repulsive because they have been drained of their pus."

- Larry Neal's article *A Different Bag* tries valiantly to explain the way African Americans relate to the Beatles phenomenon "The Beatles come across as young boys (because) the most consistently asserted value in the black community is the necessity of maintaining one's manhood"
- Acid guru Timothy Leary's over the top piece entitled *Thank God for the Beatles* states "This essay is a logical exercise to prove that the Beatles are Divine Messiahs...the wisest, holiest, most effective avatars that the human race has yet produced. The Beatles were sent to the Maharishi to teach him. They are the most powerful force in the world".
- Hillary Rollins' surprisingly puts down their first appearance on *The Ed Sullivan Show* "The Beatles seemed neither good nor bad nor even especially interesting"
- Ed Davis dismisses the band's place in the 80's pop scene with "Lennon's bones moldering in his grave, McCartney's double chins, Ringo's alcoholism, and Harrison's disappearing act."

There are also two stone classics included here. Noted intellectual Greil Marcus' *Another Version Of the Chair* tells how *I SAW HER STANDING THERE* starts "...with Paul's one-two-three-fuck opening-how in the world did they expect to get away with that?" In addition, white suited Tom Wolfe depicts the Merry Pranksters' time digging the band at the Cow Palace ("...thousands of teeny bodies hurtling toward the stage"). Call me a perfectionist but I prefer consistently excellent books where you don't have to separate the wheat from the chaff.   B-

IN MY LIFE: The Brian Epstein Story by Debbie Geller (2000 Thomas Dunne)

As the new century began the five year wait for the official Beatles' oral history ended. *Anthology*, the book, finally came out to well-deserved critical acclaim. Lost in all the hoopla was the release of another oral history that was originally published in merry old England under the title *The Brian Epstein Story*. Unlike *Anthology* it wasn't lavishly illustrated (though it does boast one great photo of Epstein and John relaxing together) and unlike *Anthology* it has hardly any quotes from who the book was about. That's right, despite the plethora of interviews given in his last few years of life and a best-selling autobiography (ghosted by Derek Taylor) we only get a smattering of thoughts from the man himself. Still, the inside look at his troubled existence comes through vividly from stories relayed by intimates such as his chauffeur Bryan Barrett, personal assistant Joanne Peterson, and chef Lonnie Trimble (rumored to have written his own memoir, probably entitled *I Was a Cook for the Beatles Manager*).

Despite the through-the-looking-glass nature of this little book, it is a fine supplement to the aforementioned *Anthology* if not as the *Financial Times* put it "One of the most...engrossing Beatle books ever written."

McCartney contributes his memories to this book, as is his wont, but Starr and Harrison passed on the chance. Paul wonders what many have wondered since August 27, 1967, "...was he killed? Did he kill himself, or what?"   B+

INSTAMATIC KARMA: Photographs of John Lennon by May Pang (2008 St. Martin's)

Fun? Wow! Back in 1972 George McGovern got trounced by Richard Nixon in the race for United States president. John and Yoko were at a party and Lennon was not very happy about the outcome. He grabbed a young woman and dragged her into a room to "make love." For Yoko this was the last straw. She had been putting up with John's bullshit for six long years and enough was enough. By the time 1973 rolled around she told John to hit the bricks. Yoko sent him to LA in the care of their assistant May Pang. You take care of him now, Yoko commanded. May was only too happy to oblige. Growing up in the 60's she was a Beatlemaniac. May was one of those crazy little girls who worshipped at the altar of those four lads from Liverpool. In 1971 when Dick Cavett had George Harrison on his show they had a little Beatle trivia quiz before the taping of the interview. May Pang was the winner.

For two years May took care of him. Their time together was one in which Lennon hit the booze, hit the drugs, and hit a waitress ("It's not the pain that hurts. It's finding out that one of your heroes is a big asshole"). They also went to Disneyland, Disneyworld, the set of *Happy Days*, and a *Monday Night Football* game at Candlestick Park (the same place the Beatles played their last gig for the paying public in 1966). May even appeared on John's top ten hit *NUMBER 9 DREAM* (it made it to number 9 on the Billboard charts).

But the two most important activities they indulged in together were sex and photography, though as far as I know not simultaneously. They both enjoyed the physical intimacy and John loved having his picture taken because he was an egomaniac. He also liked his buddies to be photographed with him. So in this average collection of snapshots we get the last photo of Lennon and McCartney together. Plus, candid pics of superstars who just happened to be hanging around the house in Santa Monica like Ringo, Keith Moon (aka Baron Von Moon), and Harry Nilsson.

If you're in the market for slightly blurry photos of Dr. O'Boogie doing nothing very exciting you have come to the right place. You get John blowing his nose, sucking down soup, swimming in water, dancing in Central Park, giving the finger, eating pizza, scratching his face, sticking his tongue out, and sucking on a camera lens. This is history folks.

If that's not enough to get you salivating, at no extra cost, you get one of those boring introductions by twenty fifth Beatle Larry Kane ("John was rich in material terms, but he was richer still as an individual who respected the good in people"). B-

I WANT TO TELL YOU: The Definitive Guide To The Music Of The Beatles Volume 1: 1962/1963 by Anthony Robustelli (2014 Shady Bear Productions)

I used to think that 1962-1963 were the simple years of the Beatles. Before they hit America and began to grow in leaps and bounds I thought they were recording some decidedly non-complex tracks like LOVE ME DO or HOLD ME TIGHT or LITTLE CHILD. But I must defer to the expert. In this case that's Anthony Robustelli. Robustelli has turned my head around. These early years were actually chock-full of thoughtful musical visions. From the one-chord drone (a single tone, or possibly two tones, sustained continuously against a moving melodic part) in I WANNA BE YOUR MAN to the primarily pentatonic melody (a five-note scale in which the tones are arranged like a major scale with the fourth and seventh tones omitted) of NOT A SECOND TIME to the non-typical secondary dominant utilized in ASK ME WHY the Beatles were obviously doing more than the layman such as myself could comprehend.

I used to think that Ian MacDonald's *Revolution in the Head* was the last word on the analysis of the canon. Now I think Robustelli's series of books could be the definitive guide to the music of the Beatles...for trained musicians anyway. I on the other hand don't know an Aeolian mode from a relative minor, a Barre chord from a Chromatic scale, a dotted note from an ostinato. But if you do, gentle reader, adjust my grade accordingly.   B+

JOHN by Cynthia Lennon (2005 Crown)

John used to be cruel to his woman. He beat her and kept apart from the things that she loved. Now tit for tat she's written a book about him. This begins with a foreword by Julian Lennon, who like most kids in the 60's came out of a bottle of whiskey on a Saturday night. Cynthia wants to tell the real story of the real John. Finally, a book about Lennon that gives us the truth we've been waiting for. I'm sick to death of all these neurotic, psychotic, pig headed writers like Albert Goldman who are feeding us lie after terrible lie. Cynthia feels that John believed in the truth and would want nothing less. Funny, I could have sworn that John tried to stop her first tell-all book from coming out back in the late 70's.   D-

JOHN LENNON by Bruce W. Concord (1994 Chelsea House)

This is a rock bio aimed at children. So you get none of the comprehensive details of John's orgies or heroin addiction or woman abuse or anorexia or cheating or insanity or neurotic compulsion or primal scream therapy or delusions of grandeur or kowtowing to Yoko or pissing on nuns from a rooftop or wearing a toilet seat on stage or beating Stuart Sutcliffe nearly to death. For those fun facts fab listeners, you'll have to wait until you grow up and out of it.   D-

JOHN LENNON by Richard Wooten (1985 Random House)

Please don't confuse this with the other unimaginatively titled kiddie book called *John Lennon* by Bruce W. Concord (1994). Youngsters tend to confuse them because they're both 128 pages and both are equally lifeless. This is the one whose chief selling point is that it has more than 45 photographs. My god, that's almost fifty! The other one by Mr. Concord has an introduction by *Entertainment Tonight's* fabulous hostess Leeza Gibbons. If anyone knows about rock and roll it is Leeza.

Anyway, about this book by the great Dick Wooten, turn to page 90 and experience the whole damn thing in microcosm. Beneath a photo of the famous rooftop concert is some very helpful captioning. The person "... playing drums" is identified as "Ringo." Paul is helpfully described as "bearded Paul." "George, with mustache, is on the right." John has no facial hair and so is described as "in the center." Thanks, Dick. That's so helpful. He's all about teaching our children.

If you really want to teach our children and also reward grownups here's an idea:

At this point in the 21st Century with the 5,000 channel TV universe in full swing shouldn't there be a network devoted to these guys? I'm talking 24 hours a day. It could be called *The Beatles Channel* (TBC). It could be a combination of old school *MTV, CNN, TCM* and the *History Channel.* You could look at fab video every second of every day on *YouTube* but what about us old people who still watch cable TV on our giant high definition plasma sets? What about us lonely people who love *VH1 Classic*? Don't we deserve our own fab channel? So when we're not watching *Bonanza* or *Gomer Pyle* on *TV Land* we can surf on over to the fab four. Every hour on the hour they could have news updates complete with anchor desk. Then the VJs would come on and introduce the videos. In prime time you could have a learned Robert Osbourne type who introduces the films *TCM* style.

Next up on *TBC* at 8:00 p.m.: *Caveman* from 1981 starring Ringo, his beautiful wife Barbara Bach in a loincloth, John Matuszak from the Oakland Raiders, Shelley Long from Cheers, and Randy Quaid's brother Dennis. Then at 10:00 p.m. it's the Harrison produced cult classic *Withnail and I* from Britain in 1987. It's the movie that the late Roger Ebert declared one of the top 300 of all time. To be followed at midnight by John in *How I Won the War* from 1967. This was the film that *Rolling Stone* featured on their first cover. This is the picture Lennon references in memorable fashion during *A DAY IN THE LIFE*. Then at 2:00 a.m. the clunker that makes *Magical Mystery Tour* look like *Casablanca*. It's Paul with a little help from Ringo in the box office bomb *Give My Regards to Broadstreet* from 1984. Leonard Maltin reported, "Some of the music is good but mostly it's a big snooze." We concur.

This would have a lot more commercial appeal than some of the crud I see on the tube every day. *Beatles Jeopardy* would be a fantastic show as would the *100,000 Pyramid* with only mop top clues. The possibilities are endless!

Back to the book I'm supposed to be reviewing. Don't waste your time kids. Grow up a little and read Albert Goldman's

Lennon bio or if you don't like nasty, horrifying, and lurid stuff then check out Ray Coleman's writings on the accidental martyr.

D-

JOHN LENNON: All I Want is the Truth by Elizabeth Partridge (2005 Viking)

Elizabeth Partridge can try to get away with something by calling this a "photographic biography" of JWL but it's just a coffee table rip off. All of the few dozen poorly chosen photos are in black and white. I guess that makes it artsy. Brigitte Bardot makes the cut (John wanted to sleep with her), so does Winston Churchill (John's middle name was a tribute to the Prime Minister), and so does Marlon Brando in *The Wild One* Ms. Partridge lies to her readers by telling them the Beatles name came from Lee Marvin's reference to the Beetles in this classic film despite not having one shred of evidence that it is the truth. Anybody who subtitles her book *All I Want is the Truth* should really be a little more careful about throwing around bullshit. Also, why the hell do we get a photo of George and Zimmerman at the Bangledesh concert and a picture of George and Lorne Michaels and Paul Simon at a *Saturday Night Live* rehearsal? Did she run out of Lennon photos?

As for the text there is no way it could be any worse. Not for one moment does it do justice to the Man of the Century. The most interesting moments aren't even about him. Her coverage of the Vietnam War and the war protesters of the era (complete of course with accompanying photos) isn't anything to write home about but it did make me sit up and think *what does this really have to do with John Lennon?*   D

P.S.: On page 111 I did find out an important tidbit. Freddie Lennon (the bastard that abandoned John in the early 1940's) sold his life story to *Tit Bits*. I thought this might be a typo but I was surprised to learn there really was a *Tit Bits* magazine. Will wonders never cease?

JOHN LENNON AND THE JEWS: A Philosophical Rampage by Ze'ev Maghen (2011 Bottom)

There is a sucker born every minute and I am that sucker. I was looking around for interesting sounding Beatle books to review and lo and behold I saw the provocative title *John Lennon and the Jews*. What was it about? Was it about a secret love affair with Queenie Epstein? Had Yoko taken up Judaism ala Sammy Davis Jr.? Was it about the Lennon/McCartney B-side BABY YOU'RE A RICH FAG JEW? Imagine my disappointment when I got it in the mail and discovered it had almost nothing to do with Lennon.

Bottom books and Ze'ev Maghen wanted big sales for his fourth book and what sells better than the Beatles (Jesus and JFK if you must know)? What a great marketing idea! I always said you could put out any book with the fab four on the cover and it would sell. This proves my point. It has only a handful of pages related to the John but that didn't stop Maghen from selling it as a Beatle book.

Maghen found a photo of Lennon where he looks like an Orthodox Jew (from the Beatles' last photo session no less) and stuck it on the front cover. Then to make sure saps perusing it in a bookstore would buy it, he puts a photo of the whole band on the back cover. Call the Better Business Bureau! To cover himself, Maghen calls the first section of his work My Sweet Lord and ends the book on the words imagine that. Imagine that.

Go right to page 25 and hear "peerlessly loyal Lennon lover" Maghen state "I'm going to kill him all over again." Is that even possible? Then he says he loves IMAGINE ("it's a great song" and "his masterpiece") before letting us know "...John's beautiful ballad is in reality a death-march, a requiem mass for the human race. His seemingly lovely lyrics constitute in truth the single most hideous and unfortunate combination of syllables ever to be put to music. The realization of his dream- even in large part- would inevitably entail the wholesale destruction of the dreams, hopes, and very reason for living of yourself and every single person you know. If we-who have for so long unthinkingly admired Lennon's words- were to see his wish come true, the result would be more staggeringly horrific and more devastatingly ruinous than you could ever possibly imagine." Thankfully Maghen then clears things up: "I don't really mean to say that John Lennon is the Anti-Christ. It's just a device, OK? Cut me some literary slack!"

Go right to page 77 and find out "John Lennon desires that you live in space but not in time, in breadth, but not in depth, he urges you most melodiously to shed all profundity and become two dimensional , he pleads with you to be superficial, to be skin deep, to be flat." "Our lilting limey...wishes upon you the Bhagavad-Gita's famous 'disengagement', in this case from both the vertical and horizontal planes of human interaction and enrichment, leaving you to live out the rest of your superficial and circumscribed existence-ignorant of how very much more there is to be had in life-stuck inside the four walls of isolated and ever-contracting one-dimensionality."

I think I'll wait for the movie.

THE JOHN LENNON FAMILY ALBUM by Nishi F. Saimaru (1990 Chronicle)

This photographic journey was first available in 1982 as a Japanese import. We yanks had to wait till the tenth anniversary of the murder to get an easily affordable stateside edition. It was well worth the wait. This really captures the fun and frolic of Sean's early years with his parents as they traipse all over the world looking for love and feeling groovy. One fascinating color shot after another. A couple of them so weird you've got to see them to believe.

When you track this down you will get a chance to enjoy:

1. John and Sean sledding in Massachusetts.
2. Father, mother, and son at the Ringling Brothers circus.
3. Mick Jagger unexpectedly dropping in to say hello at said circus which put me in the mind of John and Yoko bringing Julian to Mick's 1968 TV special (unreleased until 1996) *The Rolling Stones Rock and Roll Circus*.
4. J and S at the Tiger Balm Garden in Hong Kong.

5. John strolling around Hong Kong being asked by tourists from the west, "Aren't you John Lennon?" and replying to them, "I get told that a lot."
6. John posing with all five dozen of Yoko's relations at the Ono family reunion in Tokyo. This reminds me of the time my parents dragged me to a family reunion when I was 16 though I don't why. Lennon's smiling face seems to radiate contentment.
7. Checking out the elephants at the Tokyo zoo.
8. John taking Polaroids of Sean while Yoko's mother looks sternly on.
9. John posing with Yoko's mother while she stares sternly into the lens.
10. John teaching Sean the art of Frisbee tossing.
11. John playing guitar at a picnic, giving us visual proof that he touched a guitar between *ROCK AND ROLL* and *DOUBLE FANTASY.*
12. J&Y and visiting Julian all on one big sled going downhill in Central Park at Xmas 1977.
13. John and Sean's double birthday party at the Tavern on the Green.

Plus, the two weird ones:

14. In Monterey, Massachusetts in 1977 J&Y and their friend George Maciunas dress up in Old West costumes. John wearing a Little House on the Prairie type dress with a flower on his shoulder, a bonnet on his head, a fan in his hand in case he got a little warm, and a satisfied smile on his face.
15. Christmas 1977 in Central Park and J&Y and Julian are all posing with ski masks on. I hope my mega delightful

fellow Beatlemaniac Mr. Ski-Mask has seen this photo. It would make a great Christmas card to send him.

At no additional cost you get the complete text of the open letter to the world sent out via the *New York Times* in May of 1979 in which John and Yoko let us know they and the three angels over their shoulders were doing fine watching shadows on the wall. A-

JOHN LENNON: The Beatles and Beyond by David K. Wright (1996 Enslow)

John Winston Lennon was born October 9, 1940 in a small town on the cast iron shore of Great Britain. It was a lovely little place known for being the city of good neighbors. He grew up in a district called Penny Lane, under blue suburban skies. He had two wonderful and caring parents named Fred and Julia. They made his childhood years a pure pleasure. They doted on him and pampered him. Consequently he was a well-adjusted and happy young boy. He wanted for nothing. He had all the love and tenderness a youngster could want. While other teenagers of the 1950's embraced the rock and roll music of Elvis Presley, smoked cigarettes, and drank alcohol John was content to spend his years drinking tea, eating biscuits , playing bridge, and reading history. He never felt the need to express himself artistically because he was always blissful. He never felt strong emotional pain. Everything was hunky and dory.

In the 1960's John became a man and he decided to go out into the world to see what was up. He found out a lot of people were sad and neurotic basket cases and he tried to figure out how he could help them. He decided to spend all his nights and days working on a new medicine that would help the rest of humanity feel the way he did: satisfied, confident, and serene. After many years of struggle, on June 1, 1967, all his hard work came to fruition. That fantastic spring day he discovered the formula for the love pill. One pill a day and you'd be feeling right as rain. No matter what problems beset you the love pill would allow you to feel peaceful, joyful, and gay. Wasting no time he got ahold of some big shots in the pharmaceutical industry and soon the entire world was taking the love pill. People no longer felt depressed, violent, or distressed. Everything was beautiful. There would be no more wars between nations because all the world leaders were now content with their lot in life. You say you want a revolution? No need. John Lennon's love pill stopped all the mental and spiritual anguish that had haunted human beings since the beginning of time.

But there was still one little issue. People got sick, got injured, grew old, and died. So Mr. Lennon went back to the drawing board and came up with up a new drink. It tasted like the nectar of the gods and when you sucked it down you never aged, never felt physical discomfort, and you could never break a bone or have a heart attack or get high cholesterol. He called the drink Mountain Dew. The 1970's were a glorious time. The whole world was happy and feeling fit. It now seemed like anything was possible. Lennon looked around and around and thought, "Is this it? Have I done everything I can to make the make the world a better place? Can I get some me time? Don't I deserve that? Who was I before I changed the world? I can't even remember. It was so long ago." Mr. Lennon called a press conference in 1975 and announced to the world that he was taking a five year sabbatical to recharge his batteries. He felt perfectly fine mentally and physically but he just thought it would be nice to live like a regular person again. The person he had been before the love pill had made him the world's most admired man. It would be nice to walk down the street without women screaming in joy and trying to tear his clothes off.

So John sailed across the Atlantic to be where he belonged. It was the land of the free and the home of the brave. He settled in a luxurious apartment building in New York, New York. It was the town so nice they named it twice. There he was, of course, still one of the most famous and beloved men on Earth but people gave him a little more space in Manhattan. He could go out to a movie or a restaurant without being accosted. Sometimes people would want his autograph or want to ask him questions about the love pill and Mountain Dew. But it was all very low key. He blended in with the crowd. Some said he was a dreamer but he had made his vision of peace and love a reality. Unfortunately, all things must pass.

Unexpectedly, in 1980, the love pill and the Mountain Dew stopped working. Somehow they had lost their potency. Within months the whole world was in chaos. People were going insane. People were aging and getting sick. People were feeling down. They were so low in spirit that nothing could cheer them up. The international press reached out to John Lennon. He tried to answer their questions the best he could. But he had no idea what had gone wrong. "I'll have to start again", he said as he rolled up his sleeves. But try as he might he could not recapture the essence of that magical period. The dream was over. The world had to reawaken to so-called reality and no one was happy about it. The last 35 years have been a tough time for our planet. The children of today can hardly believe that there was once a time when all you needed was love. C+

THE JOHN LENNON LETTERS edited by Hunter Davies (2012 Little, Brown and Company)

I don't know about you but I've always been fascinated by A.J. Weberman. The way that obsessive maniac went through Bobby Zimmerman's garbage looking for clues to Bob's lyrical genius. He found amazing things: a ripped up photo of Jimi Hendrix the day after the guitarist bit the dust, coffee grounds, and dirty diapers (presumably used by Bob's children not the great man himself). In the same investigative spirit we get the Beatles' official biographer giving us a collection of Lennon's letters.

Amidst all the unnecessary padding there is a lot of worthwhile stuff:

- A four page letter to Cynthia right after Stuart Sutcliffe's death,
- Part of a seven page letter to Cynthia in 1965 in which he admits the obvious, "What a thoughtless bastard I seem to be."
- A letter to his father Fred in 1967 who abandoned him when he was a kid which states, "It will be a bit

awkward when we first meet but there's hope for us yet,"
- An open letter responding to *Black Dwarf* magazine's John Hoyland in 1969 which asks, "Who do you think you are? What do you think you know?" Then keeps the pedal to the metal all the way through
- The classic punk off letter to Todd Rundgren in 1974 (Lennon refers to him as Sodd Runtlestuntle) in which he tells Todd, "I did act like an ass in the troubadour...so shoot me!" and "violence comes in mysterious ways it's wonders to perform,"
- Two masterpieces sent to Paul and Linda in the early 70's that feature comments like, "The cunts (Paul and Allen Klein) asked me to keep quiet about it," "Have you ever thought that you might possibly be wrong about something?" and "If you're not the aggressor, who the hell took us to court and shat all over us in public?"

Some of the low lights that scrape the bottom of the barrel include:

- Letter 62 to Liz Bravo in its entirety reads, "Thanks for a great year."
- Letter two to his Aunt Harriet in its entirety reads, "I have taken David's bike. I will return it tomorrow (so as not to break into the 1 pound)."
- Letter 25 to Irene in its entirety reads, "Thanks for your letter, the L.P. comes out in 2 weeks (approx.). It's called "Please Please Me" for obvious reasons."
- Letter 115 in its entirety reads, "THIS IS IT! PRIMAL SCREAM"

- Letter 140 to Ray Coleman in its entirety reads, "50,000 people are expected at Yoko's museum show running from Oct-? (3 weeks). I thought you was with disc?"

These five above are just the tip of the iceberg, we also get:

- John's letter to his laundry, "What is your excuse for turning my brand new white shirt yellow?"
- his supermarket list which include, "milk, eggs, and grapenuts (not flakes)"
- a critique of a local pastry shop, "loved dat croissant"
- A note to remind everyone that, "The HBO guy is coming between 3-5. BE THERE."   B+

JOHN LENNON LIFE IS WHAT HAPPENS by John M. Borack (2010 Krause)

If you're looking for a sumptuous visual feast you've come to the right place. John M. Borack's takes us through John's ups and downs, through his records and his movies, through his life and his death. You'll learn how Lennon mesmerized his fans and how he influenced musicians. In page after page of beautiful imagery we see the objects and artefacts that helped shape worldwide pop culture.

For fab fans this is the next best thing to owning a LISTEN TO THIS button, a container of With the Beatles talcum powder, a flame retardant Lennon Halloween costume, a TWO VIRGINS 8-

track, a stereo copy of ROOTS, a Beatles buttons vending machine, a signed copy of *Grapefruit*, a sealed WEDDING ALBUM, a Beat Time pinball machine, a War is Over promo poster, a *Yellow Submarine* bicycle seat, a baseball signed at Candlestick in 1966, or a Beatles Kaboodle Kit.

Borack's text is also right on, that is I tend to agree with his opinions. Borack finds POWER TO THE PEOPLE to be "…completely lacking in subtlety and nuance." Correct. Borack believes LET IT BE "…was a rather inglorious way for the foursome to wrap up their storied career." Correct. Borack thinks GOD is "…the centerpiece of (PLASTIC ONO BAND)" and "One would be hard pressed to find a more powerful, personal statement in the annals of rock." Correct.

Then again I disagree with him (and practically every other Beatlemaniac I know) about the merits of SOME TIME IN NEW YORK CITY. While I find it to be a riveting and at times enchanting piece of work (I'm referring to the studio record) Borack feels "The album was a sprawling, heavy-handed, overtly political mess" and "an enormous failure musically, critically, and sales wise."

Borack's right about it being overtly political and an enormous failure sales wise but what kind of critic would I be if I didn't stand up for what I believe in, say what's on my mind, and do what I feel is right, consequences be damned! A-

JOHN LENNON: The Life by Philip Norman (2008 HarperCollins)

This is not as well written as Albert Goldman's hatchet job but it is a nicer view of Lennon's legend. It is a take on Lennon from famed McCartney hater Philip Norman, author of *Shout!* The very humble Mr. Norman feels that *Shout!* was "the definite work on the Beatles." Wrong. The very open minded Mr. Norman feels Goldman's *The Lives of John Lennon* can be "totally discounted." Wrong. The very liberal Mr. Norman calls Billy Preston "their first black American auxiliary keyboards player" which I guess makes George Martin their first white British auxiliary keyboards player. The brilliant and discerning Mr. Norman tells all us ignorant rabble that the *PLEASE PLEASE ME* LP was so mind blowing that "almost every one of its fourteen tracks now seems fresh and surprising enough to have been issued as a single." What? I guess that would mean nearly everything the Beatles put out between 1962 and 1970 was 45 rpm worthy. That might be going a little too far.

The empathetic Mr. Norman feels for Lennon because "The rich and famous discover it is not the storybook happy ending they always thought but merely a threshold to unimagined new problems, pressures and dissatisfactions." All I can say to that is, thank God I'm not rich and famous. Sounds like a horrible drag.

C+

JOHN LENNON: The New York Years photos by Bob Gruen (2005 Stewart, Tabori, and Chang)

Every time I see John's face it reminds me of the places he used to go. But all I've got are these photographs and I realize he's not coming back anymore. I thought I'd make it the day he went away but I can't take it until he comes home again to stay. I want him here to have and hold as the years go by and I grow old and grey. But all I've got are these photographs and I realize he's not coming back anymore. B+

LENNON: The Man, the Myth, the Music – The Definitive Life by Tim Riley (2011 Hyperion)

Only three years after Philip Norman's 851 page biography tried to get the taste of Albert Goldman's book out of our mouths, comes good old Tim Riley with this 766 page biography. Just in time! I think we were all starting to worry.

Tim feels for Lennon, "He seemed to spend almost two thirds of his Beatle tenure surrounded by people he wished to avoid," "he became a target of U.S. authority in ways few could fathom," "his inner life roared with emptiness," and "his mental state plumbed dangerous new levels of concern."

Tim understands Lennon's music better than we ever can, "The reviews (of PLASTIC ONO BAND) tended to be uninformed raves," "Lennon's late themes were suffused with deeply felt quietude," and "...by admitting defeat to a show business legend that was always bigger than celebrity, Lennon seems to have found a stillness worth singing about." Right... and I am the Eggman. B-

THE LENNON COMPANION edited by Elizabeth Thomson & David Gutman (2004 Da Capo)

I hope I'm not damning with faint praise but this is much better than *The Starr Companion*. The afterword is almost worth the price of admission just by itself. In it they discuss all the "rushing out to buy books and CDs as if the handing over of money demonstrates our love." That's the kind of attitude I'm counting on from Beatlemaniacs to sell my book! The afterword also features an astute analysis of Fab Four books that have been flowing out like endless rain into a paper cup. They feel that "few people want their heroes...knocked from their pedestals like so many soviet statues." I'm more of the mindset that heroes are meant to be built up and then torn down. How else could we have so many comebacks?

The meat of the book has a variety of pieces by an eclectic group of authors. Where else would you find a collection of Lennon articles by Gloria Steinem, Tom Wolfe, Pauline Kael, and Noel Coward? Nowhere, man. A-

***THE LENNON PROPHECY*: A New Examination of the Death Clues of the Beatles** by Joseph Niezgoda (2008 New Chapter)

Sometimes reading into the Beatles lyrics/album covers/recordings can go a little too far. Like when Charlie Manson thought they were sending him personal messages to mass murder people. But I think we can all get behind the whole Paul is killed in a car accident and then replaced by a look-alike/sound-alike for the last few years of the Beatles career thing. It's been fun for the last four and a half decades to look for clues to this incredible hoax.

Just when you thought things had run out of steam we get *The Lennon Prophecy* that explains we had it wrong all along. Those were John Lennon is going to die in 1980 clues. That's right, folks. They were clues about the future. For instance, did you know that the *MAGICAL MYSTERY TOUR* double EP booklet that features a photo of Lennon standing in front of a sign reading "The best way to go is by MDC" was released in England on December 8th?

Please check out these other clues:

1. The words "lose their soul" are printed directly across the beltline of John on the back cover of *SGT. PEPPER*. This proves he sold his soul to Satan.

2. *REVOLUTION 9* played backwards distinctly mentions a "dead man." Of course, we all know the driving force behind this track was Lennon who 12 years later distinctly became a "dead man."

3. As a boy John Lennon placed his dreams and hopes in magic, in a wish or a spell that would offer him a better life. Then he became a big star.   Was this a coincidence? Yes.

4. *REVOLVER* was the title of a Beatle album. John was killed with a revolver. Was this a coincidence? Yes.

5. John's favorite number was 9. He died on the 8th. 8 is only one number away from 9. Hard to believe but it's true!

6. On page 185 of this so bad it's almost good book Joseph Niezgoda points out correctly that if a written contract between Lennon and the Devil were found it would be proof that John sold his soul to the devil. Sadly, he also points out that historically few of these contracts have ever been discovered.

7. Stay with me on this one. James Joyce's *Finnegan's Wake* was written as a harbinger of the future death of John Lennon, who was not even born when the book was published. To prove this amazing claim would seem to be a hard undertaking. But check this out, in the book James Joyce writes, "he hade to die it, the beetle" and in the video for *(JUST LIKE) STARTING OVER* a copy of *Finnegan's Wake* is seen on a bookcase. Well, that's enough for me. I'm sold. B

LENNON REMEMBERS: The Famous Rolling Stone Interviews by Jann Wenner (1971 Staight Arrow/2000 Verso)

John told Wenner not to put the infamous *Rolling Stone* interviews out as a book. Lennon must have realized they made him look bad. But Jann did anyway. Thank God for that. It's the most deliriously insightful of all the Lennon interviews. John puts down everybody in Beatles lore (except fellow death by gun-shot Mal Evans and Yoko). He excoriates everyone around him, lies a lot, and trashes the fans. Fun!

John comes across as an arrogant prick. How getting shot to death transformed this guy into Saint John I'll never know. John is insecure, insensitive, and obviously a fucking genius who wishes he could just be a simple fisherman. How dare his teachers try to beat him into being a fucking dentist? How dare the fans try to beat him into being like Englebert Humperdink. Just in case you were wondering:

1. "It's no fun being an artist. It's torture. If they had psychiatrists, we wouldn't have had Gauguin's great pictures. These bastards (referring to his fans) are just sucking us to death; that's about all we can do, is do it like circus animals. I resent being an artist, in that respect, I resent performing for fucking idiots who don't know anything. They can't feel. I'm the one that's feeling, because I'm the one that is expressing. They live vicariously through me and other artists...I'd sooner be in the audience but I'm not capable of it."

2. "I don't want to die. I don't want to be hurt, and please don't hit me."
3. "I wouldn't let Eastman (Linda McCartney's father Lee Eastman nee Epstein) near me; I wouldn't let a fuckin' animal like that who has a mind like that near me. Who despises me, too, despises me because of what I am and what I look like."
4. "These people like Eastman and Dick James and people like that, think that I'm an idiot. They really can't see me; they think I'm some kind of guy who got struck lucky, a pal of Paul's or something. They're so fuckin' stupid they don't know."
5. "Eastman is a Wasp Jew, man, and that's the worst kind of person on earth."
6. "Paul thought he was the fuckin' Beatles and he never fucking was, never."
7. "I always wondered 'why has nobody discovered me?' In school, didn't they see that I'm cleverer than anybody in this school? That the teachers are stupid, too? That all they had was information I didn't need? I never forgave her (Aunt Mimi) for not treating me like a fuckin' genius or whatever I was, when I was a child.
8. "Acid will box your head open."
9. "Yoko's pain is such that she expresses herself in a way that hurts you- you cannot take it. That's why they couldn't take Van Gogh, it's too real, it hurts; that's why they kill you."
10. "I was an emperor. I had millions of chicks, drugs, drink, power, and everybody saying how great I was. How could I get out of it? It was like being in a fuckin' train. I couldn't get out. I couldn't do anything about it. I was

just going along for the ride. I was hooked, just like a junkie."
11. "George insulted Yoko right to her face...you give off bad vibes that's what George said to her. We both sat through it. I didn't hit him. I don't know why."
12. "Fuckin' big bastards, that's what the Beatles were. You have to be a bastard to make it, that's a fact, and the Beatles are the biggest bastards on earth."
13. "A lot of the things Manson says are true: he is a child of the state, made by us, and he took their children in when nobody else would. He's balmy, like any other Beatle-kind of fan who reads mysticism into it."
14. "One has to completely humiliate oneself to be what the Beatles were, and that's what I resent. I didn't know. I didn't for see. It happened bit by bit, gradually until this complete craziness is surrounding you, and you're doing exactly what you don't want to do with people you can't stand- the people you hated when you were ten."
15. "Form and not substance, that's McCartney." Paul: "I thought... he's right. I'm a turd."
16. "Marcel Duchamp would put a bike wheel on display and say this is art you cunts."
17. "I record with Yoko, but I'm not going to record with another egomaniac."
18. "Yoko is as important to me as Paul and Dylan (Zimmerman) rolled into one." Who can forget a pop classic like Ono's *I FELT LIKE SMASHING MY FACE INTO A CLEAR GLASS WINDOW*?
19. "Fans are under a delusion of awareness by having long hair. And that's what I'm sick of. They frighten me.

There's a lot of uptight maniacs going round wearing fuckin' peace symbols."
20. "The Beatles was nothing."

So called Beatle expert Wenner did an excellent job of interviewing except when he asked John, "*COME TOGETHER* – was that you?" He also let Lennon get away with some weird statements:

- John claimed he stopped writing with Paul in 1962. I think Wenner should have called him on that one.
- John said Paul always imitated him. For the record: Paul wrote songs first, married his soulmate before John got hitched to his soulmate, did a non-Beatle album first (*THE FAMILY WAY*) beating two great saints to the punch, and got into the avant-garde first. To be fair Paul and Linda's musical collaborations were a copycat version of John and Yoko.
- John outrageously declared Yoko's *DON'T WORRY KYOKO (MUMMY'S ONLY LOOKING FOR HER HAND IN THE SNOW)* the greatest rock and roll record of all time. Yeah, it usually makes number one on all the lists I've seen.

John "All you need is love" Lennon uses "fag" as his favorite insult throughout the sessions. He uses it to show his fondness for Brian Epstein ("He was a fag"), rock and roll fans ("fag middle class kids walking around London in long hair and trendy clothes"), Andy Warhol ("I don't dig all that junkie fag scene and all that he lives in."), and Mick Jagger ("I think Mick's a joke with all that fag dancing"). He uses it to explain how he has fun when hanging out with fags like his manager ("I like playing a bit faggy"). He lets it be known that his anti-war anthem *GIVE*

PEACE A CHANCE was not written for those kind of people ("I hope it's for workers and not for tarts and fags").

For you eerie coincidence aficionados: These interviews that appeared in the January 21 and February 4, 1971 issues of *Rolling Stone* took place in New York City on December 8, 1970.

A+

LENNON REVEALED by Larry Kane (2005 Running)

Larry Kane is an Emmy award winning journalist, from all accounts a wonderful gentleman, and a casual friend of the Beatles. But he's not much of a writer. I think Larry must realize this (at least subconsciously) because he always packages his books with bonus DVDs. The video extra here is decent enough in a scraping the bottom of the barrel way. It features John and Paul being interviewed in 1968 about their new company Apple. It's too bad it's not *The Tonight Show* interview conducted by baseball player Joe Garigeola that very same week, the holy grail of fab television appearances. NBC TV in their infinite wisdom taped over it. It also includes the time Lennon did the weather report in 1975 on WPVI in Philadelphia.

This book was sold as a manifestation of divine truth but I searched and searched and didn't find any. It's funny when Lennon calls Larry a fag ass (1964 at the San Francisco Hilton) and Larry calls Lennon a slob. It's imaginative when Larry conflates *CRIPPLED INSIDE* with *HOW DO YOU SLEEP*. It's touching when Mr. Kane remembers the tragic murder. But there are no revelations to be had here.   C+

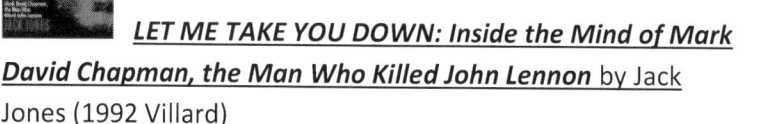

LET ME TAKE YOU DOWN: Inside the Mind of Mark David Chapman, the Man Who Killed John Lennon by Jack Jones (1992 Villard)

Jack Jones went to Attica and interviewed Chapman for two hundred hours. That's 198 more hours than Mark gave to Larry King and Barbara Walters combined. So this is a nearly comprehensive look at "a man in the grip of madness and malice." It is almost a full account of the jerk of all jerks. My mother gave it to me for Xmas and I threw it away. I did not want to know about him or his warped mind. Twenty years passed and in 2012 while in Miami (the city from which Howard Cosell announced Lennon's death to the nation) my wife and I came up with an idea to make our own movie about the assassination. Suddenly, I was ready to confront the demon and find out about him. I felt that enough time had passed. I also felt that knowing about MDC would help me immeasurably with our movie.

I learned a lot of things and I surmised a lot of things:

1. Mark's favorite artist was Todd Rundgren who he never wanted to meet because he had too much respect for him. Lucky, Todd! He left an 8-track copy of Todd's second solo album *RUNT THE BALLAD OF TODD RUNDGREN* for the authorities to find. It's the one

where Todd is at the piano with a noose around his neck. The album features several lyrics about shooting guns.

2. Chapman heard the words "Do it, do it, do it" over and over in his head as he shot John. John sings these words on BRING ON THE LUCIE (FREEDA PEOPLE), a song that is ironically about stopping killings.

3. He also left a copy of *The Bible* for the police, open to the Gospel According to John and wrote in the word Lennon next to it.

4. His favorite movie was *The Wizard of Oz*, which has even less to do with shooting a stranger than *The Catcher in the Rye*.

5. As he left for the Dakota on December 8th Mark felt, "I was going to go through a door, the poet's door, William Blake's door, Jim Morrison's door."

6. "When he shot John Lennon, Chapman robbed us all of an opportunity to better understand ourselves." I disagree with this and so did Lennon, "I can't wake you up. Only you can wake yourself up."

7. Mark was glad that a prostitute he ordered up on the phone had a green dress on. Holden Caufield had an encounter with a prostitute wearing a green dress. "Synchronicity," he said to himself.

8. When he bought *Catcher in the Rye* on that fateful Monday he leafed through the book and "felt a chill of meaning" when he saw the sentence "It was Monday and all, and pretty near Christmas."

9. John Lennon interviewed on December 8, 1980 said, "It was like I lost myself. Not that I purposely set out to be a hypocrite and a phony."

10. Chapman claimed to see Rosemary herself cross the street in front of the Dakota on 12/8. Mark felt it was an omen, "This has to be the day." Mia Farrow had played the lead in Roman Polanski's *Rosemary's Baby* (released in 1968) which had been shot at the Dakota. Mia then broke up with her husband Frank *"The Manchurian Candidate"* Sinatra and went to India to be with the Beatles. In India the Beatles wrote the songs for *THE BEATLES* including *HELTER SKELTER*. On the day the band was photographed for the cover of *ABBEY ROAD* (featuring the single *SOMETHING* that Frank Sinatra would cover) Charlie Manson sent out his bloodthirsty robots to Roman Polanski's home and brutally murdered everyone in the love house.
11. Lennon said in September 1980 he felt, "Guilt for being rich, and guilt thinking that perhaps love and peace isn't enough and you have to go and get shot or something."

It's no surprise that this book has 27 chapters but I was a little surprised that one of the chapters was a look at Mark's fan mail during his first decade behind bars. To say some of the people writing him were not really fans is to put it mildly. Here's a sample of what was sent to him:

A. "I can't believe I wasted a whole stamp on such a nothing!!!!"
B. "You sicken me. I hope you know how many lives you have wrecked and how many people out here in the real world hate you."
C. "I hope they never let you out. If they do let you out someone will kill you and I would die laughing."
D. "My only wish for you is that your pathetic soul burn in hell."

E. "You'll go down in history as one of the world's most hated and cowardly killers of all time."

What is amazing to me is the people who were really fans:

A. "I am a great fan of yours. The good Lord only knows what havoc Lennon would have wreaked had you not eliminated him when you did. I'm trying to get a Mark David Fan Club organized. But few people if any share our moralistic values."
B. "I do feel you have had a 'rough deal' because it was a 'celebrity' you shot and I would like to befriend you and help if possible."
C. "Please don't keep on condemning yourself when God does not."
D. "You were used as an instrument of divine will, nothing more, nothing less."

The one thing that I have to criticize author Jack Jones about comes on page 212. Mark re-read *Catcher* while he was being held in Bellevue after the murder and Chapman spotted things in Holden Caufield's story that were like, " …a blueprint of what had happened to me." One thing was that Mark was in NYC between Saturday and Monday and so was Caufield. But there were at least 49 other similarities that Chapman noticed between his behavior over the three day period and Holden's over the same amount of days. MDC admitted to making up, "…a list of fifty total coincidences, things that were pretty frightening because there was no way that they could have been planned, no way that I could have set them up. It was like the whole killing was set up by destiny, just something that was meant to be. It was eerie, like something more was going on than I ever envisioned. Like it was out of my control."

Jack Jones never bothers to find room in his 200 plus page book to tell us what these things were. Did he even ask Chapman in 200 hours of interviews what they were? Did he even ask if Mark kept the list or if he could recreate it? It seems to me that it would have been, by far, the most interesting chapter in this whole "biography." B+

LIGHT FROM WITHIN: Photojournals by Linda McCartney (2001 Bulfinch)

Do we need another posthumous bunch of photos from the love of Paul's life? Wouldn't it be a better world if Little, Brown, and Company put out a $50 hardcover for some struggling photographer who could really use the exposure rather than dumping these unmemorable images into the marketplace simply because devout Beatlemaniacs will buy anything with one of Paul's trademark forewords? I don't get a feeling that Linda was a talented artist. I get the feeling she married a talented artist. D-

LINDA McCARTNEY: A Portrait by Danny Fields (2000 Renaissance)

I don't believe there was ever a need for a Ringo biography, so you can probably guess how I feel about this one. But the rabid Linda fans out there demanded this, so here it is. I'm not kidding. I talked to both rabid fans and they assured me this was an important cultural document of an underrated pop musician. They've got a point. Though I never noticed her keyboard playing and I don't recall her writing any songs (though Paul did give her co-credit for half of the tracks on *RAM*), I do have a soft spot for her harmony vocals in Wings. She wasn't a bad singer at all for a photographer.

Linda hit on John first. If he had not already been carrying on an affair with Ms. Ono who knows what would have happened? We could have been treated to *John and Linda: A Love Story*. D

LINDA MCCARTNEY ON TOUR by Linda McCartney (1998 Bulfinch Press)

Finally, Linda spills the beans about all those crazy tours. We're going to get the dirt on the orgies, the drugs, and the somewhat loud music. Nope, it's a cookbook. I recommend the recipes for Vietnamese-style spring rolls, crispy rice noodle and tofu salad, and spicy lentil soup with sausages. That's good eating. The way to a rock star's heart is through his belly. A really good vegetarian meal can turn his will into jelly.

For maximum enjoyment I recommend listening to Linda sing the classic *COOK OF THE HOUSE* (available on *AT THE SPEED OF SOUND*) as you peruse these fine recipes.   D-

LINDA'S PICTURES by Linda McCartney (1976 Knopf)

We have here the first and by the far the best of Mrs. McCartney's photography books. Linda was a groupie and a shutterbug before she made a love connection with Paul at The Bag O'Nails. She was out there in America getting up close and personal with the cream of the crop of young rockers. This beautiful coffee table work features suitable for framing portraits of Jim Morrison, Jimi Hendrix, and the Brian Jones Era Stones. But the greatest picture of all is one she took Saturday August 9th 1969 of the Beatles sitting outside in London. John and Paul are looking at each other as if to say this is the end. It really should have been an album cover. Thank God the bootleggers had the sense to use it. It would have been an absolutely perfect choice for a gatefold sleeve ala *PEPPER* if they had designed *ABBEY ROAD* that way.   B+

THE LIVES OF JOHN LENNON by Albert Goldman (1988 William Morrow & Company)

This is the much maligned biography. Paul McCartney, Yoko Ono, and Jann Wenner all urged the public to not read it for it did not show John in the most favorable light. There were horrible things divulged about him and they didn't want people to see the ugly side of the man. As Paul McCartney told official Beatles biographer Hunter Davies, "Since John died people want to make out like he was Martin Luther Lennon. But he wasn't. He could be a maneuvering swine."

The same time this book came out so did the Yoko approved theatrical documentary film *Imagine*. It shows his peace loving side. The book and the movie are always linked together in my mind. *Imagine* kind of bores me but I love *The Lives of John Lennon*. Lost in the backlash toward the book was the fact that Albert Goldman was a great writer. He knew how to get inside the heads of his subjects. Mr. Goldman did it with the Who, Lenny Bruce, and Elvis. He also started a bio on Jim Morrison but unfortunately God struck him down before he could finish it. I never have cared about that *David Copperfield* crap where you learn all about a man's childhood and why he became who he was except when reading Albert Goldman. He makes Lennon life in the 40's and 50's seem as interesting as his experiences in the 60's and 70's. No mean trick. There are so many great moments in this book. Here is a sampling:

1. "Inside John had always felt the pain of being a freak but he had fought to maintain a normal appearance, which was why he resisted wearing glasses with such fanatical determination."
2. "In seeking to buttress his frail but aggressive ego with a gang of onstage henchman John Lennon had initiated a complicated chain reaction that resulted eventually in his being swallowed up by his own creation."
3. "A typical mama's boy of the pet lamb variety, Brian Samuel Epstein had been shaped since birth by the anxious ministrations of his mother."
4. "John established the pattern of his life…from infatuation to disillusionment."
5. "The rock hero must be like a lion tamer who every time he enters the cage is prepared to impose his will upon the will of the beast."
6. "John Lennon would suddenly snap out of his trance and thunder up at the control booth: 'What the fuck are you doing up there! You're not supposed to be taking tea breaks! You're supposed to work straight through because we're the fucking Beatles.'"
7. "That a man as paranoid as Lennon was able to endure such a promiscuous crush of people was another of the miracles wrought by acid."
8. On writing *I AM THE WALRUS*: "Though this method of writing courted the accidental and the ephemeral, the song brought to burning focus every resource of Lennon's mature art, commencing with Lewis Carroll nonsense and including childhood recollections, ambient noise, acoustic collage, and the inevitable Mersey beat."

9. "John rose and addressed the other Beatles, 'I've got something very important to tell you all. I am Jesus Christ come back again.' They sat there stunned for a moment; then they all agreed this was a most important announcement."
10. Yoko recalled that she and John lived on a diet of champagne, caviar, and heroin. John said that they lived in, '...a strange cocktail of love, sex, and forgetfulness."
11. On Arthur Janov's primal scream therapy, "Janov believed if he could trip a patient back to his early childhood and make him scream forth the pain he had experienced when his wants were not fulfilled ,all the distorting and deadening defenses that the patient had subsequently built up to avoid feeling this original pain would be blown away and a new man would start forth, free again to feel the bliss and grief of life."
12. Fall 1980 John, "I just fired my bodyguard." Jesse Ed Davis, "Why?" John, "It's my rationale. That if they're going to get you , they're going to get you anyway. First, they kill the bodyguard."

This might be blasphemy to some Lennonheads but this is a mesmerizing read. Put it on the shelf next to *Lennon Remembers, The Playboy Interviews,* and *The Words and Music of John Lennon.*   A

THE LONG AND WINDING ROAD by Neville Stannard (1982 Virgin)

Here is a jaw droppingly comprehensive illustrated discography covering the first two decades of Beatle records. It's all here, you Beatle nuts! Not just a review of all the legitimate stuff but also an interesting sample of the bootlegs, a list of the 21 songs Paul and occasionally John gave away in the 60's, a run-down of British chart statistics, a look at the wonderful Xmas discs, a guide to who's who on PEPPER, and an overview of the always fun "Paul is dead" clues.

As is only proper, this is separated into two main sections: British and American. As everyone knows those are two different worlds. The British releases are the way the Beatles wanted their music represented. The American releases are the way Capitol records wanted to represent the British masterpieces to their captive audience in the States.

Neville Stannard, I take my hat off to you. If my book can even be mentioned in the same breath with *The Long and Winding Road* I'll be eternally grateful. A-

P.S.: Recommended to me by John Dalton of West Hollywood, California. Thanks John.

LONG AND WINDING ROADS: The Evolving Artistry of the Beatles by Kenneth Womack (2007 Continuum)

In the grand tradition of Ian MacDonald comes this razor sharp analysis of how the Beatles went from the simple LOVE ME DO to the masterful collage of side two of ABBEY ROAD. If you're looking for a fab tome that weaves in Bjornstjerne Bjornson, Ford Madox Ford, James Earl Ray, Margaret Atwood, Lee Marvin, Rufus Wainwright, T.S. Eliot, e.e. cummings, Marcel Proust, Oscar Wilde, John Cage, Edith Bouvier Beale, and the Gideon Bible then you've come to the right place.

Womack goes through the work piece by piece and comes up with these insights:

1. EIGHT DAYS A WEEK "exudes charm from every nook and cranny."
2. SHE SAID SHE SAID "threatens to refute the reality of childhood bliss."
3. PENNY LANE "not surprisingly... finds its origins in 'Fern Hill' Dylan Thomas's beloved poem about the halcyon days of childhood."
4. DIG A PONY is "a masterpiece of whimsical nonsensicality."
5. CARRY THAT WEIGHT shows "that we inevitably shoulder the past's frequently irredeemable burden for the balance of our lives."
6. GIRL suggests "that in the end, we all too frequently serve the desire the desires of the self before ministering to the needs of others."

7. TOMORROW NEVER KNOWS "reminds us that the act of living implies that the past never really dies."
8. GETTING BETTER "features Lennon's confessional lyrics about his violent treatment of women in the past."
9. STRAWBERRY FIELDS FOREVER has a "false ending in which the music effects a return, in the circular fashion of Joyce's *Finnegan's Wake*."

I learned a lot from Mr. Womack but I didn't always agree with everything he had to say...especially when it came to my favorite album THE BEATLES (referred to by Womack for some reason as THE WHITE ALBUM... maybe it has to do with the color of the cover).

1. WILD HONEY PIE is a "trifle." That's being way too kind. As Lennon would have put it: it's a piece of garbage.
2. ROCKY RACCOON ends up "a surprisingly moving tale about the nature of nostalgia and loss." The only thing ROCKY RACCOON ever moved me to do was fast forward to the next track (unfortunately the next track is a Ringo composition).
3. WHY DON'T WE DO IT IN THE ROAD features "a throat-gnashing vocal commonly assumed to belong to John." That's news to me. I always thought it was James Paul McCartney wailing.
4. JULIA is "arguably his most powerful and fully realized composition." I think it is inarguably tied with GOODNIGHT for his lamest song on THE BEATLES. I just hope to God that Womack doesn't mean it's Lennon's most powerful and fully realized composition ever because there are at least a half

dozen tracks from PLASTIC ONO BAND that would be in the running not to mention these two from THE BEATLES: HAPPINESS IS A WARM GUN and I'M SO TIRED.

5. HELTER SKELTER "witnesses the Beatles in the act of invoking the sound and mettle of pure unadulterated terror." It is a noisy slab of rock but I believe that divorced from the Tate/ LaBianca murders there would be no listener hearing/feeling the sound and mettle of unadulterated terror.
6. SAVOY TRUFFLE "doesn't really go anywhere." It might be because I'm always jonesing for a sugar fix but I find this to be a charming confection. George never spoke so directly to my spiritual being as he does here.
7. CAN YOU TAKE ME BACK is "an unlisted outtake." It is unlisted but it's not an outtake. All songs released officially are intakes. Otherwise it would have wound up on ANTHOLOGY 3 with NOT GUILTY.   A-

THE LONGEST COCKTAIL PARTY by Richard DiLello (1972 Playboy, 2014 Alfred)

There have been books about the Beatles by their wives, chauffeur, manager, personal assistants, offspring, friends, and critics. This memoir beats them all. It is by their house hippie. Richard DiLello was the low man on the totem pole during Apple Records notorious three year non-halcyon period. It was anything but calm and tranquil in the fab kingdom during the years 1968-1970. There was nothing peaceful about this time in their lives except, of course, for John and his wife's campaign to stop the war. Apple was the backdrop for dissension, tension, erosion, explosions, pilfering, drugging, drinking, philandering, and the break-up of the act you'd known for all these years. With the end of the Beatles on Apple fresh in Richard Dilello's marijuana and alcohol soaked mind he put down the facts as he recalled them about the first of the big time rock star vanity labels. Others would follow in the fab foursome's footsteps. There would be Rolling Stones Records. Mick always copied what the Beatles did. There would be Swan Song, which seemed like a horrible choice of names for Led Zeppelin when in short succession after starting the company Robert Plant's life fell apart. He would be in a terrible car crash in 1975, have his son die in 1977, and best friend pass away from too much booze in 1980. It's no wonder he always resisted a permanent re-union with John and Jimmy. To this day fans associate the logos from these labels with the three famous acts. I think of the shiny green Granny Smith apple when I think of the Beatles, the big red lips and tongue when I ponder Mick and Keith, and the angel with a broken wing when I remember Bobby Plant's humanity. There would also be surprising companies from George (Dark Horse) and Ringo (Ring 'O Records). Didn't those two learn their lesson with Apple?

Hugh Hefner has always been famous for knowing two good things when he saw them. As the 1970's dawned and the Age of Aquarius was shattered on dawn's highway bleeding Mr. Hefner was presented with two proposals at his Chicago, Illinois mansion. One was from Holocaust/Manson Family survivor Roman Polanski. To clear his palette post Helter Skelter he thought he would follow up his light comedy smash *Rosemary's*

Baby with something a little darker. It would be his adaptation of the classic Bill Shakespeare chestnut *Macbeth* complete with bloody violence and one actor cast simply because he resembled Manson. After this cathartic purging Roman would go back to romantic comedy with the fun romp known as *Chinatown*. Jack Nicholson grew up thinking his aunt was his mother so Jack's buddy Robert Towne made sure to allude to that kind of wackiness in his *Chinatown* script. Hef jumped right on *Macbeth* and out it came as a *Playboy Films* production. Then before Hugh had time to catch his breath Richard Dilello came to him with the behind the scenes true life tale of four millionaires and their mansion headquarters in the heart of a major metropolis. Feeling sympatico with rich men living the high life with booze and broads Hefner published Dilello's masterwork post-haste though he always maintained that *Playboy's* decades long debauchery fest was the real longest cocktail party.

In the 1970's before John was murdered there was a lot of irreverence about the Beatles. After all, with their love they had not saved the world, if they only knew. So before there was the comedy of Tony Hendra's amazing Lennon rip MAGICAL MISERY TOUR (1972), Lester Bang's dream is over "Dandelions in Still Air: the Withering Away of the Beatles" (1975), Susan Winslow and Russ Regan's tasteless documentary (with a score of Lennon/McCartney songs by a cavalcade of rock superstars) *All This and World War II* (1976), Mark Shipper's satire *Paperback Writer* (1978), the *National Lampoon's* all Beatle issue (1977) and Eric Idle and Neil Innes' mockumentary *All You Need is Cash* (1978) there was the house hippie's expose of 3 Savile Row London, England.

You can tell this book has its tongue in the right place just by a look at selected chapter titles:

1. Chapter 13: For a penny you can buy a book of matches and set yourself on fire.
2. Chapter 16: LSD conditions and beautifies troubled hair in seconds.
3. Chapter 25: Art is long, life is short, judgment difficult, opportunity fleeting.
4. Chapter 31: Like Brinsley Schwartz over troubled waters.
5. Chapter 38: Play the album cover and throw the record away.
6. Chapter 55: Chopped liver, wherever you're going, I'm going your way.
7. Chapter 61: In the name of the Father (John Lennon) and of the Son (John Lennon) and of the Holy Ghost (John Lennon) Amen.
8. Chapter 85: There's a hot dog stand on the corner of the United States of America and it's calling me back home.
9. Chapter 87: It's a great place to get stoned but I wouldn't want to work there.

Thrill to the hilarious adventures of Press Officer Derek Taylor and his Client Liaison Officer as they handle all the Beatle mischief thrown at them. It's a lot like Robert Altman's *MASH* minus the blood. Find out about Apple failures like James Taylor and White Trash. Be excited by the every silver lining has a dark cloud success story of the Iveys. Enjoy George Harrison personally inviting the Hells Angels over to London and then realizing his mistake and having to ask them to please leave. Get a kick out of the Angels threatening John Lennon (dressed as Father Christmas!) at the 1968 Xmas party because the largest turkey in Great Britain wasn't ready to eat yet. Watch Harrison run away from a child fan who is screaming "George!" at him at the top of his lungs. Have fun with Lennon vetoing McCartney's decision not to release White Trash's cover version of a song Paul wrote (*GOLDEN SLUMBERS*) with the words, "That's a good imitation of us! It's going out!" Learn of art director Gene Mahon's ahead of his time thinking in regards to the Apple label, "Listen, why don't we have the A-side of the record as a completely whole apple with no writing on it whatsoever." Unfortunately at the time it was a legal requirement that each side of a record have contents clearly stated on both sides In the 70's this law went out the window and famous bands such as Public Image Ltd. released vinyl with one side of the record featuring no information. This was copied by many groups including my favorite punk band the Fems on their *GO TO A PARTY* EP. Hear about Harrison's protégé Brute Force who was known for his little ditty *THE KING OF FUH*. See the photo of Jimi Hendrix at the Post Office Tower as Mary Hopkin is celebrated with a barrel of guess what.

There's a lot of stuff to savor here. Derek Taylor's 1968 goodbye to Los Angeles party invitation stands out as a wonder of its kind. Derek was quite a good writer (remember *A Cellarful of Noise*?). He refers to the early 1968 Byrds as "older Byrds" I wonder what the remaining members are now...almost dead Byrds, I guess. This was during the period when Gram Parsons was in the band. Don Van Vliet is referenced as "dear deadpan Captain Beefheart." Derek charged for the party. "It is regretted that having given all my money to the Black Panthers, the El Monte Geranium Fund, and the Friends of Elks, I have to charge $5.50 per ticket."

There's the time when Spider, the Hell's Angel asked George a simple question as Harrison asks them to move along. Spider, "Do you dig us or don't you?" George, "Yin and yang, heads and tails, yes and no." Spider, "All right, man, I can dig it. We'll be out of here in ten minutes."

There is the dope about John and Paul appearing on *The Tonight Show* Starring Johnny Carson at Rockerfeller Center (Carson was the host before Jimmy Fallon took over). Unfortunately Carson was not available to talk to hippie freaks like Lennon and McCartney so Major League Baseball catcher Joe Garagiola subbed for him. Unfortunately, NBC TV taped over this episode so there is no video available of this historic event.

There's the time a mega celebrity showed up in the lobby. "Adolf Hitler is in reception." The response from Derek Taylor, "Oh, Christ, not that arsehole again! All right, send him up!"

There is the house hippie's patented way to get laid. "I'll ball you if you introduce me to Paul McCartney." "All right." Two days later. "Hey, I thought you were going to introduce me to Paul McCartney." "That's what I tell all the girls." "You bastard!"

There is the question of how to handle a tasteful album sleeve like the one for *TWO VIRGINS*. "He's sticking his c--- out a long way on this one, and now they've really got an excuse for going after him and her."

The staff at Apple always looks lazy. "It seems that every time George Harrison walks into this office, I'm eating a pizza, Carol is fixing her eyelashes, and you're rolling a joint. I wonder what he thinks," said Mavis Smith.

The house hippie wearing his trademark white afro is dawdling at the Rupert Street market when he hears somebody hiss at him, "Get your 'air cut!" It's Paul McCartney.

Oddly enough, the chapter on 1969 mentions the rooftop concert only in passing. I guess DiLello went out to lunch that day or maybe he called in sick. It's a weird event to miss when you work in the building where the gig takes place.

The first three parts of this book are gold. But Part Four mars the presentation a little. It is two dozen pages of reports from *The Times* in 1971 about the court proceedings that would lead to the end of the band and the final nail in the coffin of Apple Corp Mach 1. It's like watching *Interiors* after an afternoon of *Take the Money and Run, Play it again Sam,* and *Love and Death.*

Full disclosure: This is the first Beatles book I ever read or should I say the first Beatles related book. My brother Mark shoplifted it from a drug store. For the record I shoplifted the *Rolling Stone* issue from the late 70's that featured the Village People on the cover and a lengthy interview with George Harrison. How the mighty had fallen! A

THE LOST BEATLES INTERVIEWS by Geoffrey Giuliano (1994 Dutton)

Finally somebody gives us the truth about Richard Starkey, "The consistent twaddle that he is any way stupid or inept is just that. An engaging little man with a penchant for transforming the mundane into the magical, Starr may turn out to be the most subtly brilliant of the lot." I was positive that Lennon was the most subtly brilliant but live and learn.

Finally someone spills the beans on George, "Positioned dead center as the group's searing spiritual heart, Harrison became the conscience of a generation, pushing the perimeters of our life experience to include the concepts of innate spirituality and the possibility of unquestioning, uncompromising, unalloyed love." Thank you, Georgie. Thank you, Lord.

Finally we find out what Ono really did to John, "Once Yoko settled in for the duration…things quickly changed and Lennon became forever entangled in her wacky, often self-indulgent, artsy head space." Well, maybe not forever. "Towards the end John had pretty much rejected Yoko's influence over his work in favor of the straight-ahead pop/rock idiom that reached out and grabbed him as a kid back in Liverpool." I guess we only have J.O. L. to blame for _ROCK 'N' ROLL_ and _DOUBLE FANTASY_.

Finally, we find out about Giuliano's real feelings about Paul's songs, "…a long string of pretty, toe-tapping, largely inconsequential ditties tailor-made for the undemanding international top ten. Staunchly denying the deep river that runs through him, McCartney could have been a hell of a musician but settled on triple-platinum rock stardom instead. Pity." That is the most scathing assessment of P.M. I have ever seen from an alleged Beatle worshipper. I guess Giuliano is not the fan I always thought he was.

Geoffrey's painting of Ringo as brilliant while putting Paul down as an "inconsequential" hit maker is certainly a perverse way of looking at things. I have to give Geoffrey credit for not taking the obvious path. But two questions remain: when he met Paul did he tell him what he thought of his pretty toe-tappers and when he met Yoko did he let her know how wacky and self-indulgent she was and how her being that way screwed John up for quite a long time? I'm already sure he told George when he talked to him that he was an inspiration to us all. Lest we forget George said this about the great Giuliano, "This guy knows more about my life than I do." Is there any chance that Krishna lover Geoffrey holds Harrison in the highest esteem of the four because he was also a Krishna devotee? I'm just asking.

That's not all, folks. There's a special bonus treat in this interesting book of interviews. Dr. Timothy Leary shows up with eight pages of why we should "Thank God for The Beatles."

1. The fab four were: "Young evolutionary agents sent by DNA, endowed with musical powers to sing about a new breed of humans."
2. "The Beatles are inspired Psalmists. Wise, slick Divinity Agents who come along exactly when we needed to be reminded about what's happening."
3. They were "joyful young messiahs who dispel our fears and charm us back into the pagan dance of harmony."

4. "Of course if you were born after 1970 you will find it incredibly uncool when your parents babble on about Woodstock and the Hippie Days."
5. "Believing in God is a mind-blower, baby."
6. "You are God coming back in human form... So whom do you address? The adolescents."
7. "How do you announce the revelation to the fresh flower heads? Proclamations? Nope. Pass laws and resolutions? Nope. Books? Nope. You use music. The mythic voice of the epic minstrel."
8. "Are they really Divine Agents? How can anyone know? What's the criterion? Miracles, of course. And so it came to pass that in one year the Four Evangelists, brash, uneducated carpenters' sons from Liverpool, became the most powerful VOICES the world has ever listened to. Holy minstrels. Electronic instruments of the divine current."
9. "The *SGT. PEPPER* album...compresses the evolutionary development of musicology and much of the history of Eastern and Western sound in a new tympanic complexity."
10. "The Beatles were sent to the Maharishi to teach him...that if you keep traveling east you'll end up back home where you started from. The planet is round."

This blasphemous nonsense comes from a man who sued John Lennon for turning his gubernatorial campaign slogan into a Beatles' song (*COME TOGETHER*) so you might want to take it with a grain of salt.

As for the meat of this book there's some good stuff here that I'm glad was collected from the cutting room floor:

- The transcript of John apologizing for his, "We're more popular than Jesus" remark.
- Selected quotes on how they feel about God and getting high.
- John and Paul renouncing the Maharishi while promoting the launching of Apple (John, "We made a mistake." Paul, "We thought there was more to him than there was, but he's human and for a while we thought he wasn't").
- An opportunity to eavesdrop on J&Y and Harrison while they rap with His Divine Grace A.C. Bhaktivedanta Swami Prabhupada and Devotee (John, "Why isn't Hare Krishna or something similar in the Bible?" Devotee, "It's in the Bible. In Psalms it says 'Praise the Lord with every breath. Praise the Lord with drum and flute." John, "But they haven't got very good tunes.")
- Most importantly there are words to live by "What does each Beatle consider his most valued possession?" John replied, "Our lives." B

THE LOST BEATLES PHOTOGRAPHS: The Bob Bonis Archive, 1964-1966 by Larry Marion with photographs by Bob Bonis (2011 HarperCollins)

It's nice to see all these pictures from 1964-1966 that have been collecting dust for close to half a century. Bob Bonis was the U.S. tour manager during those legendary years and he was also an amateur photographer. So he took these snaps and then he put them up on the walls in his house. Thankfully, somebody finally realized there was money to be made and presto we get this lovely book for only $29.99 plus tax. I don't know if I would pay that much for it but it's certainly worth something. Particularly fun are the photos where the others try to drown Paul in the pool (the first Paul is dead clue?), the ones where Ringo fools around with a toy gun putting it to his head in a mock suicide pose, the one where John plays the organ with his elbow (what a kidder!), the ones where Lennon does his infamous imitations of the disabled (what an asshole!), and the one where roadie Mal Evans shoves a gun in Ringo's face (in 1976 Evans was shot to death by the Los Angeles police).

Not much in the way of text but there is a boring foreword by 55th Beatle Larry Kane who seems to have spent most of the last 50 years telling everybody he can that he knew the Beatles personally and that he was their friend and confidant. Got it, Larry! Thanks for the memories!   B

THE LOVE YOU MAKE: An Insider's Story of the Beatles by Peter Brown & Steven Gaines (2002 New American Library)

I never liked this book. I didn't like it in 1983 when it first came out. I didn't like it when it was re-released in 2002. I don't like it now. It takes the most exciting story in the history of rock and roll and makes it seem boring. It has no spark. It has no soul. Its sin is its lifelessness. Even the new 2002 forward by Anthony DeCurtis is terrible.

Peter *"THE BALLAD OF JOHN AND YOKO"* Brown gives us useless tidbits:

1. "Ringo complained of the roughness of the toilet paper in the EMI john, it made headlines in several daily papers."
2. When they first meet at the Indica art gallery John asks Yoko, "Where's the orgy?"
3. "It was hard to tell what part of the Beatles madness was drug induced and what part was pure whimsy."
4. George swore in 1967 he would stop taking drugs "a promise, of course, he would not keep."
5. *THE END* is "The last song on the last Beatles' album." No, that would be *HER MAJESTY*.

If you want to read their story you should start with Nicholas Schaffner's splendid *Beatles Forever*. D-

MAGIC CIRCLES: The Beatles in Dream and History by Devin McKinney (2003 Harvard University)

This is not your usual mop top book. It is the Beatles in dream and history. It scrubs under the surface of the Tate/LaBianca murders. They're creepy and they're kooky, mysterious and spooky, they're all together ooky, the Manson family. It presents the unintelligible truth of the counterculture. It shows us the elevation of the group from human to god. It tells us of the weariness and loathing implicit in the Beatles' relationship to the world. It lets us know why only Paul was wearing a black carnation (they ran out of red ones). It features a really nice annotated discography. It compares the lyrics of Manson's song *CEASE TO EXIST* (recorded and released by the Beach Boys!) with Lennon's *TOMORROW NEVER KNOWS*. It seems that both tunes are "blatant instances of crypto-spiritual, psycho-cultic indoctrination in a pop context." I did not know that. In fact, I didn't know a lot of this stuff but it's always nice to learn. It says on the dust cover that author Devin McKinney is an independent scholar living in Brooklyn. I think I'll go visit him and find out the secrets of the universe. Something's going to change my world. B+

THE MAMMOTH BOOK OF THE BEATLES edited by Sean Egan (2009 Running Press)

The best $13.99 you'll ever spend. This is hands down the best entry in the Mammoth Book series. It contains some junk but you can skip right over it because this book is huge. By all means ignore Gary Hall's brain dead "Living life without loving the Beatles", Dave Simpson's tone deaf "Penny Lame" (*"STRAW-BERRY FIELDS* and *HEY JUDE* are marvelous. But if I ponder the rest-all I think is Help!" Right, Dave. They only wrote two classic pop songs. Better get your hearing checked.), Ken Sharp's interview with Astrid Kirchherr, and Paul Gambaccini's beyond simple "Masters of Rock."

That still leaves you with Sean Egan's superlative assessment of the canon, the ridiculously self-serving self-interview from McCartney in 1970 (slipped in to the reviewers copies of his first solo LP *McCARTNEY*) in which he kind of announces the end of the band (Q: "Is this album a rest away from the Beatles or the start of a solo career? A: "Time will tell" and Q: "Is your break with the Beatles temporary or permanent? A: "I don't really know."), and the delicious treat of Lester Bang's hilarious "Dandelions in Still Air: The withering away of the Beatles" (1975).

See if you don't agree with these on the ball observations from the great Sean Egan, rock writer par excellence:

1. *LOVE ME DO*: "…did not prove that all the record companies who had turned the Beatles down had been wrong, nor did it indicate that they would become the most celebrated entertainers of the twentieth century."
2. *P.S. I LOVE YOU*: "…a song that would have impressed those who had never heard of the Beatles more (than *LOVE ME DO*)."
3. *PLEASE PLEASE ME* 45: "…when early on in the Beatles' career they decided on this joint credit (Lennon/McCartney that changed to McCartney/Lennon at the beginning of their recording career then back to Lennon/McCartney) there was no reason not to help the other as best they could, rather than hold back good riffs, hooks and ideas for their own work."
4. *PLEASE PLEASE ME* LP: Their first 12 inch "…was the last album of this type that the Beatles would ever make."
5. *FROM ME TO YOU*: "…fairly cynically made sure that their third single had a harmonica riff like the previous two."

6. *SHE LOVES YOU*: "The band was very aware of the way the record was stuffed with hooks and gimmicks."
7. *WITH THE BEATLES*: "...lived up to the impression given by the sleeve of serious artists..."
8. "There is just something indefinably lovely and warm about *CAN'T BUY ME LOVE*."
9. *A HARD DAY'S NIGHT* 45: "...the aching unhappiness implicit in the lyric is washed away by the music."
10. *A HARD DAY'S NIGHT* LP: "...if the Beatles had not been so rushed they would have striven for more sophisticated lyrics."
11. *I FEEL FINE*: "...radio listeners swung their heads toward their radio sets in alarm or surprise as it emitted a peculiar humming sound that throbbed, then flared into an almost painful crescendo."
12. *BEATLES FOR SALE*: "The Lennon/McCartney songs are accomplished but to a large extent strangely dejected."
13. *TICKET TO RIDE*: "... an arrestingly disconsolate presence on the hit parade."
14. *HELP!* 45: "...(they) engage not in call-and-response but –delightfully-response-and-call with George and Paul anticipating John's lead vocal lines."
15. *YESTERDAY*: "...Paul's brooding lament for a departed female as a subconscious pining for his deceased mother...Paul gave quotes indicating he agreed."
16. *WE CAN WORK IT OUT*: "...is an exercise in elegance."
17. *RUBBER SOUL*: "...(they) added another layer of admirers with this record: the hipsters and the folkies."
18. *RAIN*: "...is distinctly un-Beatley in its disinterest in being ingratiating." Something that Lennon would later turn into his trademark.

19. *ELEANOR RIGBY*: "…there is an undeniable feeling of distance."
20. *SGT. PEPPER* LP: "Though nobody suggests that *PEPPER'S* brilliance was a completely illusory product of a heady time, the album has fallen down the esteem scale in recent years, both as a piece of art and as a part of the Beatles oeuvre."
21. *ALL YOU NEED IS LOVE*: "The philosophy was incredibly naïve of course but, as with just about everything in life, you could only recognize its shortcomings by working your way through it in the first place."
22. *MAGICAL MYSTERY TOUR* double EP: "…feels very much like (*PEPPER*), only not as good."
23. *LADY MADONNA*: "For all its good intentions…remains a bit unimpressive."
24. *REVOLUTION*: "The gun blast of grimy guitar at the beginning…is one of the most exciting intros of any record."
25. *IT'S ALL TOO MUCH*: "…is a featureless affair that comes perilously close to being as interminable as *BLUE JAY WAY*."
26. *DON'T LET ME DOWN*: "Whatever one's feelings about Ono…it can't be denied that she was a good muse."
27. *LET IT BE* 45: "…is one of those phrases that has the smack of ancient wisdom and feels like we have heard it all our lives." It was definitely a poor choice for Paul to sing at Live Aid but *GET BACK* would have been even worse.
28. *LET IT BE* LP: "Had it been issued by any other rock artists, (it) would have been regarded as great-to-classic."

29. *THE LONG AND WINDING ROAD*: "Had Paul kept his gob shut, we would have been able to enjoy the harp and choir without worrying that we might be knuckleheads easily impressed by manipulative schmaltz."
30. *THE BALLAD OF JOHN AND YOKO*: "Despite the ultra-modern sacrilege and the fact of it being the first single mixed in stereo, the track is actually quite retro."
31. *COME TOGETHER*: "John adds to the vague air of menace with a vocal issued between gritted teeth."
32. *ABBEY ROAD*: "…having taken it as far as it could go, the Beatles bowed out."

Sean Egan also makes good points about *LIVE PEACE IN TORONTO* ("a worthwhile side and an atrocious one"), *ANTHOLOGY 1* ("Where the hell is the recording of Lennon playing with the Quarry Men the day he met Paul?"), *ANTHOLOGY 2* ("surely only those not familiar with Beatles music would be able to sit through this…without recurring feelings of dismay and irritation at the way the greatest catalogue in history is being cheapened."), and *ANTHOLOGY 3* ("After sitting through three double set CDs of wildly varying quality, one can't help but feel that this whole exercise could have been profoundly truncated").

There's also a nice wrapping up of Egan's feelings about the solo years, "The Beatles as an entity lived fast, died young and left a beautiful corpse. Their reputation is unsullied by music that is a grotesque parody of their former glories. For that mercy, we can bear all the mediocre and disappointing solo albums in the world."

But Sean does go overboard at times like when he tells us that *PAST MASTERS VOLUME TWO* "constitutes the greatest collection of music ever assembled." After all, that compilation features the throwaway B-sides *THE INNER LIGHT* and *YOU KNOW MY NAME (LOOK UP THE NUMBER)*.

The biggest surprise is what he doesn't like. *I WANT TO HOLD YOUR HAND* ("Cynicism of motivation in no way precludes great art, especially in popular music, but here the note that is struck is totally false."), *STRAWBERRY FIELDS FOREVER* b/w *PENNY LANE* ("...both sound not like the bold, arresting statements required of singles but, more than anything, like good album tracks."), *I AM THE WALRUS* ("The track's radicalism has earned it greater kudos than it perhaps deserves."), *HEY JUDE* ("...frankly this critic has never been able to listen to it without beginning to gaze out the window well before the end."), *WHILE MY GUITAR GENTLY WEEPS* ("One feels that one should like this evocatively titled Harrison rumination...Yet it's clunky, and Clapton's solo is unimpressive.") and the universally regarded best fab album ever *REVOLVER* ("To this critic...large parts of it will always sound like the Beatles as approximated by a computer.").

Plus, his least favorite album by them is *THE BEATLES* which just happens to be my most favorite. As you might have guessed he agrees with big George Martin that it would have been great if you had just eliminated a long player's worth of tunes. Also, he doesn't like the tone of the set ("The Beatles were presenting themselves as they really were-people susceptible like all human beings to boredom, horniness, hatred, even suicidal depression-and the results were not necessarily pleasant to contemplate." Precisely the reason I love the album. It seems like their most honest.). To show us the way he breaks down *THE BEATLES* into four distinct categories.

Number 1: Ephemera, doodles, sketches, and rubbish

Number 2: Failed experiments

Number 3: Material that is quite enjoyable but which in your heart of hearts you know is not quite good enough to merit space on a Beatles' album in normal circumstances

Number 4: The very good-to-classic

If Mr. Egan had it his way it would have been one record with fourteen songs just the way they usually sequenced their LPs before *PEPPER*. Thank God, that is just his fantasy. I agree with Sir Paul McCartney who felt that the reason it was cool was because it had so much stuff on it. It is also why I love *SANDINISTA!* (a three record sprawling mess) and *WINGS OVER AMERICA* (a three record approximation of a concert). If any album is too long it's *ALL THINGS MUST PASS*. There is absolutely no excuse for *APPLE JAM*.   A

MAN ON THE RUN: Paul McCarney in the 1970's by Tom Doyle (2013 Ballantine)

There are several books on Paul that cover his life in the 70's. There are several books on John that cover his life in the 70's. There are no books on George and Ringo that cover their lives in the 70's. As a public service I will now give you all the pertinent details of the sitar player and the percussionist in the 70's. George had one album that people loved in 1970 and then made five more albums that people barely cared about. He organized one great benefit concert and went on one tour which the public and the critics hated in equal measure. His wife left him for his best friend. He let Ringo help him write *PHOTOGRAPH*. As for Mister Starkey: he made two albums that people ignored and /or despised in 1970 and then made the universally adored *RINGO* long player and then made four more albums that people didn't care about at all. He shaved his head. He allegedly helped George a little with *PHOTOGRAPH*.

I was hoping this book would have revealing info on Paul's greatest achievement in the me decade and I struck gold. There were a full two pages on the behind the scenes machinations of the legendary *THRILLINGTON* album of 1977. On a par with Orson Welles' *The War of the Worlds* prank in 1938 the *THRILLINGTON* album was Paul's greatest joke. According to the British press there was a posh society figure/amateur musician named Percy "Thrills" Thrillington who had decided to release an orchestral version of *RAM*. It turned out it was actually commissioned by good old Paulie who wanted to have a lightweight Muzak version of his music on the market. Some wags have been known to say that all his post-Beatles recordings have had a lightweight Muzak feel to them but I think that's a little harsh.

What distinguishes this bio from others is that Tom Doyle interviewed Paul recently and parts of the conversations are peppered throughout the book. It's much better than just getting the writer's opinions. There are a few nice nuggets from our favorite bass player:

1. "I'm the world's worst analyst of me. Fans can tell you exactly what was going on in the 1960's, and I

kinda go, Oh yeah, that's right." It must be weird when you're living your life and all kinds of freaks are living vicariously by studying your life and commenting on it. Not that I consider myself a freak.
2. On his use of the thumbs up gesture, "I have been chastened by the world opinion on that. You will not actually see me do it. 'One thing you must not do is put your fucking thumbs up, you twat!'"
3. After a fan shook his hand and kept Paul in a vise grip for what seemed like an eternity, "That was fucking big of him to let me go, wasn't it?"
4. On Wings' reputation for making lite piffle, "There's a lot of dubious stuff." Tom Doyle, "Which records do you think were dubious?" Paul, "I'm not damning myself."

Still, I can't wholeheartedly recommend *Man on the Run*. In 2015 I need something more than just a pat rundown of events that took place 36 to 45 years ago. All the old Beatlemaniacs know this stuff already and I'm sure young Beatlemaniacs care much more about the Beatles than they do about Wings. After all, there is no such thing as a Wingsmaniac. At least I hope not.

B

THE MAN WHO "FRAMED" THE BEATLES: A Biography of Richard Lester by Andrew Yule (1994 Donald I. Fine)

Here we have the biography of acclaimed film director Dickie Lester from the author of books on Sean Connery and Al Pacino. By default, the one about the godfather must be better than this one. I couldn't find one anecdote worthy of passing along to all you *Hard Day's Night, Help!, How I Won the War,* and *Get Back* (the Paul 1989-1990 comeback tour video) fans. This is much stronger on Lester's work involving the three musketeers, Superman, and Julie Christie playing a tuba.

So I have two questions:

1. Does any book that has the word Beatles in its title qualify as a Beatle book? If the answer is no, maybe I'm wasting valuable time here. But then again don't Beatlemaniacs lean toward comprehensive coverage of their heroes?
2. If *Petulia* is my favorite Richard Lester film by far does that mean I have to turn in my Fab Fan Club badge?

On the plus side McCartney wrote the introduction for this thing and he reveals a couple items I never knew before:

1. The band was offered as their first film something called *The Yellow Teddy Bears* with all songs written for them. I'm sure that would have been way out!

2. After *Hard Day's Night* they were compared to the Marx Brothers so amongst the group they figured out that, "John simply had to be Groucho, George was the definite Chico, Ringo was a natural for Harpo, which left me, I suppose, as Zeppo. Oh, well." Makes some sense because Zeppo was the brother designated for the romantic scenes but wouldn't the quiet Beatle be Harpo? C-

THE MAN WHO GAVE THE BEATLES AWAY by Allan Williams and William Marshall (1975 Macmillan)

Here is a very sad story. Get out your handkerchiefs. This broken man was the manager of the band before Brian Epstein. Can you imagine how sick this guy must have felt the rest of his life? I mean, sure, he got a book deal but could that ever make up for the pain and regret of giving up the most lucrative act in music history? Ironically, he broke with them over money they owed him and refused to pay.

According to Beatle fan Nicholas Schaffner, "Lennon gave Williams' lurid memoir a rave review and high marks for accuracy; McCartney dismissed it as a work of fiction."

From Allan's own pen: "I dropped the Beatles when they were on the very brink of becoming the biggest thing show business had ever seen. And if you think I lose a lot sleep over this, you are on the right track- because, brother, I often wake up at night and stare at the wall, and I can feel my teeth grinding together. They make a gritty noise in my skull and the sweat starts to pop out my brow, as I think of how I let the band and a million quid slip through my fingers. I know I'm not the only sucker who didn't realize that the Beatles were to become the biggest stars in show biz...I'm not the only guy who paces the floor at night wondering: Where did I go wrong? Why aren't the millions all mine? We can't all be right all the time."

A report that the suspicious locked door drug overdose in 1967 of impresario Brian Epstein was in reality a homicide has yet to be confirmed. C-

THE MAN WHO MADE THE BEATLES: An Intimate Biography of Brian Epstein by Ray Coleman (1989 McGraw-Hill)

I love biographies of rock star managers. I treasure my copies of *Colonel Tom Parker: What a Scumbag*, Allan Williams' *I'm Going To Hang Myself Because I let that Faggot take over Management of the Beatles*, Courtney Love's *Just When Things Were Going So Well*, Allan Klein's *I'm Gonna Suck Every Last Cent Out of These Guys No Matter What McCartney Says*, and, of course, the classic *Let's Get Some Drugs in Here for Mister Jackson, he's going to need all his strength for his upcoming shows*.

But seriously, here is what I think of this book. It's nice to get the real story of Epstein. That autobiography of his didn't ring true. There are a lot of sweet stories here about his pill popping rough trading ways. Plus, the rumor that he faked his own death so he could take a teaching post in Australia is put to rest. He actually went to run guns in Africa.

On July 7, 1967 they issued a B-side in which Lennon continued his many years of heaping abuse on poor Brian by pointedly singing on his song about the beautiful people: "Baby, you're a rich fag Jew." It was the last straw for Epstein. On August 27, 1967 he was gone.   C-

McCARTNEY YESTERDAY & TODAY by Ray Coleman (1996 Dove)

I was trying to figure out why I like Ray Coleman's Lennon biography way more than this one on Paul. Both books feature the same decent writing style, the same here-are-the facts approach, and the same "Isn't it impressive that I know the band personally?" tone. Then it hit me. John is much more interesting than Paul. As Ray Coleman points out "Paul's public image as a cheery, thumbs-up, lightweight man-of-the-people pop star has irritated him as much as his critics." Be careful what you pretend to be because that's what people will think you are. Even though we know about Paul's bossy and egomaniacal attitude, even though we know the Beatles and Wings all quit on him because he was overbearing, even though we know he can write blistering rockers like *I'M DOWN* and *HELTER SKELTER* many of us still think of him as the charming guy who sang such piffle as *MY LOVE, WITH A LITTLE LUCK,* and *SILLY LOVE SONGS*.

John cheated on Yoko and then broke up with Yoko. Paul stayed at Linda's side every second. John posed nude with Yoko. Paul had cucumber sandwiches with Linda. John vomited all over Paul in *HOW DO YOU SLEEP?* Paul fought back gently with *LET ME ROLL IT*. John starred in one solo movie *(How I Won the War)* where he ends up bleeding to death. Paul starred in one solo movie (*Give my Regards to Broad Street*) where he ends up putting the audience to sleep.

The main thing that makes a Lennon bio better than a McCartney bio is the quotes from the men themselves. Lennon said any number of horrible things about the other three while McCartney mostly goes the safe public relations route. Paul tends to be more subtle which doesn't make for exciting reading. C+

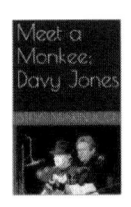

MEET A MONKEE: DAVY JONES by Steve Marinucci (2013 Smashwords)

I remember seeing photos of Mike Nesmith with Lennon and Micky Dolenz with McCartney but I always kind of figured the late, great Davy Jones must have felt some connection to the Beatles, him being English and all. Meet a Monkee confirms my suspicions.

I've always believed the Monkees were a "manufactured" group while the Beatles were "real." Davy Jones felt ,"...the way (the Beatles) presented themselves was of a manufactured nature." It made me stop and think. Brian Epstein did take them out of leather, made them stop cussing, kept the lid on Lennon, and for all intents and purposes cleaned them up for public consumption. Does that mean the Beatles were "manufactured"? Of course not ….When Colonel Parker put Elvis through one silly Hollywood movie after another did that mean Presley was "manufactured"? …Of course, not. So why disparage the Monkees? I mean, how the heck did Kiss make the Rock and Roll Hall of Fame and not the Monkees? What could be more "unreal" than Kiss?

Turns out Davy also had insight into Yoko. Instead of chastising Ono for breaking up the band Jones though we should laud her because John, "…wouldn't have been able to do the things he did later on if he hadn't moved into the next phase (with her)." Correct. We wouldn't have all that amazing early 70's solo stuff from Lennon if not for Yoko's influence. I salute her!

Weird Davy Jones trivia: when I saw him live in the early 21st Century he and his back –up band stopped for a few minutes to do a tribute to ALL IN THE FAMILY. Strange days indeed/Most peculiar mama. B

MEET THE BEATLES: A Cultural History of the Band that Shook Youth, Gender, and the World by Steven D. Stark (2005 HarperCollins)

Allegedly, this is a cultural history of the band that shook youth, gender, and the world but it reads more like another slapdash bio of the foursome's time together plus the requisite postscript chapter that jumps us right to Lennon's death and how that signaled the end of an era. Steven D. Stark does try a little to make points that haven't been made ad nauseum. He compares their hair to Oscar Wilde's, John's art college to the counterculture that came soon after it, and the screams of their female fans to the emotional upheaval of feminists yearning to break free from male oppression.

The first line of the book is "Why on earth would anyone need another book about the Beatles?" It makes sense to me that Mr. Stark is defensive right off the bat. His book is certainly one the world doesn't need. C-

MEMORIES OF JOHN LENNON edited and introduced by Yoko Ono (2005 *Harper Entertainment)*

In which musician (debatable) and multimedia widow Ono continues her seemingly endless outpouring of revisionist history. Some of the many fine stars that grace these pages actually met John Winston Ono Lennon MBE (returned). Reginald Dwight writes, "He was warm, sweet, and very funny." Billy Preston writes, "His legacy is grand and a true treasure." Jann Wenner writes, "John is obviously one of the great composers, songwriters, singers, and social critics of all time." Mark David Chapman writes, "He was always nice to me, signed an autograph and everything." Never is heard a discouraging word and the sky is not cloudy all day. C-

MISS O'DELL: Hard Days and Long Nights with The Beatles, The Stones, Bob Dylan, and Eric Clapton by Chris O'Dell with Katherine Ketcham (2009 Touchstone)

If you ever wished you were a fly on the wall when George was having an affair with Ringo's wife, this is the book for you. If you ever thought about what it would be like to snort heroin with Derek and the Dominoes, this is the book for you. If you ever wondered what it would be like to have Bob Zimmerman make a pass at you (and haven't we all wondered about that), this is the book for you.

Miss O'Dell also lets all of us music fans in on picking out outfits with Mick Jagger ("He loved suits that clung to his little butt"), the Beatles rooftop concert ("It was a bitter cold January day and the wind was blowing like crazy"), and scoring Keith Richard's "supplies" from his drug dealer ("It never occurred to me to say no"). Just say no. D+

THE MOURNING OF JOHN LENNON by Anthony Elliott (1999 University of California)

A whole book on fans still crying about the loss of Dr. Winston O'Boogie does hold for me a certain morbid fascination. Freud used to distinguish between "normal mourning" and "batshit we'll never see his likes again mourning." This is the latter. Freud would describe what has been going on for 35 years as an "open wound." Liverpool named their airport after him and the fans go and cry at Strawberry Fields and Strawberry Field. That's okay. That's normal.

But what Yoko has done can't be good. Year after year she tells us how John would feel about the world after his passing. Then she translates these feelings into product. There was a Broadway musical. There are John Lennon vintage 1974 action figures. There is a long running Las Vegas schlock fest. Yoko even put out a book (*Skywriting by Word of Mouth*) that John didn't want released because he felt it was, "not quite right." Ono let the rest of the Beatles pull AN AMERICAN PRAYER on FREE AS A BIRD and REAL LOVE. She won't let Paul credit his fab songs as McCartney/Lennon although Lennon let him do it on the WINGS OVER AMERICA live album. It's a travesty. Is this really what John would have wanted? How the hell would she know?

To her credit she sometimes tells the bitter truth about John instead of giving us candy coated memories. In the Yoko sanctioned *American Masters* episode entitled *Lennon NYC* she admits on camera that on Nixon/McGovern election night 1972 John dragged a girl into another room at a party and, "I guess you would say made love to her" and the girl was so loud that somebody turned up a Zimmerman album on the stereo to attempt to drown out her moaning but not even Bob's cow caught on a barb wire fence voice at maximum volume could do the trick.

I wish Anthony Elliott had written his book in the same jocular spirit as Greil Marcus' hilarious *Dead Elvis* but unfortunately it's very deep and very serious. Mr. Elliott feels bad that "Lennon is largely filtered through the oppressive ideology of celebrity, the dreary constraint of myth." But then he turns around and says "Lennon's murder spells not just the death of an individual but the death of an era…the era of peace, love, and understanding." I can't imagine how one rock star's passing could stop humanity's hope for a better tomorrow. Still, the deeper you go the higher you fly and despite its solemn nature Mr. Elliott's study did make me think. That's more than I can say about a lot of the Beatle books. B+

THE MUSIC OF GEORGE HARRISON: While My Guitar Gently Weeps by Simon Leng (2003 Firefly)

This does for George's solo years what *Revolution in the Head* did for the band's recorded output. Only the hardcore Harrison fan will care deeply and I am not one of those. Still, it does have a certain something. It's so well written it almost makes me feel like dusting off my copies of DARK HORSE, EXTRA TEXTURE, and GONE TROPPO and playing them for the first time in 30 years. Almost, but not quite. The author inevitably tries to make a case that George was a "major artist" despite the fact that "…his music is largely overlooked and passed over as unimportant." Can 50 million Beatle fans who don't give a damn about George's post-*ALL THINGS MUST PASS* career be wrong? B

NOWHERE MAN: The Final Days of John Lennon by Robert Rosen (2000 Soft Skull)

I'm a sucker for writings about Lennon's last days. What was he doing in the Dakota for five years? John said he was raising Sean but we all know he had nannies and assistants doing that. John said he never touched the guitar for half a decade but then cassettes of new songs from that period started appearing. Paul, George, and Ringo even made two singles out of these songs that Lennon claimed didn't exist. John was always part lies and part brutal truth telling (whatever made good copy). He was less a house husband than a burned out rock star who was taking drugs, having affairs, viewing a lot of TV in his room, watching his weight, and calling his wife, "Mother." Granted, Yoko was a mother but she wasn't his mother, at least not literally.

Robert Rosen does a great job in this slim volume of giving us his version of the final days. He's the Woodward and Bernstein of rock. This is well written and entertaining. It's 90% Lennon and 10% fascinating coda about Chapman. Rosen imagines himself in John's head and Mark's head. In 2014 Mark's wife Gloria urged Paul McCartney to get Chapman into his life. That's insane. Gloria also urged Yoko to forgive Chapman. That's insane. That's like asking Bobby Kennedy and Jackie O. to not be mad at Lee Harvey Oswald. Gloria said, "Paul would like Mark if he visited him because Mark always puts other's needs before his own." No, not always.

This book has sex ("John hooked up with Louise...She was really into getting him excited"), put downs of friends ("John was delighted that he had driven Peter Boyle over the edge...John felt emotionally and spiritually superior"), and apologies to Yoko for making her watch Reverend Billy Graham, on the tube, teach his flock about the proper way to live.

But my favorite part is John in Palm Beach answering the door when two kids show up. "'Does John Lennon live here?' one of them asked. 'No,' said John closing the door. He was in no mood for such intrusion. Real fans would have recognized him immediately. They'd have reacted as if Jesus Bloody Christ had opened the door."

This is kind of like Albert Goldman's *The Lives of John Lennon* but with less of an axe to grind. So beware all you dreamers who want to picture John as some sort of morally upright social activist. To all others, I heartedly recommend tracking this book down. A

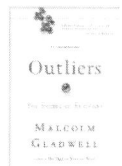

<u>OUTLIERS: The Story of Success</u> by Malcolm Gladwell (2008 Little, Brown and Company)

I feel duty bound to inform you that this is one of those products that my wife would say is not a Beatle book per se. The thing is, she would be right. But it does deal with the fabsters as an example of how to have success in life. Malcolm Gladwell's theory is this: to be a success it takes practice, ten thousand hours of practice. He has a valid point.

Lennon, McCartney, and Harrison were together for six/seven years before breaking in America in 1964. They played hour after hour, year after year, in Hamburg and at the Cavern. The Nurk twins discarded many a song (plus, Jane Asher threw some out while spring cleaning) before they arrived at the breakthrough of the *PLEASE PLEASE ME* single.

"What was so special about Hamburg?" asks Mr. Gladwell. "It was the sheer amount of time the band was forced to play." By 1964 "They had performed live an estimated twelve hundred times. Do you know how extraordinary that is? Most bands today don't perform twelve hundred times in their entire careers. The Hamburg crucible is one of the things that set the Beatles apart."

Unfortunately, Malcolm goes on to admit it's not just experience that makes one a success. Guess what, kids? You also need exceptional talent and good luck. I knew there was a catch. B-

PAPERBACK WRITER: The Life and Times of the Beatles, the Spurious Chronicle of Their Rise to Stardom, Their Triumphs and Disasters, Plus the Amazing Story of Their Ultimate Reunion by Mark Shipper (1978 Ace)

Greil Marcus said this was "The finest novel about rock and roll, it is certainly the funniest." I agree but is there a lot of serious competition in the rock and roll fiction department? There's David Littlejohn's *The Man Who Killed Mick Jagger, Spider Kiss* by Harlan Ellison, and Gerald Duff's *That's All Right, Mama: The Unauthorized Life of Elvis's Twin* but not much else.

Paperback Writer and *All You Need is Cash* came out the same year. They both twist the Beatles' legend until it cries uncle. Ringo gave an interview to Shipper about the life and times of the group. Shipper lost his notes and was forced into making up his own version of history. It's a lot like Nicholas Meyer's revisionist Sherlock Holmes stories from earlier in the 70's. In *The Seven-Percent Solution* and *The West End Horror* Meyers takes Arthur Conan Doyle's Holmes and Watson and puts them into contact with Freud, Stoker, Wilde, Gilbert, and Sullivan. In *Paperback Writer* Shipper gives us the Beatles cavorting with F. Stop Fitzgerald, God (only George can see him), KC & the Sunshine Band (the fab four did SHAKE YOUR BOOTY as a ballad complete with string quartet), Lenny Bruce, Cher, Peter Frampton, and John Lydon.

It's a magical ride from their first LP WE'RE GONNA CHANGE THE FACE OF POP MUSIC FOREVER through the butcher cover of MEAT THE BEATLES up to their 60's swansong BREAK UP. Hear about the time the very wasted John and Paul wrote a song with Bobby Zimmerman entitled PNEUMONIA CEILINGS ("Elephant guns blazing in my ears/I'm sick and tired of your applesauce tears!"). Check out Yoko's breakthrough art piece *Milk Bottle in a Blanket of Snow* (1961). Dig George giving head to an excited female fan on Carnaby Street. Find out the truth about John's, "...bigger than Jesus" quote. Lennon merely meant they were taller than our Lord. Read *Rolling Stone's* vicious pan of the band's late 70's reunion album GET BACK ("The Beatles are back and I think we all wish they'd stayed away"). There were several similar reviews of DOUBLE FANTASY written for real.

The Beatles were bigger than America or as George Harrison said, "I think we might be bigger than Pittsburgh." A

PAUL McCARTNEY: A Life by Peter Ames Carlin (2009 Touchstone)

Just like John Lennon, Paul's mother died when he was a teenager. But unlike John he didn't view it as the defining moment of his life. He didn't write any songs about how it felt. He didn't write any lyrics that conflated his soul mate with his mom. He didn't hit the bottle to try and cover the pain. Paul mentioned his mother Mary in *LET IT BE* and the fans thought he was talking about Jesus' mother. Paul went through as much turmoil as Lennon but you'd never know it. McCartney ended up going through a tremendous amount of pain. He was the one Beatle who couldn't get out of bed when they broke up. *EVERY DAY* gives us a blow by blow account of this emotional tumult. Paul sued the other band members to dissolve the partnership and the fans and the press turned on him for breaking up the Beatles. Paul had to deal with Lennon's murder, Linda's death from cancer, George's death from cancer, and Heather Mills dragging him through a horrible divorce. How does it feel to know that John and George were attacked at their homes by weapon wielding psychopaths bent on murdering them? It can't give you a serene sense of safety. Yet through it all he (mostly) keeps his head up high.

Peter Ames Carlin does a pretty good job of telling the standard McCartney story. :

1. Paul is born.
2. Paul's mother dies of cancer.
3. Quarry Men drummer Colin Hanton remembers that Paul was, "very clean."
4. John Lennon remembered "I ruined Paul's life. He could have gone to university. He could have been a doctor. He could have been somebody."
5. Paul was very critical of the Beatles bass player "commenting loudly when Stu missed a cue or fluffed a note."
6. Paul's first serious girlfriend Dot "miscarried his baby, and all talk of marriage came to a speedy halt."
7. The Beatles went to Hamburg, Germany with handsome new drummer Pete Best. "Was Paul jealous of Pete's appeal to the female fans?"
8. Pete was kicked out of the group. "They merely instructed manager Brian Epstein to break the news to Pete when the rest of them were a long way away. None of them ever spoke to him again."
9. Brian talked Paul into changing the songwriting credits from McCartney-Lennon to Lennon-McCartney. Paul later had reason to regret it.
10. John F. Kennedy died and "So it came to be that where a youthful, seemingly magical president once stood now emerged a youthful, seemingly magical foursome."
11. "Seen together Paul and his actress girlfriend Jane Asher were, simply, beautiful."
12. "Paul with all his charm knew how to bend people to his will."

13. Paul thought Allen Klein was "...ill dressed and ill mannered, a screamer and finger pointer."
14. "John Lennon's moods were like London's weather in the spring. If you didn't like what you were seeing, just wait ten minutes, and it would change."
15. When the band broke up Paul felt "the existential angst of the redundant man."
16. Paul wrote on the back cover of the first Wings album *WILD LIFE*: "can you dig it?" and "most people didn't."
17. "Wings wasn't a democracy as much as a benevolent dictatorship."
18. Publicist Tony Bramwell told Paul his new album *LONDON TOWN*, "...doesn't sound finished." Paul responded, "What the fuck do you think you're talking about? You fucking work for me!"
19. "Was Paul a genius or a loser? Was it possible for him to be both at the same time?"
20. Paul is booed at Live Aid because a technical glitch meant "they couldn't hear him." McCartney thought "had it really come to this?"
21. Heather Mills did "modeling for photographs, some of which were what you might call soft-core pornography."
22. "Paul works overtime to maintain his own currency in the post-millennial age. He provided a vocal to a performance by Jay-Z and members of Linkin Park."   B+

PAUL McCARTNEY: Many Years From Now by Barry Miles (1997 Henry Holt and Company)

Miles has written better psychological portraits of Ginsberg and Burroughs but this is best look at the mind of a Beatle. When he got older McCartney got angry about the fact that dead John Lennon was getting all the praise for being the edgy avant-garde member of the songwriting team. So he rang up old 60's compadre Miles and had him write this authorized account of how out there he was before he turned his life over to cucumber sandwiches at the country club. Paul's memories might be a little shrouded by the haze of marijuana smoke getting in his eyes if this quote from him in 1994 means anything, "I feel like the sixties is about to happen. It feels like a period in the future to me, rather than a period in the past." Here's another clue for you all: the pothead was Paul.

Still, this is worthwhile because Paul gives us his long overdue recollections of writing those wondrous hits of the 60's. He also throws out some fun quotes like:

1. "I remember at the time feeling a little bit empty…it was probably just staying up all night and doing too many drugs."
2. "It was the sixties… I'd been doing a bunch of drugs."
3. On his mother Mary, "At night there was one moment when she would pass our bedroom door in underwear…and I used to get sexually aroused." Let it be, Paul.

4. "I remember I had a girlfriend called Layla, which was a strange name for Liverpool." Did McCartney mention this bird to Clapton when they were recording *WHILE MY GUITAR GENTLY WEEPS*?
5. "It seemed very normal to us to be smoking a lot of pot and flying around very late."
6. When he asked Harrison to let him off Apple Records, "George ended the conversation, and as I say it now I almost feel like I'm lying with the devil's tongue, but I swear George said to me, 'You'll stay on the fucking label, Hare Krishna.' That's how it was, that's how the times were."
7. "Lest it be seen that I'm trying to do my own kind of revisionism, I'd like to register the fact that John was great..." Protesting a little too much.
8. "When George Harrison wrote his life story *I Me Mine*, he hardly mentioned John. In my case I wouldn't want to leave him out." Hare Krishna!   A-

PAUL McCARTNEY: The Legend Rocks On by James Kaplan (2012 Time)

More accurate alternate title for this work: *Paul McCartney: The Legend Pops On.* This special keepsake from Time/Life does a decent job of capturing the reasons we all love Sir James Paul McCartney, without ignoring his dark side. Paul is charming, witty, cute, and cuddly. We'd love to take him home with us, we'd love to take him home.

He is the most successful musician of all time but he's still out there busily entertaining the world. Every time you look up there he is. One minute he's at the Grammys, then he's rocking out at Moscow's Red Square (performing *BACK IN THE USSR* of course), then he's slyly making jokes about Ringo on *The Tonight Show* or showing up at the last Shea Stadium concert to play with Billy Joel. You'll find him playing on the marquee of the Ed Sullivan theatre, doing a show at Amoeba records in Los Angeles or riding a bus in Manhattan (he's just a regular guy!). Fans crossing Abbey Road sometimes find him jumping out of his minivan to take photos with them. According to reports he keeps his shoes on.

Time/Life has always been an important media player in the McCartney saga. *Time* had the famous cover of the Beatles as psychedelic puppets and the famous post-psychedelic cover of Paul's first U.S tour by artist Peter Max. *Life* was the periodical that tracked him down in Scotland in the fall of 1969 when the whole world thought he was dead. Paul screamed at the writer and photographer that showed up uninvited at his farm and told them to leave him alone (much like the time, a few months later, when he kicked Ringo out of his London apartment when Starr came there to discuss album release date problems). Paul threw a bucket of water at the pair and took a swing at the photographer, who caught the moment on film. Paul came to his senses and posed for photos with his family in exchange for the offending roll of film. Besides being charming, witty, cute, and cuddly Paul has a bit of a temper.

Time magazine reporter James Kaplan writes in what I would call an opinionated style:

1. "LSD brought out the prissy workaholic in Paul."
2. Linda McCartney had a "brass bound self-assurance."
3. Paul had a "melting, masculine beauty that made his female fans swoon."
4. Why had Paul not invited the Beatles to his marriage to Linda in 1969? Paul, "Why not? I'm a total bastard I suppose."
5. Gold digging second wife Heather Mills is a "piece of work, to put it mildly." Before her tragic accident she "had been nobody special."

Along with the text we get a nice selection of photos and a thought provoking list of Paul's 40 greatest songs by Bob Spitz. All in all, this is not a bad stocking stuffer for Macca fans. B

***THE PLAYBOY INTERVIEWS WITH JOHN LENNON AND YOKO ONO** by David Sheff (1981 Playboy)*

I have a hate/love relationship with this important, informative, poignant, and downright fun classic. On the one hand it captures John right before the shooting in all his glory.

- He tells lies claiming he never picked up a guitar in five years and he's just been spending all his time, "...baking bread and looking after the baby".
- He talks about the band ad nauseum but claims he doesn't enjoy doing so, "This Beatles talk bores me to death."
- He gets defensive about his subservient relationship with Yoko, "You think I'm being controlled like a dog on a leash...then screw you...fuck you brother and sister."
- He blames McCartney for screwing up the recordings of some of his best work, "He subconsciously tried to destroy songs, meaning that we'd play experimental games with my great pieces, like STRAWBERRY FIELDS- which I always felt was badly recorded" and "the same thing happened with ACROSS THE UNIVERSE...the guitars are out of tune and I'm singing out of tune 'cause I'm psychologically destroyed and nobody's supporting me or helping me with it and the song was never done properly."
- He hates when people worship celebrities who are no longer with us, "I don't appreciate the worship of dead Sid Vicious or of dead James Dean or dead John Wayne...making Sid Vicious a hero, Jim Morrison-it's garbage to me."
- He is not a fan of the Beatles, "I am dissatisfied with every record they ever fucking made...I feel I could remake every fucking one of them better."
- He makes a plea for rock fans to not live in the past which obviously many Beatles fans do, "I think that's pathetic. I mean forget about that. Listen to the Beatles records, but dig Queen or Clash or whatever is going on now."

- He gets sick hearing about the need for a fab reunion, "For those who didn't understand the Beatles and the Sixties in the first place, what the fuck are we going to do for them now? Do we have to divide the fish and the loaves for the multitudes again? Do we have to get crucified again? Do we have to do the walking on water again because a whole pile of dummies didn't see it the first time or didn't believe it when they saw it? You can't do things twice. You can never go home. It doesn't exist. It's not that we're withholding it from you; we don't possess it to withhold it. It was never ours in the first place. It existed of its own. The moaning about Beatles is the same as our parents who never stopped talking about the goddamn Second World War."
- He can't make sense of peaceniks like himself getting shot to death, "Gandhi and Martin Luther King are great examples of fantastic non-violents who died violently. I can never work that out. We're pacifists, but I'm not sure what it means when you're such a pacifist that you get shot. I can never understand that."

On the other hand, self-proclaimed big Beatles fan David Sheff, ("*STRAWBERRY FIELDS FOREVER*...haunted me when I was a teenager") doesn't seem to know Lennon and the Beatles as well as he thinks he does. Some of Sheff's mistakes during the interview sessions are embarrassing and make me wish that all conversations with John had been conducted by journalists who were also bona fide Beatlemaniacs. These are some of the things in this book that bother me:

- Sheff makes the point that his favorite Lennon number is *STRAWBERRY FIELDS* but then asks this question when discussing the famous Paul is dead clue at the end of that track, "What about the line in *I AM THE WALRUS*: 'I buried Paul'?" John answers, "I said 'cranberry sauce. That's all I said."

- When going through a list of Beatle songs with John to get his comments on whether a song was written by McCartney or by him Sheff brings up *CRY BABY CRY* which is one of Lennon's most loved masterworks (*The Rock Snob*s Dictionary* tells us that "the cool Beatles song for Snobs to like is *CRY BABY CRY*"). John answers, "Not me. A piece of rubbish." Any Beatlemaniac would have jumped in and said something like, "But you sing it, John and it doesn't sound at all like a McCartney song." Instead, Sheff just moves on without comment.

- The defining moment of John's life (as any Lennon head would tell you) was the passing of his mother Julia when he was a teenager. He wrote a few very emotional songs about her. There's *JULIA, MOTHER*, and of course the upbeat *MY MUMMY'S DEAD*. So you would hope that any professional interviewer would know about her and her untimely death. But 22 years after the accident that took her life genius David Sheff asks Lennon, "She's not alive, is she?" If I was John I would have said this interview is over but instead Lennon just answered, "No, she got killed by an off-duty cop who was drunk." This is akin to doing a major interview with your idol Jackie Onassis and asking her, "Your first husband, the president, he's not alive is he?"

- As John complains about how McCartney used to record songs for Beatle albums all on his own ("We came in and he'd made the whole record. Him drumming. Him playing the piano. Him singing...I was always hurt when Paul would knock something off without involving us.")

stupid git David Sheff asks, "You never just knocked off a track on yourself?" John answers, "No." (Lennon was probably forgetting that it happened one time with the song from *THE BEATLES* called *JULIA*). Then in the very next breath Sheff brings up *JULIA* and to add insult to injury asks, "Who was Julia?" If I was Lennon I would have said this interview is over but instead he just said, "Julia was my mother." This is akin to doing a major interview with Elizabeth Taylor and asking, "Richard Burton, who was he?"

- Every Beatle fan worth his salt knows that Epstein was in love with Lennon so pop historian David Sheff mentions, "Brian Epstein's secret love of Paul" and John has to correct him, "He wasn't in love with Paul. He was in love with me."

Despite these major gaffes this is a must own as the most important document of Lennon 1980. Just the fact that John comments on the vast majority of his songs (he also did that for *Hit Parader* in 1972) makes it what Lennon said it would be ("This will be THE reference book"). 　　　　　　　A

POSTCARDS FROM THE BOYS by Ringo Starr (2004 Chronicle)

Not to be outdone by John; George; and Paul; little Richard Starkey of Los Angeles, California comes up with his own book. Harrison gave the public his memoirs, McCartney gave us a hand-picked selection of his poetry, and Lennon gave us three works of anarchic nonsense inspired by Lord Tennyson, Lewis Carroll, Edgar Allan Poe, and Peter Sellers. Ringo gives us some cards they sent him.

In an effort to encourage Ringo to reach a higher reading level his three mates began sending him postcards in the 1960's and continued to do so until their deaths. These missives are what Mr. Starr shares with us, with all the profits going to charity. The cards are very revealing of how they felt about him.

Ringo was feeling badly about his lack of percussion skills in 1968 and he said, "I was playing like shit." John and George both sent telegrams to him that reassured him that he was the best (interesting choice of adjective considering who he had replaced in the band). They may have gone a little overboard in their praise. Starkey was certainly not a musician who exceeded all others in quality or excellence. Neither was he the most suitable, desirable, or useful man for the task. James Paul McCartney did not want to be outdone. As the GET BACK sessions wound up he sent a card echoing J and G that read, "You are the greatest drummer in the world. Really" I think Sir Paul doth protest too much. After all, he was the one that made Ringo quit the group briefly during the recording sessions for THE BEATLES, by letting him know in an authoritative manner that he was not playing correctly on Paul's Beach Boys tribute BACK IN THE USSR. Paul played the drums on the track while Ringo sulked at home. Then when Starr returned posthaste Paul did not have him redo the drums but instead left the fabulous McCartney percussion in the final mix.

To add insult to injury, after he sent the postcard, Paul repeated the trick in the spring of '69 by playing on THE BALLAD OF JOHN

AND YOKO while Ringo was out of town filming *The Magic Christian*. When Ringo returned to London two days later Paul again deemed his own work good enough for the 45 release and told Starr not to bother replacing it because it was just fine as it was. No wonder they broke up that year (George, "I'll play whatever you want Paul or I won't play at all. Whatever will make you happy I'll do it." John, "I can't speak for George but I can say we were pretty well fed up with being back up musicians for Paul.").

To keep things simple for the ring man other postcards from the boys ranged from the ridiculous Paul's, "Woof! Woof!" to the extremely ridiculous John's, "Did you know we were the youngest bores of the year!?!?" to the fun loving John's, "Wild Goose yippie I aye! Great disco" to the sublime George's, "A little turtle groupage from the Barrier Reef."

I would be remiss if I didn't also mention my favorite card, from Lennon and his missus, "Thanx a lot for coming to my birthday chaos Love bonnie John & Yogurt." I am eagerly awaiting the follow up book of Ringo's postcards to himself.   B

THE PRIMAL SCREAM by Arthur Janov (1970 G.P. Putnam's Sons)

Good news folks. If you suffer from neurosis you can be cured. You can relive all the trauma of your childhood with a trained doctor of psychology. They can guide you as you scream, "Mama!" while you are rolling around on the floor. Let it all hang out. Don't think for a moment that you have to live in pain and fear. Remember when you were young and all the people seemed so tall? That's because they were adults and you were just an unimportant and needy little runt. You didn't get what you wanted out of life. Your parents kept telling you what to think and where to go or worse yet they ignored you and all your fine ideas. The sun was shining but not for you. They didn't tell you as they packed you off to school that God was simply a concept by which we measure our pain, our unhappiness, and our complete dissatisfaction with spinning around on a globe in outer space.

Arthur Janov discovered primal pain one lovely spring day. During a therapy session Janov heard "...an eerie scream welling up from the depths of a young man lying on the floor." Arthur compared it "...to what one might hear from a person about to be murdered." Think of that. If you take this cure you will emit a sound from your writhing body that will sound like you are about to have your life taken by another human being and you're not too happy about it. The great thing is you get to do hundreds of hours of this wonderful kind of catharsis before you get sent back to your office fully healed. What could be better? Oh, did I mention you might also be recorded on video shouting your guts out so the doctor can have evidence for future historical study. You might wind up on YouTube!

I'll let Janov explain further "Patients quickly learn during their therapy how to get into feelings. A patient may discuss a dream from the night before, tell it as though it were happening right then, feel the feeling of fright or helplessness, and quickly be out of control and connecting the feeling to its source. Being totally out of control permits connection because self-control always means suppression of self. The patient wants that Pain because he knows that is the only way out of his neurosis. It's me hurting, said one patient, and if I can feel me, that is all I want."

When we are children we have what Janov refers to as minor Primal Scenes. These are countless minor experiences in which we are "…ridiculed, rejected, neglected, humiliated, driven to perform." At some point we then experience the major Primal Scene of our life. This is "…the single most shattering event in the child's life. It is that moment of icy, cosmic loneliness, the bitterest of all epiphanies. It is the time when he begins to discover that he is not loved for what he is and will not be."

Just in case you think you're special this book will disabuse you of that notion. Arthur tells us "We are all creatures of need. We are born needing, and the vast majority of us die after a lifetime of struggle with many of our needs unfulfilled." But you can be helped. Sure, you might be thinking you're functioning pretty well. But as Janov's patient Laura points out, "…functioning is not necessarily an indication of feeling well….Right up to the moment when I was most ill, the moment when my mind and feelings separated completely, I had performed beautifully on my job and was a model housekeeper." Don't be fooled, ladies and gentlemen. You might think you have it together. You might think you're centered. But your life is just a catastrophe waiting to happen.

Find out if screaming a scream to wake the dead is right for you. Read this book and see if you're ready to vomit all that sadness right out of your system. See if you're willing to let down the defenses that have been propping you up your whole life. Neurosis is merely symbolic behavior in defense against excessive psychobiologic pain. You couldn't walk and you tried to run. A-

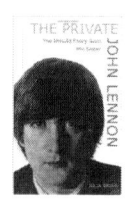

THE PRIVATE JOHN LENNON by Julia Baird (2008 Ulysses)

The untold story from his sister proclaims the front cover. Julia is actually his half-sister, so right off the bat I doubt this memoir will give me the truth. If the two books about John by his first wife, the two books by his mistress, the countless books authorized by his second wife, the two dozen books by his assistants, and the three books Lennon wrote himself (mostly gobleygook) have not been enough for you then by all means, check this one out.

You're not going to believe this but John was abandoned by his parents and left to live with his aunt when he was only five years old. No wonder he was always so pissed off. Then get this, just as he was reestablishing a relationship with his mother, she got killed in a car accident when he was 17. No wonder he was always so pissed off.

Julia doesn't tell us anything new about John Lennon. By her own account she barely spoke to him in his last 20 years so she wouldn't know behind the scenes stuff from his famous years. Even the pre-Beatle years focus not on his private life but hers. It seems like her whole existence has been a struggle and maybe it has been but the fact that she was related to John doesn't make her story fascinating. It's like reading a dreary diary of somebody you don't know and don't want to know.   D-

READ THE BEATLES edited by June Skinner Sawyers (2006 Penguin)

Perfect for a day at the beach, catching some rays and digging some great Beatle writing from a variety of fab related and unrelated authors. Highlights include excerpts from *Helter Skelter*, *The Playboy Interviews with John Lennon and Yoko Ono*, and *The Rolling Stone Illustrated History of Rock and Roll* (all of which are worth checking out in their entirety). Further highlights come from such esteemed periodicals as *The New York Times* (Richard Goldstein's much derided pan of PEPPER) that let us know PEPPER was "...dazzling but ultimately fraudulent", *The Evening Standard* where John tells us that, "Christianity will go. It will vanish and shrink...Jesus was all right but his disciples were thick and ordinary. It's them twisting it that ruins it for me", and *Q* where Paul brings up the obvious question about the Anthology CDs, "If it wasn't good enough to release then, why is it good enough to release now?"

Being a compilation of prose from pros (plus poetry) the quality does tend to vary but it's hard not to recommend this. After all, the contributors include Robert Christgau, Greil Marcus, Andrew Sarris, Simon Frith, Phillip Glass, Allen Ginsberg, and John Winston Ono Lennon. That reads like a who's who of 20th Century pop culture artists and commentators. This ranks right up there in variety with the list of scribes in *The Lennon Companion*. A-

REVOLUTION: The Making of the Beatles' "White Album" by David Quantick (2002 A Cappella)

This book is about *THE BEATLES*. It is the double album that came with four suitable for framing color portraits. The package also included a big poster with a collage of stills ranging from the early years to the middle years to the later years. Still, it is the amazingly eclectic selection of fantastic musical tracks that draw many fans back and back to this endeavor. Just imagine it could have been even better. If we were living in a perfect material world then the album would have contained these other 1968 recordings: *HEY JUDE, REVOLUTION, ACROSS THE UNIVERSE, and HEY BULLDOG.* All of them gems. Then the band could have dropped these four substandard pieces: *WILD HONEY PIE* (a useless noisy doodle), *PIGGIES* (a misanthropic view of the human race from a man besotted with the love and acceptance of Indian mysticism), *ROCKY RACCOON* (in which Paul adopts a horrible redneck accent), and *DON'T PASS ME BY* (the Ringo song that should have stayed hung up on the fridge).

Unfortunately, side two features those last three clunkers in a row. Great sequencing! This book is basically a 200 page album review. Normally, I would think that's going a little overboard but in the case of the band's best recording ever I think it's a little too short. There's nothing startling in David Quantick's examination but he writes fairly well so it's a pleasure to ride along with him. Just in case anybody is coming in cold he points out to the novice listener who was the actual writer on each Lennon/McCartney song. Here's a clue for you all: John sings lead on the songs he wrote and Paul sings lead on the ditties he composed.

Mr. Quantick also describes the atmosphere. It is "melancholic, cautionary, sleepy, wise, and angry." Correct, and he does point out one thing I never noticed before. Paul's horny rocker *WHY DON'T WE DO IT IN THE ROAD* is followed by Paul's pretty answer *I WILL*. B+

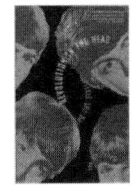

REVOLUTION IN THE HEAD: The Beatles Records and the Sixties by Ian MacDonald (1994 Henry Holt)

This is the analysis I was waiting for since I became a student of the Beatles. I had been studying them since I was a child and I thought I knew it all. I understood all their songs and I understood them as people. I had read the interviews. I had seen the photos. I had memorized their lyrics. I could see why John chose Yoko, Paul chose Linda, George chose Olivia, and Ringo chose Barbara. I had watched them on the big screen and tuned in to catch them on the small screen. I had bought *SOMEWHERE IN ENGLAND, MILK AND HONEY, OLD WAVE,* and *PRESS TO PLAY* but I couldn't bring myself to listen to them. I didn't like the cartoons about them but I loved Ron, Dirk, Stig, and Barry. I felt they were better than the Stones, the Kinks, and the Pistols but I thought the Who might be just a little bit better despite Roger Daltrey's average vocal stylings. I bought *Creem* and *Rolling Stone* when they made the cover and I would have done the same with *Sports Illustrated* but it never happened. I put *Mad's* Don Martin poster on my bedroom wall. I debated the merits of the *MIND GAMES* album with my brother. I skipped a gig with a band I was in to travel to another country to see Paul's 1989 comeback tour. I went to the Dakota every time I was in New York. I immediately bought tickets for Ringo's first solo tour. Starr kept telling the audience in downtown Buffalo, "Hello, Boston." We were not amused. Knowing Ringo I couldn't tell if he was joking or if he really thought he was in Massachusetts. I thought Paul was dead. I wished John wasn't dead. I despised Todd Rundgren's stilted version of *STRAWBERRY FIELDS FOREVER*. I was sickened by the Bee Gees and Peter Frampton. I found it hard to sit through the ending of *How I Won the War* when I saw it in 1981. It was too soon. I threw out the biography of Mark David Chapman that my mother had given me for Christmas. I saw *Rock Show* on its road tour complete with sound system. I told myself it was the next best thing to being there. I paid for my brother's ticket to *History of the Beatles* so he would take me to scary downtown to see it. I thought Apollo C. Vermouth was one hell of a producer. I believed there should be a biography of Jimmy Nichol. I knew that the fifth Beatle was Harry Nilsson. I went to midnight mass and prayed for the soul of Allen Klein. I regretted not purchasing *VERSUS THE FOUR SEASONS* when I saw it. When I was twelve years old I bought a used copy of *MAGICAL MYSTERY TOUR* for $2.50, complete with 24 page color booklet, and I still own the damn thing. I listened to *COLD TURKEY* on headphones at maximum volume. I wondered what Yoko playing wind meant. I wondered why John and Yoko had claimed they were shy yet had released an album cover where they were both stark naked. I tried to get into *DOUBLE FANTASY* but it seemed to me to be a great historical document without artistic value. I knew the dream was over but I wasn't too happy about it.

Then, out of nowhere, sent down from heaven above, there was the book that answered all my questions, even the ones I didn't know I had. *Revolution in the Head* became my Bible. I read it the same way theological scholars read the Old Testament and the New Testament. The footnotes alone would have made a great article. I put it on my turntable and played it backwards. I realized you couldn't take Ian MacDonald at face value. He was obviously sending the tuned in beautiful people secret messages on how to live and to love. You couldn't take him seriously when he was denigrating the poetic beauty of *ACROSS THE UNIVERSE*. He couldn't actually think the song was, "boring… insipid… babyish… shapeless… listless… lethargic… directionless," could he?

I envy all of you out there who have yet to read this magnum opus on the Beatles' records and the sixties. You have so much enjoyment ahead of you. This was a new phase Beatles book. In came the warmth and the freshness of a live performance. It's the book equivalent of being given a seat next to Maureen Cox on the top of 3 Savile Row London, England at lunchtime on January 30, 1969. It's almost as good as finding yourself on a boat in a river surrounded by tangerine trees and marmalade skies. It's nearly as invigorating as going out for burgers with John and Yoko after a refreshing afternoon of primal screaming. It will enliven your senses like getting on a bus with the McCartneys and the Dennys and hitting the college circuit in

1972. It will make you as blissful as being at the feet of the Maharishi with Mia Farrow and Mike Love. You'll need a dump truck to unload your head.

If there is such a thing as a genius then Ian MacDonald was one. He was the kind of pop critic who really was a classical music expert. His other full length musical analysis was on Shostakovich for Christ's sake. I couldn't understand that guy if I lived to 99. So we all should be grateful that MacDonald would deign to share his wisdom on the magical decade of the sixties with us and at the same time teach us about the fab four's output so we can hear it like we're hearing it for the first time.

Ian MacDonald's words will fill your head. You won't forget them.

1. *LOVE ME DO*: "A new spirit was abroad: artless yet unabashed-and awed by nothing."
2. *PLEASE PLEASE ME*: "...contrived hysteria only fails if the material is weak and the Beatles had done a thorough job of covering every crack in the facade."
3. *FROM ME TO YOU*: "...Lennon's abrasive voice turning a trite lyric into something mordantly sardonic."
4. *SHE LOVES YOU*: "The contour of the melodic line fits the feeling and rhythm of the words perfectly-and where it doesn't, the singers make a virtue out of it by altering their inflection (e.g., the cajoling emphasis of 'apologize to her')."
5. *I WANT TO HOLD YOUR HAND*: "Harbouring no conscious subversive intent, the Beatles, with this potent record, perpetrated a culturally revolutionary act. As the decade wore on and they began to realise

the position they were in, they began to do the same thing more deliberately."

6. *CAN'T BUY ME LOVE*: "The Beatles' ability to be two contradictory things at once-comfortably safe and exhilaratingly strange-has been displayed by no other pop act." A nice way to sum up the Lennon/McCartney dynamic.

7. *A HARD DAY'S NIGHT*: "The mighty opening chord…has a significance in Beatles lore matched only by the concluding E major of "A Day in the Life", the two opening and closing the group's middle period of peak creativity."

8. *A TICKET TO RIDE*: "The word sad here carries a weight graphically embodied in the track's oppressive pedal tonality."

9. *TOMORROW NEVER KNOWS*: "Among the commonest of the altered states induced by LSD is depersonalization or ego-loss. In this condition, awareness of self as a separate entity dissolves in what Jung termed, 'oceanic consciousness": the sense that all things are one and individual awareness an illusion…That LSD was Russian roulette played with one's mind must have been clear to Leary, yet so excited was he by its revolutionary potential that he threw caution to the wind by advocating it as a social cure-all."

10. *RAIN*: "Lennon's rain and sun are physical phenomena experienced in a condition of heightened consciousness, the record portraying a state of mind in which one is peacefully at home in an integrated universe."

11. *I'M ONLY SLEEPING*: "...dismisses the empty activity of the mundane world with an indolence that holds the seeds of Lennon's later heroin addiction."
12. *ELEANOR RIGBY*: "Often represented as purveyors of escapist fantasy, the Beatles were, at their best, more poignantly realistic about their society than any other popular artists of their time."
13. *STRAWBERRY FIELDS FOREVER*: "While there are countless contemporary composers capable of music vastly more sophisticated in form and technique, few if any are capable of displaying feeling and fantasy so direct, spontaneous, and original."
14. *A DAY IN THE LIFE*: "A song not of disillusionment with life itself but of disenchantment with the limits of mundane perception."
15. *I AM THE WALRUS*: "A trace of the more peaceably philosophical Lennon remains in the song's opening line, but the rest is pure invective (including a swipe at the mechanical mantra-chanting of the Hare Krishna movement to which his friend Harrison was amicably disposed)."
16. *REVOLUTION 9*: "Intentions apart, the actual experience of listening to this track, where not merely boring or baffling, often inclines to the sinister, an effect ascribable to the twin driving forces behind it: chance determination and drugs."
17. *GLASS ONION*: "It goes without saying that the late sixties were drenched in mind expanding drugs with all the unwarranted 'creativity' this entailed....Who set up chains of suggestive self-reference in their lyrics for the explicitly avowed fun of confusing people?...The essence of the confrontation between straight society

and the counterculture was a clash between logical/literal and intuitive/lateral thinking."
18. *THE BEATLES*: "Certainly no other product of the noon-bright idiom of Sixties pop offers as many associations of guarded privacy and locked rooms, or concludes in such disturbing, dreamlike darkness."
19. *COME TOGETHER*: "A call to unchain the imagination and, by setting language free, loosen the rigidities of political and emotional entrenchment. As such, the song continues a theme consistent in Lennon's work since "I am the Walrus"-one partly originating in his LSD-enhanced outsider mentality and partly imbibed from the prevailing countercultural atmosphere of anti-elitist anarchism as defined by pundits as diverse as Marshall McLuhan, Arthur Janov, R.D. Laing, and Herbert Marcuse."
20. *I ME MINE*: "By a poetic stroke of fate, the last track to be recorded by the Beatles was this dry lament over divisive egotism."

The Beatles were famous for not giving musician credits on their album sleeves. I guess they wanted to pretend that they were playing all the instruments themselves, that all four members were on each track, Paul wasn't recording some songs alone, and that McCartney wasn't taking over the drum kit whenever he could elbow Ringo out of the way. Helpfully, MacDonald gives us full as possible credits for each song so we can know which numbers feature Harrison or Lennon on bass, which ones John sits out, and which ones McCartney plays lead guitar on.

The band did not always issue tracks as they were recorded. They would leave things in the vault until there was a need for product. Then dust them off and presto four "new" songs available for the *YELLOW SUBMARINE* soundtrack. They started recording *YOU KNOW MY NAME (LOOK UP THE NUMBER)* in May 1967 and it didn't come out until the very end in March 1970 on the B-side of their last U.K. single *LET IT BE*. MacDonald presents the official canon in the order it was recorded and not the order it was released in. Therefore, giving us much needed context.

Of course, geniuses can be a little arrogant about how special they are. John Lennon, for example, was known for thinking he was the greatest and lauding it over people. For proof see his song *I'M THE GREATEST*. Ian MacDonald is no exception. He believed that he and the other teenagers of his era were part of a magical time called the sixties and if you missed it he could only feel sorry for you. He was one of those people who thought the music of his youth was the best ever and could never be topped. Ian would have noticed all the great rock music made after 1970, if he thought there had been some made ("...older listeners who grew up with sixties music have become steadily more disappointed by pop ever since"). Like all old fogeys hanging on to the times of their youth Ian could not let himself believe, "...that what changes in pop is not its objective level of soul and inspiration but the subjective points of views of commentators as they get older and less involved with it." People like Ian MacDonald who live in the past never glimpse the truth until it's far too late and they pass away.   A+

REVOLUTION IN THE HEAD: The Beatles Records and the Sixties THIRD EDITION by Ian MacDonald (2007 Chicago Review Press)

This is the second revised version of the greatest Beatles book ever published. Think of the original 1994 edition as the Old Testament in which the Beatles spend seven years creating a whole new world of pop culture. In the 1970's they rested. Think of this third edition from 2007 as the New Testament. Here you get a flat out dismissal of their solo careers with "The Beatles post-Beatles story is, on the whole, unedifying" and solo albums "Constraints of space, time, and interest prevent consideration of these albums." I think of the first edition as being like the Beatles classic canon of 186 original songs recorded between June 4th 1962 and April 2nd 1970 (*LOVE ME DO* which features Andy White on drums on the *PLEASE PLEASE ME* LP to *I ME MINE* which Lennon didn't play on because he usually couldn't be bothered putting guitar on the late period Harrison songs). I think of the third edition as being like the three double CD sets called *ANTHOLOGY*. Just as the *ANTHOLOGY* outtake discs are worthwhile in filling out the picture of their 60's music so is *Revolution in the Head's* third edition worthwhile because of Ian MacDonald giving us his fascinating appraisals of all the songs he missed the first time around including *LIVE AT THE BBC* (1994) tracks, the still unreleased even on bootleg legendary 13 minute 48 second 'freak out' *CARNIVAL OF LIGHT* (1967), their only Xmas song *CHRISTMAS TIME (IS HERE AGAIN)* (1967), the bootleg only

Lennon meditation number *CHILD OF NATURE* (1968), and of course *FREE AS A BIRD* (1995) and *REAL LOVE* (1996).

Ian MacDonald states the obvious at the beginning of this revised edition, "As the 21st Century advances, no abatement of popular interest has yet occurred in the Beatles." I might not even be writing this Beatle book about Beatles books if that wasn't the case. Mr. MacDonald also states many opinions in this edition that I disagree with, such as:

- "If we were to ask average listeners what the Beatles lyrics mean, they would likely say very little."
- "The Beatles' casual lyrics look slipshod beside the careful verses and refrains of the great composers of popular song before them."
- Harrison had "natural modesty." I think he had just as little as Lennon and McCartney. That is to say, George had none. Maybe MacDonald was thinking of Ringo.
- "The Beatles are, in a sense, us." If most people in the world were all originally from Liverpool and had grown up to be rich and famous musicians then I would agree.
- "They made and changed history-yet history, indifferent as ever, simply moved on, leaving them behind."

MacDonald also comes up with many ideas I deem correct:

- "Coining almost every trend which has succeeded them apart from musical mechanization, the Beatles, together and individually, amount to a veritable academy of pop cultural values and talents."
- "*FREE AS A BIRD* stands no comparison with the Beatles' Sixties music...banal...unfocused."

- On the *Anthology* DVD, "The picture of the post-1967 Beatles is too nicely forgiving, too sentimentally nostalgic to fit the facts as recorded by independent observers at the time."
- Starting in the mid 1960's , "The Christian social values of the old culture were then giving way to a life dominated by technology-driven consumer materialism, an impatient expectation of instant gratification, and a self before-before-others ethic that has since fragmented Western society."
- "The sensitivity to cultural context which enabled the Beatles to remake their career has been surpassed only by David Bowie in pop and, in their respective idioms (and, of course, over far longer stretches of time) by Stravinsky, Picasso, and Miles Davis."

All in all, this third edition is a must have for any rock music fan's bookshelf. It is right up there with *Hammer of the Gods, No One Here Gets out Alive,* and *Saucerful of Secrets.*   A+

REVOLVER: How the Beatles Reimagined Rock'N'Roll by Robert Rodriguez (2012 Backbeat)

During the magical years of 1966-1967 the fab four released only two albums. One was black and white and one was color. This is the black and white one. Sometime in the 1970's REVOLVER began to inch past PEPPER as the most acclaimed

Beatle album (as mentioned in THE BEATLES: An Illustrated Record). There was talk about how PEPPER was tied to the summer of love but REVOLVER was a timeless masterpiece which remained as fresh as the day of issue. I concur with this assessment. Still, the packaging of PEPPER is much more to my liking than the Klaus Voormann cover art for REVOLVER. I thoroughly enjoy PEPPER's cover photo which overflows with groovy celebrities (including the very creepy Aleister Crowley, Edgar Allen Poe, and Marlon Brando), and allusions to death. But when it comes to the music I'll choose REVOLVER every time. Note: Turn to chapter 8 (THERE'S SOMETHING THERE: SGT. PEPPER AND THE LEGACY OF REVOLVER) for a cogent analysis of how REVOLVER vaulted over PEPPER in the estimation of critics and fans worldwide.

Robert Rodriguez takes us through the REVOLVER story step by step. It was a heady time in pop. The same year the Beatles arguably hit their artistic peak so arguably did Robert Zimmerman (BLONDE ON BLONDE) and Brian Wilson (PET SOUNDS). Of course, and this can't be stressed enough, the REVOLVER we're talking about is the 14 track U.K. REVOLVER (first released on compact disc in 1987) not the much inferior 11 track U.S. REVOLVER. The U.S. REVOLVER omitted three Lennon tracks (!) which had been thrown by Capitol on to the fairly worthless "YESTERDAY"... and TODAY.

 Beatles' authority Rodriguez gives us the back story: they were fed up with performing live (he takes us inside their lackluster official final English concert appearance), they wanted to experiment in the studio (Q: "What's going to come out of the next recording sessions? A: Lennon, "Literally anything. Electronic music, jokes...one thing's for sure: the next LP is going to be very different."), and they wanted to utilize reversed tape as part of their sonic landscape.

Then we receive a track by track blow by blow account of the recording sessions:

1. TOMORROW NEVER KNOWS (a.k.a. MARK I): "As a measure of how far they'd come and the direction they would give to others that followed, it was an achievement of inestimable value."
2. GOT TO GET YOU INTO MY LIFE: Geoff Emerick helped to achieve the excellent sound by "going so far as to place the mics into the bell of each horn."
3. LOVE YOU TO (a.k.a. GRANNY SMITH): George records his own "khyal...a short-form modern Indian musical composition built upon an unharmonized melodic line, with distinct slow and fast movements."
4. DOCTOR ROBERT: "Having laid down two earnest evocations of his drug experience so far (TOMORROW NEVER KNOWS and RAIN)...John was now ready to offer up a tongue-in-cheek salute to a drug dispensing physician."
5. AND YOUR BIRD CAN SING: "...is a picture-perfect example of how the group *orchestrated* their parts, arranging so as to provide optimum color and detail without stepping on each other."
6. TAXMAN: On Paul's guitar solo: " His angry bloodletting sounded nothing like anything previously heard on a Beatles record, capturing the rage implicit in the lyric while simultaneously getting inside George's own head and speaking a language of which the composer fully approved."

7. I'M ONLY SLEEPING: "A considerable amount of time and labor was expended on getting exactly the right touch for John's somnambulant rumination."
8. ELEANOR RIGBY: "This was full-bore chamber music in support of a rather serous-minded lyric that went far beyond the standards of romantic sentiment."
9. FOR NO ONE: "In *Many Years from Now*, Paul relates that his and George Martin's first choice (for the French horn part), maestro Dennis Brain had been booked for the session, but was killed in an auto accident before it could take place. He was half right: Brain did indeed die behind the wheel-in 1957."
10. YELLOW SUBMARINE: "...proved that the Beatles could compete with the best of the novelty acts on the charts without compromising their integrity."
11. I WANT TO TELL YOU (a.k.a. LAXTON'S SUPERB... a.k.a. I DON'T KNOW): "It has been suggested that George was accorded a *third* composition on this album due to John not having another song ready."
12. GOOD DAY SUNSHINE: Rodriguez points out that Paul could have played the drums on this instead of Starkey "but thankfully the do-it-yourself tendencies that served to alienate his fellow Beatles in the future had not yet become fully awakened."
13. HERE, THERE AND EVERYWHERE: "Though not experimental in the usual sense, it did feature delicate harmonies, a double-tracked lead vocal, and layered melodic guitar lines."
14. SHE SAID SHE SAID: Though Ian MacDonald's *Revolution in the Head* lists McCartney as the bass player on this track Rodriguez points out that it might have been played by Harrison. Paul told Barry Miles, "I'm not sure

but I think it was one of the only Beatle records I never played on." Paul also sat out George's three Indian numbers (though he sang background on THE INNER LIGHT) JULIA, and GOOD NIGHT.   A-

RINGO STARR: Straight Man or Joker? By Alan Clayson (1991 Paragon House)

There is no need for a biography of this man. Does he even have fans who ask for this book for Xmas? "Honey, what I really want for Christmas is the new Ringo biography. I need to find out what makes that man of mystery tick. After all, he's my favorite musician." Is he a straight man or a joker? Is he a mod or a rocker? I think he is one of the luckiest men who ever lived. Half the people I know drum better than him. All the people I know write songs better than him. Everyone at Karaoke night at the corner bar sings better than him.

The countless Ringo apologists always point to his drumming on *RAIN*. How amazing it is. Come on. The real test is this: Paul plays drums on *BACK IN THE USSR* and *BALLAD OF JOHN AND YOKO* and no one listening thinks, "Where is that superb drumming we are used to?" If anything they think, "Ringo sounds adequate as usual." Can you imagine how amazing the Beatles would have been with a great drummer? If they had kicked out Richard and brought in Mitch Mitchell or Alan White? You don't really have to imagine it. Just listen to Lennon in 1968 with The Dirty Mac at *The Rolling Stones Rock and Roll Circus.* There's Mitch Mitchell on drums. Mitch sounds excellent. Then, just listen to John in 1970 with the Plastic Ono Band on their hit single *INSTANT KARMA*. There's Alan White on drums. To say he excels is to put it mildly. Alan elevates the song to another level. I wish Alan had drummed on the *PLASTIC ONO BAND* album but Lennon played it safe. That would have been startling.

Look at the facts. George Martin would not have replaced Ringo with session drummer Andy White on *LOVE ME DO* (a simple song if there ever was one) and *P.S. I LOVE YOU* if Starr was great. You don't tell the band's drummer to go play tambourine/maracas in the corner if there's not a problem.

Like the vast majority of rock star bios this is a just the facts, nothing new to say, tedious hack job. There are no new insights and no fascinating anecdotes. There is no reason to read this.

D-

P.S.: Folks, I know Lennon got shot and Harrison got stabbed but does that excuse Ringo from saying, "Peace and love, peace and love, peace and love" over and over in all his interviews? He sounds like he has Post Traumatic Stress Disorder, which I guess he does.

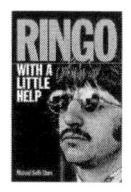

RINGO: With a Little Help by Michael Seth Starr (2015 Backbeat)

Appropriately enough the most recent biography of Richard Starkey was written by a man named Starr. He does a fine job.

Starr makes Ringo seem almost fascinating as he takes us through the ups and downs of five decades in the public eye. He explores the questions we'd all like answers to.

Is Ringo a talented actor?

1. David Essex, his co-star in *That'll Be the Day* said, "He was a natural and truthful actor."
2. Janet Maslin, *New York Times* critic, said in her review of *Caveman*, "Mr. Starr is better here than he's been in anything since the Beatles films, abandoning his former deadpan quality for something more active and engaging."
3. The *New York Times* had this to say about *Blindman*: "There's hairy Ringo Starr, snarling away and still looking like a parrot trying to thread a needle."

Is Ringo good at relationships?

1. Marriage #1 in the early days: "Ringo was the dominant force and Maureen was docile, although she could keep her husband in line when necessary."
2. Marriage #1 in the later days: "They still loved each other and always would, but the price of fame, combined with their marital indiscretions, was too much for them to surmount."
3. Marriage #2 in the courting days: Ringo told Yoko, "Barbara and I do everything together."
4. Marriage #2 in the early days: Ringo remembering October 1988 and his worst moment with Barbara after they'd been drinking around the clock for several days, "I came to one Friday afternoon and was told by the staff that I had trashed the house so badly they thought

there had been burglars, and I'd trashed Barbara so badly they thought she was dead."
5. Marriage #2 in the later days: "In 2001 Ringo and Barbara celebrated their thirtieth wedding anniversary."

Is Ringo a great drummer?

1. "What you won't find in *Ringo: With a Little Help*, are any overt judgments, from this author, on Ringo's technical skills as a drummer vis-à-vis The Beatles. That's one of the endless arguments among Beatles fans best waged in barrooms and on the Internet. It could be a book in itself, and maybe one day will be. I'm not a musician…but, for the record, I think Ringo's steady backbeat and unflashy style was perfectly suited to The Beatles and their sound."
2. "Let's face it: you can't change history. That's Ringo's drumming on all the group's immortal hits. It speaks for itself. Get over it." Ok. I will.   B+

THE ROUGH GUIDE TO THE BEATLES 2nd Edition by Chris Ingham (2006 Rough Guides)

The back cover screams…"The essential Beatles companion!" I have to say it's not too far off the mark. This book is crammed with facts and yet finds time to devote a chapter to debunking all the famous rumors. It turns out John didn't kill Stu, John didn't make love to Brian, Klaatu was not the Beatles but a bunch of Canadian musicians, and Paul did not blow his mind out in a car. It turns out he's still alive and a devoted grandfather who when he got older losing his hair married a gold digger with one leg who took him for hundreds of millions which made him so mad he married a third time and made sure she had two legs and they had one big beautiful pre-nup before tying the knot.

This book is honest up front about what's going on. In the introduction Chris Ingham points out "Nostalgia is obviously part of it…but it's the endurance of the music too." Well put. Check and mate. There is a wonderful chapter on what Mr. Ingham thinks are the best Beatle books. There is a list of best Beatle websites so you can sit at your computer eight days a week and glean more and more info until you shrivel up into a little ball and start picturing yourself on a boat in a river with tangerine trees and marmalade skies.

My only quibble is with the section on candidates for the position of fifth Beatle. I never even heard of Tommy Moore or Chas Newby but that's not the problem. Here's the issue: Yoko Ono nominated as fifth Beatle. Come on! I know nothing is real but this is something to get hung about. But the more I thought about it she:

- Was the only one to ever be shown with the band on a picture sleeve of a 45
- Appeared on a poster included in a best-selling Beatle album
- Was the only non-Beatle to "sing" a solo line on an official Beatles release (*THE CONTINUING STORY OF BUNGALOW BILL*)
- Was the real co-"writer" of *REVOLUTION 9*

- Appeared live on stage with Lennon and Harrison at their last gig together
- Had a Beatles A side written about her honeymoon exploits
- Was mentioned by name in a Beatle song title
- Was, as John admitted, the real co-writer of *GIVE PEACE A CHANCE* and if he was being honest he would never have credited it to Lennon/McCartney
- Was mentioned in COME TOGETHER
- Gave Paul, George, and Ringo the permission to use the tapes of Lennon songs so they could play along with them and then put them out as two "new" singles
- Accepted with George and Ringo at the rock and roll hall of fame induction ceremony (Paul stiffed)
- Did have to watch in horror as Mark "scumbag" Chapman gunned John down

Okay. She's the fifth Beatle.   A

A SECRET HISTORY by Alistair Taylor (2001 John Blake)

The devoted assistant, who can be heard speaking on *THE BEATLES* right before *REVOLUTION 9,* and who the Beatles never mentioned again after they had Allen Klein sack him, comes back to tell all. This book was originally called *A Secret History* but it was so secret that they renamed it *With the Beatles* to generate more sales.

It's a simple story from a simple man. Turns out he thinks he co-wrote *HELLO GOODBYE*. He was in the room at the time. Turns out he and Paul had a religious experience. A middle aged man came up to them while they were out for a walk. The man said hello and then disappeared. Blimey! Turns out when John and Yoko got married he organized the flights. Just in case you think he's making it all up there are several photos of him standing next to John Lennon. He was really there! C-

SHE LOVES YOU: Volume 3, The John Lennon Series
by Jude Southerland Kessler (2013 Penin Inc)

You might think you're the biggest John Lennon fan ever. You might think you know every last little detail of his 40 plus years. You might think you cried the hardest when he passed away. But you've got nothing on Jude Southerland Kessler. Kessler is in the process of working on a nine volume series covering in depth like never before the life and times of our favorite rhythm guitar player. She started out with SHOULDA BEEN THERE 1940-December 1961 (Volume 1). She soldiered on with SHIVERING INSIDE December 1961-Mid-April 1963 (Volume 2). Now we get SHE LOVES YOU April 1963-March 1964 (Volume 3).

To give you some idea of the magnitude of this endeavor :

1. SHE LOVES YOU (Volume 3) alone is 945 pages.
2. It includes a Scouse glossary so you can figure out what you're reading. For example: bushwa means bullshit,

spot of kip means a nap, and winklepicker means a man's low-cut boot with a very pointed toe.
3. There are over a hundred pages of endnotes.
4. Kessler concludes every little chapter with notes and sources
5. WITH THE BEATLES is illustrated by a series of lithographs by Louisiana native Enoch Doyle Jeter. If he hasn't put out a Beatles calendar he ought to.

Kessler ignited the dormant Beatlemania within me and all throughout reading this book I heard John Lennon singing early 60's recordings in my mind. I haven't felt that way since I was a kid and I used to go to sleep with John's voice ringing in my head. All the way through I felt like I was there with the band as they basked in the first wave of mania. This is the next best thing to going back in time and befriending the boys as they become world famous.

I look forward to SHOULDA KNOWN BETTER (Volume 4) and the volumes to come as we make our way into the roaring 20's like SHE SAID SHE SAID. I'm surprised, though that Kessler plans to call September 1969-May 1973 SHADES OF LIFE. I would have called it SHE'S NOT A GIRL WHO MISSES MUCH in honor of Yoko.
A-

SHOUT!: The Beatles in Their Generation by Philip Norman (1981 Fireside)

This one got extra attention from the public because John got killed right at the time Philip Norman was finishing it. It gave fans solace during the dark year of 1981 when the only new music came from Yoko, George, and Ringo (none of it very good) and we all knew there would never be a reunion of the fab four. It's a standard issue full length band biography. I suggest you get their story from Nicholas Schaffner's glorious *The Beatles Forever*.

Philip Norman has one great weapon that he uses in *Shout!* He absolutely hates McCartney and doesn't bother to disguise it. Lennon comes across as a musical genius while Paul becomes " a multimillionaire businessman who professes himself a simple, unspoiled lad...who allows his wife to sing on stage, unmelodiously...whose every lyric betrays what editing it has not had." Mr. Norman makes sure to quote George Martin on Paul's song *SGT. PEPPER*, "Just an ordinary song...not particularly brilliant." Norman feels Paul was the "most dandified Beatle." Linda Eastman, the love of Paul's life "did not arouse resentment as much as bewilderment...The Apple Records secretaries stared with frank incomprehension at Linda's shapeless dresses and flat heeled tennis shoes." Paul was in "love with his own bewitching, beguiling, melodic power."

Despite the anti-Paul bias Philip does go a little crazy when praising the group as a whole. He asserts the group "were beings such as the modern world had never seen" and eventually "The Beatles ruled over time itself." Could they also walk on water and raise the dead?   B

SOLO IN THE 70s: John, Paul, George, Ringo: 1970-1980 by Robert Rodriguez (2014 Parading Press)

If you're like me you lay awake at night for a few years humming I'M SO TIRED as you waited for Robert Rodriguez to release the sequel to his masterpiece *Fab Four FAQ* 2.0. Finally *Solo in the 70s* appeared and gave us "solo years" fans more of what we crave. Here is the lowdown on the promo films; court cases; business associates; friends; lovers; gofers; protégés; non-album B-sides; bootlegs; album cover art; outtakes; and untimely deaths of that magical 11 year period that climaxed with the passing of John.

If you're like me you're now lying awake at night hoping that Rodriguez is hard at work on *Fab Four FAQ 3.0*. Can you imagine how beautiful that would be? The life and times of Yoko, Paul, George, and Ringo 1981-2017...dare I say those 37 years contain enough material to fill two volumes? So much has happened since Christmas 1980. The assassination attempt on George; Paul collaborating with Elvis Costello; Ringo and Paul touring their little hearts out; the Traveling Wilburys; Harrison's Japanese tour with Slowhand; the mostly shoddy Ron Howard documentary; Linda's sad final months; the incessant clamor for a Wings re-union that never came; Paul's 15 year stint with the same group of guys (none of whom I can name); Paul's dreadful 2nd marriage and the tabloid fall out that ensued; Yoko's endless avalanche of Lennon re-issues and remasters; Yoko's reforming of The Plastic Ono Band (albeit without the most important member); Sean's checkered musical career; George's tragic demise; Pete Best finally getting some big money for his efforts; Stuart Sutcliffe coming out of his self-imposed retirement; Yoko hitting number one on the dance charts; the release of the first of Mark Lewisohn's long awaited trilogy; George Martin ascending to that great recording studio in the sky (unfortunately no more new *Games of Thrones* stories); Julian's painting career; Zak's stints with Oasis and The Who; the much lauded publication of *The Beatles Album Guide 1963-2016*; all three survivors on ALL THOSE YEARS AGO; and the release of ANTHOLOGY (the recordings), *Anthology* (the coffee table book), *Anthology* (the video documentary); etc.   A-

SOME FUN TONIGHT!: The Backstage Story of How The Beatles Rocked America: The Historic Tours of 1964-1966 by Chuck Gunderson (2013 Gunderson Media)

Yea though I walk through the valley of the shadow of death I shall fear no evil....because for our third wedding anniversary my wife bought me Chuck Gunderson's two volume boxed set *Some Fun Tonight!* This is the one Beatle tome you'd like to have with you on a desert island or trapped for eternity in your bomb shelter or on a 34 hour flight to Australia. This is the most beautiful fab related package since the glory days of the WEDDING ALBUM, ALL THINGS MUST PASS, and THE CONCERT FOR BANGLADESH. To say it's sumptuously designed is like saying the Sistine Chapel has a drawing on it. To say it's a work of art is like saying the Mona Lisa is a nice little portrait.

Some Fun Tonight! takes you along with the fab four on their journey through America 1964-1966. They arrive in San Francisco for their first U.S. tour in August 1964 and leave San Francisco two years later in August 1966 as they finish their last tour ever. It's full circle.

During those two years they go through a whirlwind of screaming girls, helpful policemen, autograph seekers, press conferences, plane rides, Shea Stadium twice, meeting with Robert Zimmerman, civic centers, memorial auditoriums, convention halls, and John Lennon trying to explain what he meant by: "Christianity will go. It will vanish and shrink. We're more popular than Jesus now."

All of this mayhem, delirium, and controversy are covered here in jaw droppingly comprehensive detail. Gunderson presents us with tickets, views of the venues, photos of the gigs, meetings with the press, shots of the band valiantly fighting their way in and out of the arenas, and pictures of girls screaming/crying/freaking as the boys from Liverpool descend from the sky to bring joy and meaning to their lives.

Chuck Gunderson is a charming raconteur. I know because I was lucky enough to see his audio/video presentation of this material at the Fest for Beatle Fans in Rye Brook, New York (2016). But if you don't have a chance to see Chuck live in person don't worry. *Some Fun Tonight!* brings us all back home to a time we can never forget even if we're too young to remember.   A+

SONGS WE WERE SINGING: Guided Tours through the Beatles' Lesser-Known Tracks by Kit O'Toole (2015 12 Bar)

Going against the grain Kit O'Toole disputes the standard critical response to such tracks as Mr. MOONLIGHT, FOR YOU BLUE, RUN FOR YOUR LIFE, and WAIT. She sees greatness where most of us just see cheesiness (Mr. MOONLIGHT), emptiness (FOR YOU BLUE), misogyny (RUN FOR YOUR LIFE), and lethargy (WAIT). Being a contrarian myself I felt right at home here yet the parts of this book I enjoyed the most were the times when I was nodding in agreement. I too believe that HEY BULLDOG is "an underrated rocker in the Beatles' oeuvre", SAVOY TRUFFLE "encapsulates Harrison's apparent glee in playing with language", CRY BABY CRY "still intrigues with its unusual instrumentation and cryptic lyrics", and WHEN I GET HOME is "a buried gem in the Beatles canon."

This book features a wonderful foreword from Ken Womack, a section on the less loved solo recordings, and a list of underrated Starkey drumming performances (no surprise…the critics still feel the need to defend Starr).

We also get a thorough examination of the release of the remasters in 2009. We hear from *Beatlefan* Executive Editor Al Sussman on why the remasters matter ("If the Beatles catalog is the Rolls-Royce of pop music catalogs, then that Rolls has been taken in for a complete tune-up, but not an overhaul, and a thorough cleaning/washing") and O'Toole guides us through the mono and the stereo of 2009 while looking back at the much maligned 1987 CDs.

Best of all there is a detailed look at the ABBEY ROAD medley. Some folks claim that the medley begins with YOU NEVER GIVE ME YOUR MONEY but I always thought it started with BECAUSE. I feel validated because O'Toole puts BECAUSE first.

Nitpicking: Kit asserts that BECAUSE "was the last time all four Beatles recorded a song together." Actually, Ringo was on a coffee break but it does feature the harpsichord playing of George Martin. B

SOUND MAN by Glyn Johns (2014 Blue Rider)

This one is for you folks out there who didn't feel full after reading books by and about Geoff Emerick, George Martin, and Phil "I fought the law and the law won" Spector. Glyn Johns helped to record many of the great classic rock albums such as *THE ART OF CHRIS FARLOWE, FAMILY ENTERTAINMENT,* and *McGUINNESS FLINT.* He also worked on a couple of lesser known works by some quartet from Liverpool, England that were called *LET IT BE* and *ABBEY ROAD*.

The fun begins when Glyn gets a call from Paul McCartney asking if he wants to help record them while the Beatles start rehearsing for a TV special. Glyn thinks it's his friend Mick Jagger calling as a prank so he tells him to stop messing around. It turns out it really is Paul so off Mr. Johns goes to the sessions that John Lennon said were so miserable that not even the biggest Beatles fan on earth could sit through them. The Beatles regular producer George Martin agrees with that assessment and gets the hell out leaving Johns in charge of the Beatles getting back to where they once belonged. Glyn then makes a nice contribution to pop history by suggesting they play live on the Apple rooftop. It turns out to be a wonderful time.

Unfortunately, then things got dark. Glyn presented the Beatles with his version of the *LET IT BE* album (at that point still with the working title *GET BACK*) and "The next day I got a resounding NO from each of them." Undaunted, Mr. Johns started working on *ABBEY ROAD* and then out of the blue the band asked him to prepare a second version of *LET IT BE*. This too was rejected. To add insult to injury Lennon gave the tapes to Phil Spector to work on and according to Johns Phil proceeded to, "...puke all over them, turning the album into the most syrupy load of bullshit I've ever heard...obviously I'm biased, because they didn't use my version, which upset me...but I was totally disgusted and I think it's an absolute load of garbage...I think Spector did the most atrocious job... just utter puke...mind you, the *Let it Be* film is even worse." Be honest Glyn, what do you really think?

This humble reviewer's opinion is that Spector's *LET IT BE* is much superior to the very sludgy bootlegs of the two Johns versions. But who knows? They might have been spiffed up a bit if they were released officially. As it is, they sound like they were recorded under water and Spector's version sounds like it was recorded above sea level. C-

STARTING OVER: The Making of John Lennon and Yoko Ono's Double Fantasy by Ken Sharp (2010 Gallery)

I'm a sucker for these oral memory books. Let the people involved tell the story instead of some outside journalist. The story in this case is the tale of the making of *DOUBLE FANTASY*. It's not a good album but it is a good story. Lazy rock star crawls out of hiding, forces the vinyl buying public to listen to his wife's songs on every other track, then gets shot by deranged J.D. Salinger fan. It's the circle of life.

The best part is the chapter featuring five esteemed critics telling how they felt pre and post-assassination. The only problem is Charles Shaar Murray. Charles pans *DOUBLE FANTASY* and its solipsistic complacency in 1980 then turns around in 2000 and praises its eerie immediacy. Somehow, I think if John had stayed alive and kept churning out *DOUBLE FANTASY* type slop Charles wouldn't have changed his mind about what he heard.   B

TEARING DOWN THE WALL OF SOUND by Mick Brown (2007 Knopf)

The story of the man who:

1. Wrote a song about himself called *TO KNOW HIM IS TO LOVE HIM* that the Beatles covered as TO KNOW HER IS TO LOVE HER (available on 'LIVE AT THE BBC'). Note to John M. Borack: It's a joke John, just a joke.
2. Produced a whole host of hits that the fabs dug because of the crazy sound he got.
3. Accompanied the band as they sailed across the Atlantic to be where they belonged. "He had originally planned to take an earlier flight but, paranoid as ever, had changed his arrangements to travel with the group, trusting to the fates that no plane carrying the biggest pop group in the world could possibly crash….he followed the Beatles down the gangway of the plane…into a furnace of adulation. The only problem was , it wasn't for him."
4. Produced a record for sick comic Leonard Bruce who made the cover of a little album called *SGT. PEPPER*.
5. "Took steps to turn his mansion into a fortified redoubt" with an electrified wall of sound that would deafen anyone trying to break in, after the Manson girls freaked everybody in Los Angeles out by following the orders of Paul McCartney to start helter skelter.
6. Appeared as a drug dealer in Dennis Hopper's cinematic milestone *EASY RIDER* alongside Peter Fonda, the actor responsible for inspiring Lennon's *SHE SAID SHE SAID*. You could say Peter got on John's nerves while he was trying to enjoy a pleasant acid trip.
7. Produced the greatest Lennon solo single ever (released as a Plastic Ono Band 45). It was called *INSTANT KARMA* and featured Harrison on guitar.
8. Reproduced for disc the new phase Beatles album *LET IT BE* which made him persona non grata with the cute

one for slathering his *LONG AND WINDING ROAD* with 18 violins, four cellos, one harp, three trumpets , three trombones, two guitarists, 14 female voices, and a partridge in a pear tree. Yet he still left on John "I've not really a bass player" Lennon's terrible four string thumping.

Lennon, "He worked like a pig on it. He always wanted to work with the Beatles and he was given the shittiest load of badly recorded shit-and with a lousy feeling to it-ever. And he made something out of it. It wasn't fantastic, but I heard it, I didn't puke."

9. Reproduced *ACROSS THE UNIVERSE* beautifully by ditching the horrific background vocals of Lizzie Bravo and Gayleen Pease and the irrelevant bird noises that it was splattered with when it appeared on *NO ONE'S GONNA CHANGE OUR WORLD*.

10. Thought it was ironic that McCartney picked up the Grammy for *LET IT BE* after all his complaining. I am guessing that it was to keep it out the hands of the reproducer. The complaining would go on for over three decades until the release of the useless *LET IT BE...NAKED*.

11. Co-produced the mega hit three record boxed set *ALL THINGS MUST PASS* featuring the delightful 45 *MY SWEET LORD b/w WHAT IS LIFE*. The high point of George's solo career commercially speaking even though (according to Roy Carr and Tony Tyler) his burying techniques tended to cover what little melody George came up with in the first place.

12. Co-produced John's worst solo single ever *POWER TO THE PEOPLE* which was mitigated by co-producing its

pornographic B side from Yoko, the self-explanatory *OPEN YOUR BOX*.

13. Co-produced Lennon's greatest solo LP *PLASTIC ONO BAND* as well as playing piano on it. He did not use much Wall of Sound on it but check out the way he harnesses Yoko's wind.
14. Co-produced George's dreadful 45 *BANGLADESH* b/w *DEEP BLUE*.
15. Co-produced Lennon's signature solo track, *IMAGINE*.
16. Co-produced the *IMAGINE* album as well as singing on it (*OH YOKO!*)
17. Co-produced *HOW DO YOU SLEEP?* the song that tears down McCartney in every way possible, asserting that fans were right to think he had died (Lennon, "I think he died artistically in a way."). George Harrison joins John as he performed his attack.
18. Co-produced *THE CONCERT FOR BANGLADESH* featuring the felt but not heard strummed guitars of Badfinger, the sounds like somebody tuning up of Ravi Shankar, and this man needs a vocal coach singing of Rob Zimmerman.
19. Co-produced *SOMETIME IN NEW YORK CITY* giving him the chance to finally work with Frank Zappa and Keith Moon.
20. Produced the Righteous Brothers who then promptly broke up. Worked with the Ronettes who then promptly broke up. Reproduced the Beatles who then promptly broke up.
21. Co-produced Lennon's holiday classic *HAPPY XMAS (WAR IS OVER)*.
22. Was involved in the sessions for John's *ROCK 'N' ROLL* album. During this he threatened to shoot Lennon to

death (John, "If you're going to shoot me just get it over with.") He also tied Lennon up at one point and John gave him a black eye at another point. He called his relationship with Lennon, "The perfect marriage...we just loved each other."

23. Produced the first lackluster Ramones album (*END OF THE CENTURY*), the band that was named after McCartney's old alias Paul Ramon. The first song on the album features Joey Ramone asking us if we remember John Lennon.
24. Shot to death actress Lana Clarkson who he was on a date with.
25. Was played in a TV movie by Al "the Godfather" Pacino as directed by David "Glengarry Glenross" Mamet.
26. Wore an utterly ridiculous wig to court that made him look like the ultimate mop top.

(Chapter) 27. Was convicted of murder and was sent to prison, where by all accounts he lost that loving feeling.   B+

TOMORROW NEVER KNOWS: Rock and Psychedelics in the 1960's by Nick Bromell (2000 University of Chicago)

Old hippie Nick Bromell has a head full of ideas and they're driving him insane. Lost in a terrifying acid flashback, Bromell spills his guts. It's amazing how creative you can get when you use drug trips to jumpstart your imagination. Lennon cranked out *In His Own Write* and *A Spaniard in the Works* in the throes of a hard day's drunk. Mr. Bromell looks back at the 1960's through an LSD inspired haze. The dreaded lysergic rears its ugly head and points Nick in the direction of the Beatles who inspired Robert Zimmerman who inspired Jimi Hendrix. Are you experienced? Have you ever been experienced? I think it's safe to say Nick Bromell would answer yes to both of these questions. Nick asks some of his own, "Will we ever know what really happened in the 1960's?" and "Did the 60's really take place?"

Just in case you thought the British invasion was a bunch of teenagers screaming and throwing jelly beans:

- "The beginning of the Beatles was experienced by many persons as the end of the world, of history, of life as we knew it."
- "It was obvious that they were thinking not just about the ups and downs of teenage love but about the problems and possibilities of all human encounters."
- "We stand on the shore of the Beatles' secret island even now."
- "When the Beatles asked where all the lonely people came from, I already knew the answer: they came from the way life is, from the way things have been set up…we are Eleanor Rigby."
- "I remember finding a blue comb lost beneath the leaves of a shrub in the garden…at such moments, the sheer beingness of these things flood us with light we have not yet learned to fear."
- "Our moments of naked confrontation with a formless Being cut a fissure through the surface of the world we thought we knew-a fissure that opens into another dimension, into other worlds, into the void…we are

- swept up and swallowed…at the edge of the fissure, a counterculture grew like the dense colonies of mysterious organisms that thrive only in the depths of the ocean near life-giving jets of hot gas and molten lava."
- "The intensification of life that living to music produced was the pursuit of breaking loose even if at the risk of chaos, madness, and death."
- "To sanction an adolescent vehemence that cuts through the lies of culture and steps into the region beyond the veil is to legitimize madness and mysticism and to affirm the belief that instability is more natural than stability."

This wins the prize hands down for craziest, zaniest, most out there Beatle book on the market. If you want to take a trip upon a magic swirling ship and have all your senses stripped, this is the one for you. B+

TUNE IN: All These Years – Vol. 1 by Mark Lewisohn (2013 Crown Archetype)

If you really want to hear about it you'll want to read this. Out of all the accounts of the pre-fame years this is the most comprehensive and well told. I'm not much for finding out about the formative years of any celebrities. I like to hear about them from the time they become "overnight sensations" until the time they hit their peak and on to the inevitable decline into has been status. I usually skip over the formative years in star biographies unless it's about the Beatles where I dutifully delve in. The one version of pre-1963 I liked was Albert Goldman's in *The Lives of John Lennon*. This is also the one most fans shun. So it was with great trepidation that I sat down with the number one Beatle expert's first volume of his planned trilogy. Nearly 900 pages and it's only a document of the history up to New Year's Eve 1962? That sounded ridiculous to me. But damn if Mark Lewinsohn didn't win me over. The only problem is it took him 10 years to put this together which means we'll see volume 2 in 2023 and volume 3 in 2033. Can we really wait that long for *Turn On* and *Drop Out*? Mark will be 65 in 2023 and 75 in 2033. We better pray for his good health.

"Through sheer force of personality, John Lennon changed others' lives, and many went willingly on the journey." For you genealogy lovers, first we get the family backgrounds of the four main players. Then we learn that Ringo Starr will be referred to as Richy Starkey until quite late in the narrative. Then you have their boyhood experiences. John lived in Penny Lane and played in Strawberry Field. John became a bookworm at Mendips, his childhood home. Lennon would be a fan of biographies his whole life just as long as they weren't about him. Richy spent much of his childhood dangerously ill including a burst appendix leading to peritonitis leading to ten weeks in a coma. Paul found out "things came more or less easily to him." George became a fan of the *Goon Show*, the start of his life-long appreciation of zany comedy. It was a straight line from Peter Sellers to being the producer of *Life of Brian*.

In their teenage years John forms a skiffle group called the Quarry Men and plays a gig on July 6, 1957 where he meets another young fellow called Paul. This meeting, of course, gets a whole chapter. Paul has a little buddy named George who plays guitar and soon all three of them are in the Quarry Men. "Paul and George's friendship was not a perfect fit. Paul had a need to remind to remind George, one way or another and often without much subtlety, that he was 'nine months older', ensuring George didn't forget who held the aces." Still, when John let George in the group, even though he was the youngest and smallest member, he was the only guitarist in the band designated lead.

All three of them loved Buddy Holly (the first song they ever recorded was a cover of THAT'LL BE THE DAY) but when he played in Liverpool in 1958 they skipped seeing him. That's strange. I wonder if missing Buddy Holly in '58 led John, George and Ringo to go see Bob Zimmerman in 1969 at the Isle of Wight. Maybe they had learned not to miss special events.

Paul's mother died in 1956. John's mother died in 1958. Paul was John's one friend who could relate to his situation. Paul, "We had a bond that we never talked about-but each of us knew that had happened to the other."

John's behavior after Julia's death "now seemed worse by degrees. He was the definitely gifted yet troubled young man, the mix that defined him: artistic and sarcastic, literate and cruel, brutal and tender, swift and funny, contemptuous of all pretense. His obsession with deformities, race, and religion seemed to have gone up a few notches."

The Quarry Men changed names "on a whim." One gig they called themselves the Rainbows and for a period they melded their first names together to be the Japage (pronounced as

"Jaypage") 3. That's right. We almost had Japage 3 mania sweeping the world.

Enter Brian Epstein into their lives. They'd been to Hamburg. They'd brought in Pete Best as their drummer. Now they just needed a better manager than Allan Williams. Brian managed his family's record store and he liked their trousers. Epstein would get them to George Martin and Parlophone records in 1962. One of their best pieces of luck was that Parlophone was still in existence and George Martin still worked there. "The 'Parlophone to end' rumors reached their Zenith in February 1957, having gained such strength that EMI issued a statement insisting that the story had 'no foundation' and that there was no truth Mr. Martin (would be) leaving EMI."

Richy was brought in to replace Pete Best. What a lucky guy. On meeting George Martin at EMI "Ringo lost his head and started hitting everything with everything. It did not go unnoticed…The Beatles' last drummer hadn't uttered a word, this new one was crazy."

Saying goodbye to 1962 and ushering in 1963 the band went from Hamburg, Germany to London, England "flying into a bright white tomorrow. Sometimes in life, things go right, only very rarely do they all go right, and so it was now- for them and for everyone and everything around them. The plates were aligned for a cultural earthquake that would start shaking the walls in 1963, one of the century's most remarkable years and thrilling years."

At least it was thrilling for J, P, G, and R and countless enraptured British girls. Let's not kid ourselves. It would be years before there would be as many males worshipping the Beatles as there were females.

Lewinsohn's book reminds me a little of the Vince Lombardi biography *When Pride Mattered*. As 1962 ended, the Green Bay Packers boarded a plane home to Wisconsin and nothing would ever be the same. They would change the face of professional football and become one of the most important parts of 1960's American pop culture. They would finish the decade with five NFL championships including two Super Bowl victories. In 1970 Lombardi would die.

As 1962 ended, the Beatles with new drummer Ringo Starr would board a plane home to Liverpool and nothing would ever be the same. They would change the face of pop music and become one of the most important parts of 1960's American pop culture. They would finish the decade with over a dozen number one albums. In 1970 they would break up.   A-

TWILIGHT OF THE GODS: The Music of the Beatles by Wilfred Mellers (1973 Richard Seaver)

In this masterwork Wilfrid lets us know that "When the senior critic of The Times wrote the first musically literate piece about the Beatles it was greeted with hoots of mirth both from the Beatles themselves and from their hostile critics." Then Wilfrid goes on to show how wrong everybody was. The Beatles do deserve to be mentioned in the company of Brahms, Mozart, and Stravinsky. Roll over Beethoven and tell Tchaichovsky the news. To help us readers learn how to fully appreciate the band's genius he gets down and dirty with musical terms. Don't worry musical illiterates there is a handy dandy glossary to help you grasp what's going on. In case you didn't know acciaccatura is a decorative note approaching the main note, ostinato is an obstinately repeated linear figure or even rhythm, and a melisma is an ornamental passage used in medieval times. Duh! Revelations from this stunning treatise include:

1. *SHE LOVES YOU* "...depends on contrast between upward tending sharp sevenths and the blue flat sevenths of folk tradition."
2. *NORWEGIAN WOOD (THIS BIRD HAS FLOWN)* is about a girl whose "...polished archness is satirized in an arching waltz tune wearily fey."
3. *ELEANOR RIGBY* features "...cadences that reinforce the tonal ambiguity of the submediant introduction."
4. *SHE SAID SHE SAID* has "...abrupt changes of metre from double to triple time that suggest incomprehension."
5. *TOMORROW NEVER KNOWS* "...is the first significant narcotics song...the melody alternates a non-metrical phrase on the triad of C major with a triplet on the fifth, rising to the flat seventh, then to the tonic."
6. *STRAWBERRY FIELDS FOREVER's* "...hallucinatory atmosphere is maintained through the vaguely shifting rhythms of the monotone vocal line, mumbling to itself as it sinks below consciousness."
7. *A DAY IN THE LIFE*, "Some of it is funny, more of it gives me the creeps...it is a deep little song with one of the most haunting phrases in Beatles music...it agitates nerves we hardly knew we possessed."
8. *I AM THE WALRUS* is "...a grotesque beast who lives beneath the watery depths." True. My wife and I saw him at Sea World.

9. *COME TOGETHER* is "...a portrait of a kind of hobo-outcast-messiah, written in juvenile gibberish more scary than comic."
10. *HAPPINESS IS A WARM GUN* has "...at least three satirical elements...of sophisticated cabaret song, of soul-song-cum blues, and of corny balladic waltz."

I just like to sing along to the nice tunes.   A

THE ULTIMATE BEATLES ENCYCLOPEDIA by Bill Harry (1992 Hyperion)

Bill Harry was friends in the early days with John Lennon. So I guess it's not surprising that he turned that into a career writing Beatle books. But where will the madness end? Do we really need 723 pages crammed with information on these important figures in Beatle history?

1. Joseph Ephgrave who painted the drum skin for the *SGT. PEPPER* cover and used to dress up as a mouse in his spare time.
2. Duncan McKinnon who was an elderly chicken farmer somehow involved in their 1960 Scottish tour.
3. Anello and Davide who made the famous Beatle Boots of 1964. Ask for them by name.
4. Ann Margaret, famous film star, who Ringo denied having a romance with. Ringo didn't date her. He denied dating her. How is this worthy of an entry?

5. Alf Bicknell. You remember the famous Beatles chauffeur, don't you? His worst selling memoir was of course entitled *Baby, You Can Drive My Car*. Probably the best book by a chauffeur I never read.
6. The Koobas, a band from the same town the Beatles were from. I expected every musician from Liverpool to be in here but only the Koobas made it. My favorite LP when I was a kid was MEET THE KOOBAS.
7. Bruno Koschmider who was a "small, pugnacious circus clown, fire eater, and acrobat."

You've got to be kidding me. Plus, all of this is written in the most boring dreadful manner you can imagine. This is the Beatle book that almost made me want to stop reviewing Beatle books. F

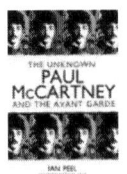

THE UNKNOWN PAUL McCARTNEY: And the Avant Garde by Ian Peel (2002 Reynolds and Hearn)

Paul must love this book. I wonder if he commissioned it. Since Lennon died he's been shouting to the rooftops, "I'm not just the cute one who writes the superficial pop songs but I was ahead of Lennon in embracing the avant-garde and I continue to this day to work outside the box by making experimental techno music, ambient soundscapes, and my own classical compositions. I am a renaissance man. I even got together with those two guys from Nirvana to form McVana and we won a Grammy for our efforts. So there!"

In 1997 Paul even got his friend Miles to write a book called *Many Years from Now* that set the facts straight on who was the avant-garde Beatle. Despite REVOLUTION 9, TWO VIRGINS, LIFE WITH THE LIONS, and THE WEDDING ALBUM giving strong evidence to the contrary it was (you guessed it) Paul who was the avant-garde beatle. I knew it wasn't Ringo.

The Unknown Paul McCartney is worthwhile. I found it fascinating. It was illuminating to find out the scope of Paul's music outside of pop and roll. It was refreshing to read a book with a new slant. It's not the usual Beatles, Wings, solo career, and duets with Michael Jackson and Stevie Wonder slant we're used to. Now the question is: Will I ever listen to any of this crazy weird "out there" stuff he's recorded? It's one thing to read about it. It's another thing to take the plunge. Maybe I'll check that stuff out another day.   A-

THE WALRUS WAS PAUL: The Great Beatle Death Clues of 1969 by R. Gary Patterson (1998 Fireside)

John Lennon had this to say about the Paul is dead conspiracy theorists, "They live vicariously." Of course, that's what fans do. I think it's great that while living vicariously they could make up a whole thing about James Paul McCartney shuffling off the mortal coil on November 9th, 1966. With no facts at their fingertips the fan base made up an incredible story about Paul dying in a car accident. Then instead of announcing the tragedy in the press the three remaining members decide to perpetrate a hoax on the public. They get the winner of a Paul lookalike contest (one William Campbell) to stand in for McCartney during photo shoots for the next three years and somehow they are able to come up with McCartney like vocals for studio recordings like HEY JUDE, LADY MADONNA, etc. When they perform live for the cameras in *Let it Be* William Campbell is able to sound exactly like Paul. Amazing! Also, as R. Gary Patterson admits "totally ridiculous." Patterson further tells us "a number of these clues are rumor or hearsay and cannot be confirmed but many of them are hilarious." He's right about that. Here are some of my favorite death clues:

1. At the end of STRAWBERRY FIELDS FOREVER John mumbles the words, "cranberry sauce." Everybody knows that when they buried bodies in ancient Egypt they used to pack them in cranberry sauce.
2. If you play REVOLUTION 9 backwards you can hear Lennon clear as day say, "Attention Beatle fans! Paul died two years ago and for a laugh we covered up his horrible death in a car accident that left him decapitated. Then we put clues on all the album covers. Check out PEPPER, MAGICAL MYSTERY TOUR, and the poster that comes with this album for all kinds of hints that Paul is a dead man. Then stay tuned for clues on our next three LPs YELLOW SUBMARINE, ABBEY ROAD, and LET IT BE. Pay special attention to ABBEY ROAD. We're putting a shitload of clues on the front cover of that one. We're going to have Paul carrying a cigarette in his right hand and he was left handed, people! Then we're going to have him barefoot because we all know that when they buried people in ancient Egypt they sent

them to the grave barefoot and covered in cranberry sauce. Nothing is real, people! Nothing!"
3. On the inside of Paul's first solo album *McCARTNEY* there is a photo of Paul picking his nose. We all know that in ancient Egypt when they buried people barefoot in cranberry sauce they also staged it to look like they were picking their nose.

I have one little bit of nitpicking about this well researched tome. Patterson goes along with the party line that Paul bit the dust and kicked the bucket in November 1966. But then he presents album cover clues in the photo section from records (*HELP!, RUBBER SOUL, REVOLVER, YESTERDAY AND TODAY*) that came out before November 1966. So unless somebody went back in time to plant those clues we have a little problem here.

Despite everything I like this book. I obviously need help and I don't mean the album. B+

WAY BEYOND COMPARE: The Beatles' Recorded Legacy, Volume One, 1957-1965 by John C. Winn (2008 Three Rivers)

Here is proof positive that Beatlemania is a disease. We need a telethon and we need it soon. Every year more books, articles, websites, and blogs pour forth from the huddled masses yearning to be free. These writers are worshipping at the altar of four guys from Liverpool who got together to play pop music. It seems like hardly any of these writings possess a sense of humor or a sense of proportion. Beatle expert Mark Lewinsohn (the man who wrote the 1,000 page biography that goes all the way up to 1962) on fellow scribe John C. Winn, "It takes a rare and special mind to shift through it all...to fit all the myriad pieces into the vast jigsaw puzzle that is the Beatles' career." I say it takes a demented mind. When will it end? Never! As long as the wind blows and the grass grows you'll find beautiful people like John C. Winn spending countless hours of their life collecting, studying, and enjoying the walrus and his three friends. THIS IS JUST VOLUME ONE! It's nearly four hundred pages on the recorded legacy from 1957-1965. Just the facts, maam. Here you'll find out about every press conference, radio interview, TV appearance, and bathroom break the band took part in over a nine year period. Plus, just to make it as dry as possible, there is not one single photograph in the whole book, not even on the cover. The first word in the introduction is WHY? That's what I'm wondering. Please give generously.   C-

"WE'RE GOING TO SEE THE BEATLES!": *An Oral History of Beatlemania as Told by the Fans Who Were There* by Garry Berman (2008 Santa Monica)

I used to love those oral history books by Studs Terkel. He would turn the tape recorder on, listen to what real people think, and then transcribe the results. It was great stuff. It was Americana. It was entertaining and you learned something from it. So why not do it with the fans who were there for the tours of 1964-1966? It sounds like it would work and let's be honest these people have one foot in the grave at this point so somebody better get their stories down quickly. As a card carrying member of the fantastic four's fan club I feel envy toward these fans who got to see them live. Damn them all to hell. I always thought my parents should have taken me in the womb to New York City for the summer 1964 tour but they didn't. What were they thinking, depriving their fetus of a once in a lifetime experience?

Digging this book depends on how sentimental, nostalgic, or curious you are about the screaming, crying, and coming that these kids went through when they went to a concert. Obviously the experience was great, exciting, and fulfilling for them but can they translate that euphoria to the reader? In my case I have to go with no. I get more out of playing *HOLLYWOOD BOWL* for the thousandth time than I do from this whole paperback.

On the bright side we also hear from promotor Sid Bernstein who booked them at Carnegie Hall and Shea Stadium. For those who have always wondered why the second Shea gig (1966) had empty seats, wait no longer for the answer. The Singer sewing machine store at Rockefeller Center did not get all the tickets they were supposed to. 2,500 were left in a box, never to be delivered to Singer. Mystery solved! Like most of the people who dealt with the group during Beatlemania Sid Bernstein spent the rest of his life basking in their glory, "The Beatles made me an international semi-celebrity. People know me wherever I go." It's true. I've had a picture of Sid on my bedroom wall since the 70's. It's right next to my Ed Sullivan and Brian Epstein posters.   C-

WHEN THEY WERE BOYS: The True Story of the Beatles Rise to the Top by Larry Kane (2013 Running)

Oh, no! Please not another badly written book about the pre-Beatlemania years. I'm begging you, please stop. I can't take it anymore. I'm only human. If you're interested in the rhythm guitarist's early years turn to Albert Goldman's *The Lives of John Lennon*. If you want to know about the whole band up to 1962 see Mark Lewinsohn's thousand page epic *Tune In*.   C-

THE WHITE BOOK by Ken Mansfield with Brent Stoker (2007 Thomas Nelson)

In the great tradition of Joan Didion's *The White Album* comes Ken Mansfield's look back at his time in the 1960's as U.S. manager of Apple (a subsidiary of Capitol records and tapes). What a lucky bastard! How I envy him his time with my heroes as they took drugs, lay in the sun, played on the roof, and counted their money. It wasn't hard working up sales for fab vinyl. As Ken candidly admits "You didn't promote a Beatles record- you just hung on when one came out." He also lets us in on other facts:

1. "Rock stars are like hyperactive children in a way, and they can only sit and be quiet for so long."
2. "Individually, the Beatles were incredible people." Even Ringo?
3. "They were a performing live in your face rock and roll band." Except for most of the last three years.
4. "I wish we could get back to that special time in the record business. For some of us it's hard to just let it be in the past."
5. "I think World War III could have started during the Paul is dead period and no one under the age of thirty would have noticed." No. The soldiers would definitely have noticed.

What this book comes down to is the usual for authors who write about their time as hangers on. They were there with the Beatles and that makes them special.

As Ken says "If the Beatles music and legend last forever, then also the people who were there are eternally ensconced in the echoes of the events that transpired."   C+

WHO KILLED JOHN LENNON? by Fenton Bresler (1989 St. Martin's)

I'm going to take a wild guess here and say Mark David Chapman. I'm pretty sure it wasn't the FBI or the CIA or the BBC or B.B. King or Doris Day or Matt Busby. Author Fenton Bresler asks us right off the bat "It was a madman who did it, wasn't it?" Yes, obviously, I mean, you don't need a weatherman to know which way the wind blew. Furthermore, Bresler asks us "How can you fathom the mind of a madman?" That is a tough one to figure but it doesn't mean that the U.S. government programmed Chapman to take Lennon out as this book contends. Nixon didn't have it done. Dick just tried to deport him. Does Carter pull the trigger on the Beatle assassination? Or are we to believe the first thing on Reagan's mind after being elected is killing Lennon?

Now that I think of it, Ronnie and Johnny were on the same episode of *Monday Night Football*. Cosell interviewed the Beatle and Gifford took the governor. Maybe, they had a dust up that night because one was a conservative icon and one was a liberal icon. Maybe, Ronnie didn't like all that nonsense about giving peace a chance and all you need is love. "Get a haircut you damn hippie!" It all makes sense now. After being elected Reagan takes a few weeks to get his plan together. He decides to have Chapman shoot John during the fourth quarter of *Monday Night Football's* game in little Havana between the Dolphins and the Patriots. This way bleeding heart liberal Cosell can be the one to break it to the nation that his good buddy Lennon is dead (Howard claimed he was the one who brought J&Y back together). What a masterful plan! What a way to usher in the 80's. It was morning/mourning in America again. Ron's vice president was George Bush. George was formerly the head of the CIA so it was easy for him to call his buddies and have them locate an unstable loser in Hawaii to use for the task. Think of it. Bush had Lennon murdered and then 21 years later his son (also named George Bush) was behind that other historic NYC moment when the two towers went down. In 1988, while running for president, Bush the elder told a cheering crowd in Texas that handgun control was, "...not the American way!" I rest my case.

On the other hand, this book makes a case not only for the CIA but the YMCA being involved. Get this: "The fact remains that, if Chapman was, indeed, a CIA-trained killer there could have been no better cover than the YMCA for his activities." We know Chapman stayed briefly at the Y before the shooting and we all know it is fun to stay at the YMCA. Mark was probably just trying to have a last good time before doing the deed.

If you've ever seen the Frank Sinatra movie *The Manchurian Candidate* you know how easy it is to program sad and angry men into killers. That's what LBJ allegedly did with Lee Harvey Oswald and maybe that's what George Bush did with John Hinkley. First Chapman then Hinkley, the wheels were already in motion. Hinkley was in the crowd at the Dakota on December 9th and had *Catcher in the Rye* in his hotel room. Do I have to spell it out? Bush might have thought: why wait eight years to become president?

If you're a fan of JFK conspiracy books this one's for you. If you're just a normal Lennon fan you might not want to waste your time on this mindless drivel about mind control.   C+

WHO WAS ELEANOR RIGBY: And 908 More Questions and Answers About the Beatles By Brandon Toropov (1996 Harper Perennial)

As a grown man who spent 50 dollars on Beatles Trivial Pursuit I am the perfect audience for this book of 909 questions about the world's greatest pop band. Why 909 questions you ask? The same reason the remastered Beatles CD catalog came out on 9/09/09. The same reason the Beatles Rock Band video game came out on 9/09/09. John Lennon wrote a simple little ditty when he was a young whippersnapper called *ONE AFTER 909*. It was a little ditty about John trying to find his baby at the train station. Not exactly *I AM THE WALRUS*. This book is a good place for newer fans to learn gobs and gobs of useless information that only an insane maniac could care about such as "Who was Eleanor Rigby." Old fans, near death, can stave off dementia by testing their knowledge of all kind of arcane nonsense. This is a book for obsessives and what's wrong with that I'd like to know. B-

WIDE OPEN by Linda McCartney (1999 Bulfinch)

Late period snaps of nature and objects taken by Linda and put out on the market for the mourners. Compared to her excellent

Linda's Pictures this comes across as nothing much. *Pictures* has wonderful suitable for framing shots of the Stones, Hendrix, Morrison, and the Beatles outside Abbey Road on August 9, 1969. *Wide Open* has three dozen nondescript tiny photos of something or other. So despite Paul's heartfelt introduction that had me tearing up I have to say close to *Wide Open*.   D

WINGSPAN: Paul McCartney's Band on the Run by Paul McCartney as edited by Mark Lewisohn (2002 Bulfinch)

Having cornered the market on great books about the Beatles, Mark Lewisohn turns his attention to that other band that resides in the hearts and minds of all lovers of popular music. This is the story of the most important and influential band of the 1970's. It is about that giant of pop and roll, Wings. It is the true tale of Paul, Linda, Henry, Geoff, Jimmy, Joe, Laurence, Steve, Denny, and Denny. Unfortunately, it's also the white washed true story because it's narrated by one man, the band's bassist. Just like Bill Wyman's Stones memoirs or Nick Mason's Floyd memories this bassist fellow spins the facts his way. So it comes across as self-serving with many glaring omissions. On the plus side it has a nice selection of photos and with Linda, Jimmy, and probably some other important dead band members, this is the closest thing we'll get to a Wings reunion. I mean, after all, it's not like Paul and the Dennys can just get together and call it Wings. That would be ridiculous. It would be like Paul, George, and Ringo playing along with some old

Lennon recordings and then releasing the results as "new" Beatle singles. We know that would never happen.   B

WITH A LITTLE HELP FROM MY FRIENDS: The Making of Sgt. Pepper by George Martin with William Pearson (1994 Little, Brown and Company)

The first sentence of this book is "Books about the Beatles must make such a big pile by now that there should probably be some sort of law against adding to it." I don't agree. There can never be enough Beatle books. It's like saying stop writing about Jesus, Elvis, Zimmerman, or the JFK assassination. Why would we want to stop? Writers love these subjects and the public can't get enough. They are addicted to entertainment and so am I. This is the second book from George Martin. Bring it on. This time Martin sticks to one album. Unfortunately it's not 1968's *THE BEATLES*, which George deems a little too much of a good thing, but it is that old classic *SGT. PEPPER*. I love *PEPPER* as much as the next guy and to go inside it's making with the producer himself should be fascinating. But it's not. With the help of professional writer William Pearson this still comes across as mundanely remembered and by the numbers. Even the John Lennon tripping on the roof story comes across flat.

 As usual Martin complains about losing *STRAWBERRY FIELDS FOREVER* and *PENNY LANE* from *PEPPER* because they went out already as a single. For the record let me state: in England *ELEANOR RIGBY* b/w *YELLOW SUBMARINE* went out on 45 and were included on *REVOLVER* so the same thing could have been done with *SFF* b/w *PENNY LANE*. They could have been on PEPPER. It's as simple as that. Just think how they would have improved it. They could have dropped *SHE'S LEAVING HOME* and *WITHIN YOU WITHOUT YOU* and substituted *SFF/PENNY LANE*. It would have been perfection. But it really doesn't matter, because if they're wrong they're right.   C+

WITH THE BEATLES by Robert Whitaker (2012 Life)

John's buddy Bob was their official photographer from 1964-1966 so he got to cover the touring from the first American jaunt to the end at Candlestick Park. Along the way he captured so many magical moments that *Life* considers him to be "...as close as there was to a Fifth Beatle". Right... and I am the Lizard King.

This is a giant size life like representation of Beatlemania from down in the trenches and between the buttons. You'll fall in love all over again.   A-

WONDERFUL TONIGHT: George Harrison, Eric Clapton, and Me by Pattie Boyd with Penny Junor (2007 Crown)

George came home with BAD VIBES. When looking back at her marriage with Eric Clapton she realized how SHALLOW and NARROW her life had become. Allen Klein was ROTUND. Do you have any idea what having your face on the front cover of VOGUE does for the EGO? She still has a weakness for SHOES and she will always love buying CLOTHES. Who would have guessed that the HUMBLE POTATO would play such an important part in her life? She had been shown the way to SPIRITUAL ENLIGHTENMENT. She was appalled when LENNON was KILLED. Me too. D-

THE WORDS AND MUSIC OF JOHN LENNON by Ben Urish and Ken Bielen (2007 Praeger)

This should be on the shelf of any fan that digs the Lennon solo career. In comprehensive detail it covers the avant-garde recordings, the live albums, the compilations, the outtakes, work on Yoko's solo records, collaborations with his rock superstar buddies, the lost Lennon tapes radio series, the singles, and the albums. There's also a nice annotated bibliography. The only thing missing is a chapter on bootlegs.

But what really makes it stand out is the very smart writing about the songs. I would keep it right next to *Revolution in the Head* because it is the logical follow up to that book. *Revolution* explores Beatles music in a masterful way and this does the same for Lennon post breakup.   A

WORKING CLASS MYSTIC: A Spiritual Biography of George Harrison By Gary Tillery (2011 Quest)

After long months of waiting here is the eagerly awaited follow up to Gary's first spiritual biography (*Cynical Idealist*, which was about John). This time he takes on a more appropriate subject. This one's about good old Georgie boy. I can't wait for his final 2 books. *Optimistic Pot Head Dreamer* (about Paul) and *Don't Know Much about Spirituality* (about Ringo).

Webster's defines mystic as, "A person practicing or believing in the spiritual discipline of communion with god." That fits Harrigeorgeson perfectly. As for the working class part, George was working class for his first 20 years. After that he was a pampered, worshipped, and more and more wealthy big shot. Good thing to be in the material world.

Just like his study of John we get a lot of mind throwing facts and ideas about curious George. "Regular meditation...brought him a sense of 'buoyancy' and 'energy' and helped him cope with the vexations of daily life" which include:

- Sutcliffe dying of a brain hemorrhage (1962)
- Epstein dying of an overdose (1967)
- Paul treating him unkindly (1955-1970)
- John disparaging his songwriting and then not bothering to participate on recordings of George's numbers in the later years (1963-1970)
- The fans booing him on his much panned U.S. solo tour (1974)
- Best friend Eric "slow hand" Clapton stealing his wife away from him and marrying her (1968-1979)
- Being sued for ripping off *MY SWEET LORD* from an old Chiffon's hit (1975-1976)
- A&M Records dropping him for breach of contract (1976)
- Being forced by Krishna to help Ringo Starr with his music (1968-1981)
- Good buddy Mal Evans being shot to death by overzealous LAPD (1976)
- Being punked off by Capitol and EMI who released *THE BEST OF GEORGE HARRISON* compilation with one side solo material and one side of Beatle tracks because they deemed his solo career so bereft of quality songs that they need to pad the LP out with something the fans like… like SOMETHING…even Ringo was not treated this way (1976)
- Only getting $750 to appear on SNL with Paul "I will later punch Edie Brickell in the face" Simon (1976)
- John meeting with a little accident (1980)
- Krishna forcing him to jam on stage with Deep Purple (1984)

- Losing so much goddamn money on his Homemade Films that he has to get involved in *ANTHOLOGY* if he wants to keep the coffers full (1994-1995)
- Throat and lung cancer (1997-2001)
- December 23 a woman breaks into his house on Maui: eating, making calls, and doing her laundry (1999)
- One week later December 30 a man breaks into his castle in England attempting to murder him and almost stabs him to the afterlife while humming that famous Prince song (1999)
- Brain tumor (2001)
- Untimely death (2001)   B

YEAH! YEAH! YEAH!: The Beatles, Beatlemania, and the Music that Changed the World By Bob Spitz (2007 Little, Brown and Company)

YEAH! YEAH! YEAH! was written for juveniles. This seems like an okay introduction for tykes age five to ten. So if you've got a youngster who you want to turn on to the fabulous 1960's this wouldn't be that bad of an idea. Ironically enough the dust jacket tells us that "When Bob Spitz was a teenager, he got beat up at school for saying the Beatles were no-talent bums." I assume he's come to his senses and now fully embraces their genius.   C+

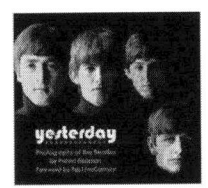

YESTERDAY: The Beatles 1963-1965 photos by Robert Freeman (1983 Thunder's Mouth)

An early example of the John is dead so the final nail is in the coffin type tome that would become more and more prevalent as the 80's and 90's segued into the new millennium. "Hey, didn't Robert Freeman shoot a whole bunch of photos including the cover of WITH THE BEATLES? We could take about 100 of those stills and slap them together with a foreword by McCartney and about ten pages of Freeman reminiscing about the 60's and bam we got a bestseller!"

And so it came to pass that in 1983 this inoffensive little picture book hit the market and became a perennial favorite, just as popular for Father's day as it was for Jesus' birthday.

Unfortunately, the photos were mostly forgettable, the foreword was completely forgettable, and the reminiscing was the kind that gives reminiscence a bad name. Bah, Humbug.   C-

YESTERDAY: The Beatles Once Upon a Time by Astrid Kirchherr and Max Scheler (2007 Genesis)

I believe a book of photos that costs $27.50 (USA) and $33.00 (CAN) should contain several fascinating images or at least one color one just for novelty's sake. Nothing here that hasn't been done to death and for chrissakes half the book isn't even shots of the Beatles. I'd demand my money back but I shoplifted this.

C-

YES YOKO ONO by Alexandra Munroe and Jon Hendricks (2000 Harry N. Abrams)

Looking for a gift for the fab four fan who has everything? How about this 20 pound 350 page coffee table book on the art of Yoko "I was married to John Lennon" Ono? It's sure to be met with screams of delight or at least screams of some sort. Originally priced at $60 (U.S.) and $90 (Canada) it's a great bargain and doubles as a doorstop. It takes you along on her journey from the beginning of the Fluxus movement through her time as prophet of the 1960's and up to the end of the 20th century. You get to read about her early objects, events and performances, advertisements, films, videos, and music.

Is there anyone amongst us who doesn't get a thrill when recalling such dazzling work as *Three Spoons* (4 spoons on a Plexiglas pedestal) which "poses a Zen-like riddle about the relationship between language, object, image, illusion, and reality?" or doesn't get excited when thinking about her 80 minute film *Bottoms* which "shows the naked, moving buttocks of a group of New York artists and friends presented in close-up" or doesn't start humming wistfully when we recall our first reaction to Ono's visionary pop music classic *RISING* which Yoko describes as "a purging of my anger ,pain, and fear?" This is the real deal. It's about an artist who has been vilified, "crucified", and mortified. It's about standing up to express yourself even as the world puts you down, grinds you up, and tears you apart. It's about a woman being told she has no talent, can't sing, and that she broke up the band. You don't take anything with you but your soul.   B+

YOKO ONO ARIAS AND OBJECTS by Barbara Haskell and John G. Hanhardt (1991 Peregrine Smith)

This is a terrific look at Yoko's constructs and concepts, arias and objects, exhibitions and cinematic visions. All your favorites are here as we walk down memory lane being followed by a camera that won't leave us alone. Thrill again as if for the first time to *A Hole to See the Sky Through, Painting to be Stepped on, Wrapped Chair, Strip Tease for Three, Eternal Time Clock, A Box of Smile, To Be Appreciated Only When It's Broken,* and *Chewing Gum Machine Piece.*

Of course, there's also a mention of her *SGT PEPPER* which everybody agrees is *Air Dispenser* from 1971. If you put 25 cents in and turn the handle you receive one capsule filled with air to do with as you please, no questions asked.

The design of this book by the great Matthew Yokobosky (surprisingly, this is not an alias for Yoko) draws you in, blind folds you, makes you walk up a ladder, and cuts pieces of your clothes off while you are wearing them. It's almost too action packed to take in. From John Cage to John Lennon we are reminded that Ono only worked with the finest Johns (though not Glyn oddly enough unless you want to count *LET IT BE*).

So get out your copies of *FLY, APPOXIMATELY INFINITE UNIVERSE, FEELING THE SPACE,* and *STARPEACE.* Put on your headphones, sing along to the hits, gaze at the book in your hand and let the evening go. You'll be glad you did.   A-

<u>YOU NEVER GIVE ME YOUR MONEY: The Beatles After the Breakup</u> by Peter Doggett (2009 HarperCollins)

This is presented as an examination of the Beatles finances from the 1960's to the 21st Century. It's actually about their socializing post-1970. It gives us a detailed account of how the fabs interacted from their breakup to the death in 2008 of noted flunky Neil Aspinall. You might remember him as the beret wearing insider in the *Anthology* video history.

Everything they did together in the 50's and 60's has been written about ad nauseum but what they did together in the 70's, 80's, 90's and beyond has gotten very little attention relatively speaking. You get Ringo telling Lennon, "That's enough John" as J&Y competed to come up with the most insulting lines about Paul for *HOW DO YOU SLEEP* and this from the man who wrote the anti-Paul single *BACK OFF BOOGALOO* Paul told Jimmy Fallon on *The Tonight Show* that this was his favorite Ringo song. There is Paul visiting John and Ringo during the lost weekend with Harry Nilsson offering McCartney elephant tranquillizer (which Paul declines). We learn of Lennon skipping a meeting in 1974 with Paul and George and instead sending a balloon over to them with a sign saying, "Listen to this balloon". George on Paul in 1989, "We don't have a relationship. You wish the other person well, but life has taken you to other places, to friendlier climes." Then there were the Threatles recording sessions about which Ringo commented, "There have been a lot of bad feelings." This is great stuff. A-

SNAPSHOTS

The three greatest rock critics this side of John Mendelsohn never wrote Beatle books. But that doesn't mean they wrote nothing about the Beatles. On the contrary, their work about the fab four is some of the most essential reading material on J, P, G, and Ringo.

Lester Bangs:

"Dandelions in still air: The withering away of the Beatles" Originally published in April 1975 in The Real Paper and reprinted in Creem June 1975 as "Who Killed the Beatles?"

This is available in The Mammoth Book of the Beatles edited by Sean Egan (2009)

1. Lester puts the Beatles' solo careers in perspective while not neglecting to pigeonhole 60's/70's greats like Lou Reed ("...a professional zombie") and Mick Jagger ("...washed up, moribund, self-pitying, self-parodying has-been"). Bangs realized that the Beatles would never again "...give off a glint of the magic they used to radiate with such seeming effortlessness."
2. On Lennon "He'll do anything, reach for any cheap trick, jump on any bandwagon, to make himself look like a Significant Artist."
3. On Harrison "George belongs in a daycare center for counterculture casualties."
4. On McCartney "Paul makes lovely boutique tapes, resolute upon being as inconsequential as the Carpenters."
5. On Starr "Ringo is beneath contempt."
6. For good measure he also theorizes that the Kennedy assassination, "...was a good thing, historically speaking" despite the fact that it left us with "...fragmentation and disillusionment."
7. Then finishes off with a clear eyed view of their record company and us old fans who don't want the dream to end "...they can be dusted off at appropriate intervals, depending on the needs of Capitol's ledgers and our own inability to cope with the present." A+

"Paul McCartney: He did it all for you?" Creem July 1976

This is Lester's coverage of the Wings over America tour. What could be more fun for the Bi-centennial than Lester Bangs report on Paul's first U.S. tour in ten years? When I was a kid reading this for the first time I thought Lester was referring to his child when he kept referencing his baby working at a clothing boutique, pushing his baby through the crowd, etc. I had no idea he was actually referring to his old lady. It was very confusing for a young lad.

From the McDonalds parody cover cartoon with staunch vegetarian Paul serving up hamburgers and fries at McCartney's to Lester's backstage chat with Paul this is a delicious treat. Lester, "Why did you bring your kids on tour?" Paul, "Kiss?" Lester, "Not Kiss. Kids!"

Bangs surmises that this looks like the biggest rock tour in history but it's really just Paul, Linda, and their children on vacation. A

"Thinking the Unthinkable About John Lennon" Los Angeles Times December 11, 1980

This is available in Psychotic Reactions and Carburetor Dung edited by Greil Marcus (1987)

- "John at his best disguised cheap sentiment..."
- "He was always the one who lived most on the existential edge..."
- "I can't mourn John Lennon. I didn't know the guy."
- "...cynical, sneeringly sarcastic, witheringly witty, and iconoclastic..."
- "Ultimately you are mourning for yourself."   A+

Greil Marcus:

STRANDED: Rock and Roll for a Desert Island (1979, 1996, 2007 DaCapo Press)

In the introduction Greil states "I'm sure if that if this book had been written ten years ago, the Beatles and Bob Dylan would have not only appeared in it but perhaps dominated it..." And, "The absence of Elvis from this book is as scandalous as the fact that the Beatles are missing, and as sensible."

Greil makes up for the missing Beatles in his epilogue entitled Treasure Island:

- *RUBBER SOUL*: "Exchanging assault for seduction..."
- *I AM THE WALRUS*: "It stands as a signpost to a future never quite reached..."
- *THE BEATLES*: "...masterpieces scattered like crumbs..."

- *DON'T LET ME DOWN*: "...their last shining moment..."
- *BAND ON THE RUN*: "Pure pop for all people..."
- *RADIO DINNER*: "The Persecution and Assassination of John Lennon..." National Lampoon assassinated him nearly a decade before Chapman did.   A-

THE ROLLING STONE RECORD GUIDE (1979 Random House/Rolling Stone Press)

- *PLASTIC ONO BAND*: "The record was a full, blistering statement of fury, resentment, and self-pity."
- *GOD*: "John's singing on the last verse may be the finest in all of rock."
- *SOME TIME IN NEW YORK CITY*: "...disastrous... horrendous..."
- *MIND GAMES* and *WALLS AND BRIDGES*: "There was no real point of view at work."
- *ROCK 'N' ROLL*: "He tried to escape a dead end by going back to his roots."   A-

"Life and Life Only" Rolling Stone January 22, 1981

- "To hear that John Lennon had been murdered by a fan, that he had been killed for who and what he was, was like watching someone you love being hit by a car."
- "As Jim Miller has written, rock & roll works as common experience and private obsession."
- "...made the last sixteen years collapse on my head as if now it was time to pay for every moment of pleasure, affection and friendship they had contained."
- "Four days after John Lennon was shot, when I woke up to find Beatles music off the radio and the story off the front page...does this mean, I thought, that's it over? That he's not dead anymore?" A+

THE HISTORY OF ROCK 'n' ROLL IN TEN SONGS
(2014 Yale University Press)

- "George Harrison died of cancer at fifty-eight, twenty-one years after John Lennon was murdered at forty...only Paul and Ringo left...was it worth it?"

- MONEY: "It wasn't pop. It wasn't entertainment. It was fun in the way that watching Michael Corleone shoot Sollozzo and Captain McCluskey is fun. It was shocking."
- "Later the Rolling Stones would be recording their own version of MONEY, but compared to the Beatles they were a skiffle band."
- "I want to be free, John shouts off the beat...and you realize the person speaking will never be free."
- "It is a record that in the years since it was made has lost none of its ugliness and none of its beauty."   A-

Greil Marcus recommends *Magic Circles: The Beatles in Dream and History* by Devin McKinney (2003) B+ (see review somewhere in this book)

Robert Christgau:

(check out his comprehensive website at Robertchristgau.com)

ANY OLD WAY YOU CHOOSE IT: Rock and Other Pop Music 1967 – 1973 (1973 Penguin)

- *RUBBER SOUL*: "...an album that for innovation, tightness, and lyrical intelligence was about twice as good as anything they or anyone else (except maybe the Stones) had done previously." Bob must have forgotten about *BRINGING IT ALL BACK HOME* and *HIGHWAY 61 REVISITED*.

- *REVOLVER*: "...was twice as good and four times as startling as *RUBBER SOUL*, with sound effects, Oriental drones, jazz bands, transcendentalist lyrics, all kinds of rhythmic and harmonic surprises, and a filter that made John Lennon sound like God singing through a foghorn."
- *THE BEATLES*: "Their most consistent and probably their worst."
- *McCARTNEY*: "Why did I give *McCARTNEY* a B plus? Because I was taken, that's why."
- *ALL THINGS MUST PASS*: "...sounds more like Muzak to my ears than *RAM* does."
- *PLASTIC ONO BAND*: "...is conceptual in the Yoko Ono rather than the *Sgt. PEPPER* sense. It is one of the few albums I admire that does not permit casual enjoyment."
- *SOME TIME IN NEW YORK CITY*: "Does Angela Davis have to be told that she's one of the million political prisoners in the world?" A+

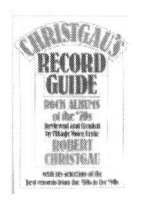

CHRISTGAU'S RECORD GUIDE: Rock albums of the 70's (1981 Houghton Mifflin)

- *PLASTIC ONO BAND*: "John wants to make it clear that right now truth is far more important than subtlety, taste, art, or anything else."
- *LIVING IN THE MATERIAL WORLD*: "If you call this living."
- *BAND ON THE RUN*: "Pop masterpiece? This?"

- *SHAVED FISH*: "Eleven shots in the dark from the weirdest major rock and roller of the early 70's."
- *ROTOGRAVURE*: "This fellow definitely sounds like he could use a band."
- *WINGS GREATEST*: "…pop for potheads. All I could ask for is a stylus-width scratch across *MY LOVE*.

A+

CHRISTGAU'S RECORD GUIDE: The 80's (1990 Pantheon)

- *STARR STRUCK: THE BEST OF RINGO STARR, VOL. 2*: "Better than Telly Savalas…"
- *SOMEWHERE IN ENGLAND*: "Twice Warners sent these sappy plaints back for seasoning. Then a former associate of Harrison met with an accident, and Harrison wrote his catchiest tune in years…"
- *MILK AND HONEY*: "Those too numbed by tragedy or hope to connect with *DOUBLE FANTASY* aren't likely to hear this one either-it's definitely more of the same…"

A+

GROWN UP ALL WRONG: 75 Great Rock and Pop Artists from Vaudeville to Techno (1998 Harvard University Press)

In the article "Why the Beatles Broke Up" Christgau explains "...because they couldn't stand each other anymore." And in "Nothing to Say but Everything, or, As Far As He Could Go" with John Picarella he tells us "But a week later Paul was in the band, and for the next decade-plus his unreconstructed boyishness, snazzy melodic ideas, transcendent harmonies, and insufferable pop treacle would clutter and inestimably enrich John's passion, calling, and way of life." A

CHRISTGAU'S CONSUMER GUIDE: Albums of the 90's (2000 St. Martin's Griffin)

- *WONSAPONATIME*: "Lennon wasn't above dabbling in religion. But he never got so down he mistook God for more than a concept by which he measured his pain."
- *RUN DEVIL RUN*: "I don't want to call McCartney the most complacent rock and roller in history. The competition is way too stiff, especially up around his age." A

Blender (2004)

THE CAPITOL ALBUMS VOL. 1: "In any self-respecting Beatles discography these four 1964 albums do not exist."

Rolling Stone (2006)

LOVE: "Played too often, this version of the world's greatest rock and roll band could give a person a tummyache."

Creem (1977)

Sgt. PEPPER: "A dozen good songs and true. Perhaps they're too precisely performed, but I'm not going to complain."

<u>GOING INTO THE CITY: Portrait of a Critic as a Young Man</u> (2015 Dey St.)

Bob's new memoir reiterates his love for PLASTIC ONO BAND: "As life turned out, there are no records I put on even monthly after their currency has eroded. Terrific ones sink to the bottom for years, PLASTIC ONO BAND I never forget…Rock-as-art figurehead Phil Spector deserves credit for once. Forbidden to ask Tchaikovsky the news, he hones his expertise to deep, durable, subliminal effect. Every minimal note reverberates…It's where I began to believe that rock proper has produced no better singer."

Bob recounts his time with John and Yoko in NYC and Syracuse: "I'd met Mick Jagger, remember, and had interviewed Janis Joplin, Aretha Franklin, Miles Davis. But there was no comparison wattage-wise-this guy was intense."

Bob writes about how he and his wife Carola Dibbell reacted to Lennon's death: "...Carola raised a question of logic: 'Why is it always Bobby Kennedy or John Lennon? Why isn't it Richard Nixon or Paul McCartney?' The front-page thousand-worder I completed at six thirty in the morning quoted her question and concluded that famous people who gave ordinary mortals hope often get blamed when hopes were dashed, and by Thursday we both had been widely accused of advocating the assassination of gifted Wings bassist McCartney. Even Carola was more bemused than discomfited by the misreading." A

SELECTED MAGAZINES

THE ATLANTIC (July/August 2014)

Joshua Wolf Shenk explains how genius works vis-à-vis Lennon/McCartney and their well-known creative tension. This is an adaption of his writing on Paul and John in his book *Powers of Two: Finding the Essence of Innovation in Creative Pairs*.

Also, covered in the book are Laurel and Hardy, Jerry and Larry, Harrison and Starkey, Glengarry and Glenross, Ross and Gwen, Sutcliffe and Best, Sterlace and Wachowiak, Bingo and Rock, Rocky and Bullwinkle, Rock and Doris, Sajecki and Viola, Stills and Young, Seals and Croft, Bob and Ray, monkeys and donkeys, Belushi and Ackroyd, Tom and Jerry, Bud and Lou, Roger and Gene, Leopold and Lowe, Donald and Walter, Paul and Gene, Pete and Roger, Mutt and Jeff, Mick and Bianca, Gilliam and Jones, Cleese and Chapman, Penn and Teller, Ray and Dave, Ian and Martin, Laurie and Fry, Amos and Andy, Gleason and Carney, Matthau and Burns, DeNiro and Grodin, Johnny and Ed, Conan and Andy, and Waters and Gilmour. B

THE BEATLES: A Pictorial History (1970 Magnum-Royal)

Jumping right on Paul's news of the break-up Royal/Magnum specials kicked out the jams with this photo essay that starts from the beginning and stops at the end. For a buck you received "Over 100 outasite pix" and as a "special bonus full color photographs suitable for framing." It's not just hype. There are two, count them two, color 8 ½ x 11 shots that would look good in 8 ½ x 11 frames. You get a cardigan sweaters and ties 1963 one and a psychedelic Epstein pepper party 1967 one. Who could ask for more? For a special this isn't very special but it is a classic historical artifact, now going for up to two dollars on the white market. B

THE BEATLES: 100 Greatest Songs by Rolling Stone (2010 Rolling Stone)

The Beatles only put out 186 originals when they were together. I'm glad *Rolling Stone* had the fortitude to eighty six the eighty six they didn't love. As it should be *A DAY IN THE LIFE* is number one with a bullet. After that, it is completely subjective. I wouldn't have *LET IT BE* or *WHILE MY GUITAR GENTLY WEEPS* in my top ten but I tend to favor Lennon when making my list.   A-

THE BEATLES: The Ultimate Album-by-Album Guide by Rolling Stone (2011 Rolling Stone)

A magazine special from *Rolling Stone* that night as well be a trade paperback. There's track by track analysis and lots of pretty pictures. The highlight writer wise is Rob Sheffield who contributes the introduction and a sharp essay on *RUBBER SOUL*.

Bonus feature: pop stars sound off on the band. Hear what Graham Nash, Steven Van Zandt (his show *Lillyhammer* is a lot of fun) Stephen Malkmus, Liam Gallagher, Colin Meloy, Wayne Coyne, James Taylor, Liz Phair, Bob Weir, and guitar god Joe Perry think of the fab four. Couldn't they get somebody who wears their influence on their sleeve like Jeff Lynne, Joe Orlowski, or Robert Schneider? A-

THE BEATLES: The Ultimate Music Guide – Issue 13 from the makers of Uncut (2013)

This "Special Collector's edition" is indeed that. We receive 148 delightful pages on the canon. Just like the Lennon issue we get up to the minute reappraisals of all the classic long players ...plus a chapter on the compilations, a gander at the *ANTHOLOGY* releases, and a quick opinion on *PAST MASTERS* volumes one and two. In the correct order we begin with:

PLEASE PLEASE ME: "...at heart a lean, hungry rock and roll band."

WITH THE BEATLES: "...32 and a half minutes of energy, invention, and unwitting cultural devastation."

A HARD DAY'S NIGHT: "Almost half a century after its release, everywhere you look there is something to enjoy, admire, and surprise."

BEATLES FOR SALE: "...was widely seen as a retrograde step."

HELP!: "LSD, Dylan, secret messages, and the irresistible rise of Paul McCartney."

RUBBER SOUL: "Their future direction quietly budding before its glorious spring."

REVOLVER: "...the continuing shift away from simplistic romantic material..."

PEPPER: "The Beatles build a new world of awe and wonder."

MAGICAL MYSTERY TOUR: "Maybe getting a little lost was part of the design."

THE BEATLES: "It's a glorious, giddy, liberating hoot."

YELLOW SUBMARINE: "...widely regarded as the runt of the Beatles' discography."

LET IT BE: "Today we're all familiar with the jaded rock band getting back to basics..."

ABBEY ROAD: "Why did the Beatles cross the road?" A

CREEM (April 1976)

America's only rock 'n' roll magazine realized they could boost sales via our heroes so we get the butcher photo on the Creem cover. The accompanying "Beatles Confidential" article leaves everything to be desired. It's just a few unmemorable stories relayed by Tony Tyler about the years 1959-1964. To make things even worse, Susan Whitall fills us in on their girlfriends and wives in a way that makes me wish we heard more from Tony Tyler. In Rock 'n' Roll News we get a nugget about McCartney looking into a hair transplant ("Did you ever wonder how he maintained that mop of black hair?").

If this issue is not particularly attractive to Beatle fans it is more than made up for by three absolute classics from Lester Bangs. We get his rave review of *STATION TO STATION*, his lengthy pan of *DESIRE* ("*DESIRE* is a sham and a fake-out.") and his "Death May Be Your Santa Claus" interview with Hendrix straight from the grave. Catching up with Jimi is a mind blower and the way Lester tears apart Zimmerman's Joey Gallo epic is an education.

A

ENTERTAINMENT WEEKLY (9/11/09)

Couldn't they have just called this the 9/09/09 issue just to play along? Only Lennon/McCartney on the front of this compact disc remasters issue, oddly in the same pose as another EW cover featuring Pam and Jim from the U.S. Office. Inside they rate *Rock Band* (it "rocks") and give it an A. Then they give us four short paragraphs on the re-masters where we are informed they have "pretty packaging", are "...not just for audiophiles", and are "cost-effective." The 1987 discs were "crapola" but these new ones "...achieve both volume and subtlety." The liner notes are "controversy-avoidant" and "the Beatles' catalog has a way of turning everyone anal-retentive." Run for the hills, everybody!

Going out on a limb, their list of the 50 best songs starts with the surprising choice of *A HARD DAY'S NIGHT*. *A DAY IN THE LIFE* is relegated to number two. Interesting... but more interesting is their list of the five worst songs. *WILD HONEY PIE* should obviously be number one (if you want to count it as a song) but it is relegated to number two and in a shocking move their 7/07/67 A-side *ALL YOU NEED IS LOVE* is voted worst song ever, despite the fact they also list it as 50th best song ever. Black is white, up is down, and in is out. We're through the looking glass here, people. DIG IT is third worst (like *WILD HONEY* not really a song...especially in its Spector vision version). Number four is Starkey's excretion *DON'T PASS ME BY*. Coming around the turn at number five is *FLYING* which is basically a doodle.

Is it possible we have uptight Beach man Mike Love to blame for McCartney's terrible *WILD HONEY PIE*? I'm guessing he took a copy of his latest Capitol platter *WILD HONEY* to India to show Paul (him being a big Brian Wilson fan and all) and it unfortunately sparked McCartney into action. Paul's excuse for putting it on vinyl was that Maureen Starkey liked it. Thanks, Mo.
                                                                                        B

LENNON: The Ultimate Music Guide - Issue 3 from the Makers of Uncut (2010)

This 148 special is like a wonderful book with a magazine look. There are rare photos, a complete discography, incendiary interviews, and a fresh twenty first century look at every Lennon album, even the three avant-garde ones and *LIVE PEACE*:

TWO VIRGINS: "It lacks the concentrated, layered nightmarishness of *REVOLUTION 9*."

LIFE WITH THE LIONS: Reviewer David Stubbs reviews all the tracks on here save *BABY'S HEARTBEAT* (though he does give it two stars out of five in the track listing) which is a five minute and ten second loop of their dead baby's heartbeat from Yoko's tragic miscarriage. The cover of the album features Yoko and John in the hospital after the sad event. I guess David Stubbs didn't want to offend any readers but as Yoko pointed out about the cover of *SEASON OF GLASS*, "there was blood everywhere."

WEDDING ALBUM: "He achieves more in the harrowing few minutes of *COLD TURKEY* than he does on all three of these albums." That's obvious.

LIVE PEACE IN TORONTO 1969: "Toronto is confronted with a sound for which nothing has prepared it... Yoko..."

PLASTIC ONO BAND: "It's completely self-absorbed and solipsistic..."

IMAGINE: "...all hippie millionaires rock stars are essentially hypocritical..."

SOME TIME IN NEW YORK CITY: "Was Lennon being exploited?" Yes is the answer.

MIND GAMES: "...comes off as a series of entries in a diary..."

PUSSY CATS: "A lost weekend special."

WALLS AND BRIDGES: "...has never been accepted as one of the classic Lennon albums." Rightly so, though noted film maker Mike Sajecki told me one time it's his favorite.

ROCK 'N'ROLL: 1974 cartoon in *Creem* asked if "John Lennon likes rock and roll so much why doesn't he get his head out of the ozone and make some?" I guess John was feeling the same way in his Boy Howdy tee shirt because the next year we were subjected to this. I wish he had cut it with Klaus, Richard, and William…….and *Uncut's* John Robinson says, "It's a good-time record, by someone who wasn't, in the end, having that much of a good time at all."

DOUBLE FANTASY: "…will forever hover somewhere between a full stop and a question mark."

MILK AND HONEY: "For many, this was a fresher record than its predecessor."

LIVE IN NEW YORK CITY: Colin Irwin from Melody Maker says, "Erratic, frequently shoddy, and often jarring."

JOHN LENNON ANTHOLOGY: "A mammoth trawl through the archives." A+

NATIONAL LAMPOON (October 1977)

They had made fun of the Beatles before. They had done *MAGICAL MISERY TOUR* in magazine form and in vinyl form. But this took the cake. Even as the Beatles laid low in 1977 (John retired, George taking time off in Hawaii, Paul relaxing after storming America during the Bicentennial, Ringo out disco dancing) the public cried out for the fab four. Into the record shops came the lackluster two record live set *STAR CLUB*, the lackluster two record throwaway compilation *LOVE SONGS*, and the fun one record souvenir of Los Angeles, California circa 1964-65 known as *HOLLYWOOD BOWL*. But the key moment of fab '77 (if you don't count the greatest selling single in United Kingdom history being issued by Wings or the release of *The Beatles Forever*) was this full length lampooning of the act you'd known for all these years.

As the years go by this issue of National Lampoon has taken on almost near legendary proportions in the Beatle fan community. Originally priced at a reasonable $1.25 it now goes for up to $1.35 in mint or near mint or very good condition. It is chock full of laughs, guffaws, and chuckles.

The cover of the issue features the band being flattened by a bulldozer as they cross Abbey Road on that hot summer day in 1969. It is an apt metaphor for what will follow, as their lives and careers are knocked down and demolished. The Beatles are not sacred cows. Anything about them is fair game for ridicule. It's all in good fun.

It starts out harmlessly enough with a Beatles trivia quiz. I got zero answers right. See how you do.

Question 1: What fruit was Apple Records, at one point, going to be named after?

Question 4: When did Paul record "Silly Love Songs?"

Question 9: Which of the Beatles was endowed with the largest manhood?

Question 16: What did George's dentist put in his and John's coffee?

Question 27: What is the name of Brian Epstein's autobiography?

Highlights of this comedy fest include:

1. "Beat the Meatles": Chris Miller gets together at his apartment with the band and Yoko to smoke a little dope and reminisce about the old days. Insightful interviewing at its finest.
Chris, "What kind of toothpaste do you use?" Ringo, "Crest."
Chris, "Paul, what's five and three?" Paul, "Eight."
2. *FABGEARBEAT* magazine October 1964: with how to understand Liverpoolian, parts of Ringo's body look-alike contest, and the Dave Clark Five crush the Beatles.
3. "The Fab Four! Adventures in Hamburg": A graphic novel like expose of the relationship between the band and Brian. Includes the time all four went to bed with him.
4. *FUCK!:* The Beatles' second movie, this time in color. Enjoy the sexual escapades of four virile young men. With Dennis Hopper, Melvin Van Peebles, and Mamie Van Doren as the Walrus.
5. "Apple Boutique Annual Near-Givaway Sale": this resembles the Beatles.com store in 2015. It is eerily prescient. Items to buy include nowhere man note pad, Norwegian wood polish, and Magic Alex's electronic penis enlarger.
6. "The Unreleased Albums": featuring *RABBI SAUL*, George's *LIFTING MATERIAL FROM THE WORLD*, and John's magnificent 1970 opus *FUCK ME? FUCK YOU*.
7. "Advertisements to Find a Cure for Beatlemania": Let's lick B.M.

8. "He Blew His Mind Out in a Car": The true story of Paul McCartney's death.
9. "Charlie – The Fifth Beatle": Manson in collarless suit with his back to Sharon Tate's Cielo Drive love house.
10. "Surprise Poster #28" "We're more popular than Jesus Christ", says humble John Lennon as a giant foot ala Terry Gilliam comes out of the sky to stomp his bandmates to death.

Now the answers to the quiz, I hope you pass the audition.

1. Allen Klein
4. 1962-1977
9. Best, Peter
16. Cream and sugar
27. *A Cellarful of Boys*

A+

NEW YORK (May 18-31, 2015)

As Ms. Ono finally gets an exhibit devoted to her work at The Museum of Modern Art in the Big Apple, the one she'd been imagining since 1971 (Imagine people taking your art seriously, it's easy if you try). Lindsay Zoladz gives us the lowdown on why women should love Yoko and her pioneering ways. Ms. Zoladz equates Ono with Joan of Arc and Courtney Love, two others who were in "A position from which a woman could offend more deeply than a man." Yoko might not be "...a radical-or a martyr-anymore" but "Maybe we're just beginning to inhabit the world that Yoko Ono always imagined." Maybe I'm amazed at how I never loved Ono before this.

In 1966 she met Lennon ("her Eve") and contrary to popular opinion she was not a "gold digger" but merely used the Beatle to complete her vision. How nice for her. Yoko's vision was realized with such works as *Self-Portrait*, her "...42 minute slow-motion film of John Lennon's penis." Talk about letting it all hang out!

Yoko is to be admired for her metaphorical blood throwing and "Her work is being lauded by people correcting a history of female erasure". Lennon stands revealed as "...laughably tame" just like "...the entire supposedly revolutionary art form of rock and roll."

Ms. Zoladz feels she "...can freely admit sacrilegious things" about such icons as Chuck Berry and John Lennon. She feels "...uncomfortable falling at the feet of both Lennon and Berry because one of them beat his ex-wife and the other was once arrested for transporting a 14-year-old girl across state lines." That's a very good point. I just wish she had mentioned Yoko's much less criminal but still pathetic return to her relationship with John after he cheated on her. In my book strong feminists who aren't gold diggers or power trippers or control freaks walk away from their husbands when they get betrayed, especially when it happens in front of a lot of witnesses at a party.   A-

THE PAUL McCARTNEY WORLD TOUR program (1989 Emap Metro)

McCartney was so psyched about hitting the road for the first time in ten years, touring the world for the first time since the Bi-centennial that he commissioned a glossy concert program and gave it away for free. It was December 7, 1989 and I was in Toronto at Skydome to see Paul and the little woman. It was one day before the ninth anniversary of you-know-what and before the show began out rang the voice of John Lennon on the sound system. On the giant video screen was Richard Lester's eleven minute film of McCartney's life and times. It was the beginning of Paul immersing himself in full scale Beatle nostalgia which has continued well into the twenty first century.

This concert program is quite nice. It only has a few ads (Coca-Cola, Almay hypo-allergenic practical skin care for men, Converse) and it has tributes to Zimmerman and Lennon from Paul. McCartney also pats himself on the back for forming Wings in 1971 ("very ballsy").

It was a simpler time back in the 1980's. All we had was MTV, compact discs, and VHS tapes. Men cared about the quality of their skin. I still use Almay hypo-allergenic to this day. I'm just old fashioned that way. B+

ROLLING STONE (January 22, 1981)

I knew Lennon had picked the right image for the cover because as soon as my father got a look at Annie Lebowitz's December 8, 1980 photo of John in the nude with his eyes closed kissing Yoko he let out a snort of disgust. "How could you bring that into my house?" he said. Even as millions mourned his death all over the world Lennon could still outrage the squares by taking his clothes off. I would have shown my dad the sleeve for *TWO VIRGINS* next but I didn't want to give him a heart attack.

Just as they had done before, Jann Wenner and company exploded into action with the death of an icon. There had been memorial covers for Jimi, Janis, Jim, and Elvis. But only Presley and Lennon got the full issue treatment.

It still saddens me to look at this. It still fills me with emotion when I read the obituaries from Greil Marcus ("Why John Lennon, and why now?") and Dave Marsh ("He was most certainly killed not by fame but by four highly unmetaphoric bullets"). The letters to the editor from *Rolling Stone* readers also leave me stunned even though it was all those years ago.

The stars share their grief and their memories. Ray Charles, Murray the K, Peter Noone, Peter Fonda, Joan Baez, James Taylor, Nicky Hopkins, Bill Wyman, Jim Keltner, John Sinclair, Richard Perry, Bobby Keyes, Roy Carr, Carly Simon, David Geffen, Norman Mailer, Frank Sinatra, and Howard Cosell are all heard from as they try to make sense of something that made no sense.

There are also Annie Lebowitz's tremendous photos from December 8th (John, "I know you wanted to photograph me in an apron but like any rich housewife I can afford a cook."). They capture John on his last day eerily going back to the future with his fresh from the barber Hamburg look. One head shot is sans glasses. One picture he's on a windowsill wearing a black leather jacket, jeans, boots (Beatle boots?) and sunglasses.

Tastefully, we get no photos of the killer. Fuck him. A+

SOUND AND VISION (November 2009)

The audiophile bible rates the remasters and goes inside the process with the Abbey Road team at Electric Lady land. "Yesterday's music meets today's technology." The CD packaging gets four stars (out of five) the booklets get three and a half stars, the extras rightly get two stars, the sound quality gets four stars and the music, of course, gets five stars.

Rock Band also passes the audition so feel free to play the game until the end of the beginning. B+

UNCUT (October 2009)

According to the fine folks at *Uncut* this is the definite review of the remasters. I agree. Turn to page 84 for David Cavanagh's ecstatic and possibly orgasmic look at the discs. For David "It is not a dispassionate experience. It is an overwhelming one." The albums "...have taken their masks off, and we didn't know they were wearing any." You know how David feels? He feels this way: "It's as if we've been visiting an art gallery to gaze in wonder at a masterpiece all these years, and then suddenly an attendant comes along with a sponge and wipes the painting from top to bottom."

I'm sold. I'm going to throw away my mint condition Parlophone/Apple mono/stereo collection from the 60's/70 and replace it with these miniature versions. I don't need any antiques cluttering up my abode. A-

WELCOME BACK BEATLES edited by Christopher May (Fall 1977 Stories Layouts & Press)

To keep pace with the demand for all things Beatle, publisher Myron Fass started a magazine series full of black and white band and solo photos haphazardly arranged. I was a kid and I didn't know any better so I plunked down my $1.50 and got ready for a good time. To supplement the wide array of pictures Myron had Christopher May (and possibly an uncredited writer) concoct a four part fantasy story about an alternative Fab universe. This is part two of that tale. It's a doozy.

It goes like this. After the release of *LET IT BE* they didn't break-up. They simply took a break. They pursued solo projects. George had the greatest success with *ALL THINGS MUST PASS*. When it came time to get back to being Beatles he opted out. Harrison didn't want to be a Beatle anymore because it would mean a return to his subservient role. The others decided to get a new guitarist the same way Brian Jones gave way to Mick Taylor who made way for Ronald Wood. They considered Jeff Beck, Jerry Garcia, Dave Mason, and Eric Clapton. "Then one day, Ringo was chatting with a buddy of his who played with the Who." It was good old Keith Moon. Keith figured why not let Daltrey and Entwistle do that solo thing for a while like they always wanted to and he and Townshend could join together with the band and become the super group to end all super groups. "To the world's amazement, all parties agreed to the arrangement." The Who would take a long hiatus. They already were on an album only once every two years schedule anyway so it would work out perfectly.

"The new Beatles (after some discussion, Peter and Keith insisted the name be kept intact) began work on their next album project in 1975." Meanwhile, *LIVING IN THE MATERIAL WORLD* had tanked and George's "...fan mail simply dwindled." As if to dig his own grave deeper Harrison then released the horrible *DARK HORSE* album which one critic called "One of the most stupendously-hyped flops in the history of entertainment." George was in a bad place but "None of the others were particularly sympathetic." While George suffered

John, Paul, and Ringo enjoyed "...very solid careers in their own right, and each man had the total security of an imminent reunion."

On December 21, 1975 the album *WHO ARE THESE BEATLES, ANYWAY?* arrived in shops just in time to reap the Christmas sales. It featured the hit single *LOOK INTO MY EYES*, which did double duty as a ten minute long album cut. When they decided to play live they eschewed concerts at "...Shea Stadium, Rich Stadium." They selected a small theatre in Des Moines. The gig was announced in the local paper right before the night of the show. Fans thought it was a hoax and only 75 people showed up. McCartney took one look at the practically non-existent crowd and jumped back in the limo. John, Ringo, Keith, and Pete played a short show as a quartet sans bass guitar.

The next stop was Columbus, Ohio. The word had got out about the Des Moines show and there was an avalanche of ticket buyers for the Columbus show. It was like a mini-Woodstock. The site was changed from a tiny theatre to the outside of the state capitol building. The tour was abandoned and they decided to do one marathon length concert. It was a four hour extravaganza. Jerry Garcia would have fit in, after all.

But that's not all, folks. George Harrison shows up backstage and rejoins the band right in front of the crowd of 100,000 people. What a magic night! It was so wonderful to have John, Paul, George, and Ringo playing together in concert for the first time in over a decade, with an assist from Keith and Pete.

Welcome back, Beatles!   A-

ONE NEWSPAPER ARTICLE

USA TODAY page 4D (9/09/09)

Edna Gundreson does a great job looking at the remasters and *The Beatles Box of Vision*. About the CDs she says, "What you hear isn't technology. It's heart." About Jon Polk's deluxe box of vision she says, "Polk was thinking inside the box when he envisioned his...200 page linen-covered book of album artwork."

Note to my devoted readers: If any of you are planning on sending me a gift for Christmas this year, I sure would appreciate if you make it one of the limited edition mint condition The *Beatles Box of Vision*. A-

APPENDIX I

Things that I wish had happened in Beatle history:

1. *YELLOW SUBMARINE* had been issued as an EP in the U.K. like God intended. *MAGICAL MYSTERY TOUR* came out as a rare double EP because it only had six songs from the soundtrack of a TV movie. *YELLOW SUBMARINE* had only four songs from the soundtrack of a theatrical cartoon. That's the perfect fit for an EP. The British wouldn't have felt ripped off. They would have received value for money and not had George Martin's useless score foisted upon them. (John Lennon, "It's a whole sort of joke. George Martin is on one side of our album.") Apple did make plans in early 1969 to issue a five song *YELLOW SUBMARINE* EP with the addition of the, at the time, unreleased *ACROSS THE UNIVERSE* but unfortunately, the plan was scrapped.

2. Stuart Sutcliffe had stayed alive and stayed in the band. He was the coolest Beatle ever. He wore sunglasses on stage, had an artist girlfriend from a foreign country five years before Lennon copied him by having an artist girlfriend from another country, and as Sid Vicious and Casino El Camino Del Reo proved bass guitarists don't have to be virtuosos as long as they project a cool band defining image. It would have been great if the Beatles had stuck with their three guitar line-up. They would have set the trend a decade before Lynyrd Skynyrd.

3. *LET IT BE* had been issued with the photo they originally took for the cover after the *GET BACK* sessions concluded. After the rooftop show John grew a beard,

Paul shaved his beard, and John suggested they recreate the photo of their first album cover for their new album cover. John figured they were getting back to where they once belonged so why not get photographer Angus McBean to come and shoot them in the exact same spot at EMI headquarters they stood at for the *PLEASE PLEASE ME* LP (The Sex Pistols aka John, Paul, Steve, and Glen also had a photo taken there during the brief time they were signed to EMI). It was genius! It was even better than John's ideas to eat chocolate cake in a bag, send acorns to world leaders, and pose naked with his thing hanging out.

When they pushed back the release date of the album and recorded and released *ABBEY ROAD* instead the idea was scrapped. This was sheer stupidity. Now that they were breaking up and *LET IT BE* would be their last album it would create a perfect bookend to their U.K. album career. They had the opportunity to put out a mirror image that showed via facial hair and rapid aging the changes that six/seven years had wrought. *PLEASE PLEASE ME* had come out in April 1963. If they pushed back *LET IT BE's* release ten days it too would have come out in April. April fools, fans! We would have had *PLEASE PLEASE ME with LOVE ME DO and 12 others songs* and we would have had *LET IT BE with GET BACK and ten other songs*. Perfection! *LET IT BE* retained the breathless early 60's notes on the back cover ("This is a new phase Beatles album. In comes the warmth and the freshness of a live performance"). They just didn't go all the way with the sleeve.

Furthermore, instead of issuing it only in stereo they could have put it out only in mono as a tribute to Phil "back to mono" Spector. Eventually, in the spring of 1973 they finally used photos from the 1963 and 1969 sessions on the two double compilation albums *1962-1966* and *1967-1970*. It worked great. They were perfect pics to show them at the beginning and the end of the 60's. I rest my case.

4. Chapman had shot Yoko instead of John. Can you imagine the raw artistic masterpieces that would have been pouring out of Lennon after seeing his soul mate murdered in front of him? He would have been cranking out albums that would have made *PLASTIC ONO BAND* sound like *DOUBLE FANTASY*.

APPENDIX II

EERIE SIMILARITIES BETWEEN THE MURDER OF JOHN LENNON AND THE ASSASSINATION OF JOHN F. KENNEDY

Ever since December 1980 the media and the fans have been making lists that point out the mind blowing similarities between the killings of Kennedy and Lennon and the odd ways their lives mirrored each other.

1. They were both named John.
2. They both had airports named after them.

3. Yoko spoke a language besides English (Japanese) and so did Jackie (French).
4. They were both no good serial cheaters.
5. They both had two sons.
6. They were both men.
7. They were both football fans though Kennedy liked the good football we call the National Football League while Lennon liked the football where they run around willy nilly and hardly ever score despite the fact that the goalie's net is huge. Hear "block that kick" on Lennon's famous pro-football audio collage *REVOLUTION 9*. Hear Lennon's famous B-side *REVOLUTION* in the late 80's pro-football Nike TV commercial.

Lennon's favorite team, naturally, was Liverpool United. JFK and Jackie rooted for the Dallas Cowboys because they became a new NFL franchise in the fall of 1960 at the same time that Kennedy was voted the new president. The devotion the Kennedys felt for the Cowboys made them America's Team, an honor they still hold to this day. During Kennedy's speech at the Berlin wall he referenced them as a symbol of America's great capitalist spirit when he said, "How about those Cowboys?"

After November 1963 Jackie inexplicably lost interest in the Cowboys and switched allegiance to the Montreal Allouetes of the Canadian Football League where at least they spoke French for Christ's sake.

8. Kennedy fought in World War II. Lennon pretended to fight in World War II (in Richard Lester's 1967 film *How I Won the War*).
9. Lennon played mouth organ. Kennedy liked women to put their mouth on his organ.
10. They were both shot to death outside during late autumn in front of their wives by a psychotic well-traveled married loser in his mid-20's.

APPENDIX III

WHERE MY WIFE AND I WERE ON THE DAY CYNTHIA LENNON DIED APRIL 1st 2015

Strawberry Fields in Central Park Imagine that.

Coincidentally, another major figure in John Lennon's life died on April 1st (in 1976). It was his father Freddie Lennon who John would sing about at the Fillmore East in 1971 when J&Y guested with the Mothers. That's right, John sang *SCUMBAG* in honor of his father while performing with the Mothers. I wonder if background singers Flo and Eddie felt like breaking in to *HAPPY TOGETHER*. Freddie was a recording artist in his own write known for his rendition of *THE NEXT TIME YOU FEEL IMPORTANT* which is what he used to always say to John right up until the time he abandoned his child.

APPENDIX IV

TOP TWENTY TWO ESSENTIAL BEATLE BOOKS

A+

1. *ANTHOLOGY* (2000)
2. *THE BEATLES ALBUM* (1991)
3. *THE BEATLES AN ILLUSTRATED RECORD* (1975)
4. *THE BEATLES FOREVER* (1977)
5. *THE BEATLES RECORDING SESSIONS* (1988)
6. *THE BEATLES: TEN YEARS THAT SHOOK THE WORLD* (2004)
7. *THE CATCHER IN THE RYE* (1951)
8. *FAB FOUR FAQ 2.0* (2010)
9. *HELTER SKELTER* (1974)
10. *LENNON REMEMBERS* (1971)
11. *REVOLUTION IN THE HEAD* (1994)
12. *SOME FUN TONIGHT!* (2013)

A

1. *THE BEATLES BOOK* (1968)
2. *THE BEATLES ILLUSTRATED LYRICS* (1990)
3. *THE LONGEST COCKTAIL PARTY* (1972)
4. *LIVES OF JOHN LENNON* (1988)
5. *MAMMOTH BOOK OF THE BEATLES* (2009)
6. *NOWHERE MAN* (2000)
7. *PAPERBACK WRITER* (1978)
8. *PLAYBOY INTERVIEWS WITH JOHN LENNON AND YOKO ONO* (1981)
9. *ROUGH GUIDE TO THE BEATLES, 2nd EDITION* (2006)
10. *TWILIGHT OF THE GODS* (1973)
11. *WORDS AND MUSIC OF JOHN LENNON* (2007)

APPENDIX V

ONE THING THAT THANKFULLY DIDN'T HAPPEN IN BEATLES HISTORY BUT WOULD HAVE MADE EERIE SYMETRY WITH DECEMBER 8, 1980

Just like the murder of John, it was a night in December (12/30/99) when a crazy and violent man came to George's house and tried to kill him in front of his wife. If Michael Abram had succeeded Harrison wouldn't have made it to the twenty first century and Prince's song would have taken on a wholly different sinister meeting. In fact, Michael Abram would be just as infamous as the jerk of all jerks rather than just a scumbag rotting away the rest of his life in state custody. Good riddance.

APPENDIX VI

THE GREATEST ALBUMS EVER MADE

Being an old white man I tried to make sure this list would feature only old (or dead) white men. Unfortunately, a few women slipped through the cracks. Linda, Layla, and two Maureens (Starkey and Tucker) made it plus John's woman from Tokyo.

For fans of *ABBEY ROAD* side two I recommend side two of Be Bop Deluxe's *MODERN MUSIC* which was recorded and mixed exclusively at EMI No. 3 Studio, Abbey Road, London during June/July 1976. It comes complete with a McCartney-style reprise of the title track.

Speaking of classic side twos: check out Liberace's groovy *LIBERACE NOW!* (1967) which is better than side two of *THE ROLLING STONES, NOW!* (1965) in every way. For fab lovers you get his version of *YESTERDAY* (relegated to side two just like on *HELP!*) and *MOONLIGHT SONATA* (the golden oldie that inspired Lennon to write *BECAUSE*). You haven't lived until you've heard Mr. Showmanship's tap dancing on *MAME* or thrilled to his glorious reading of *THE IMPOSSIBLE DREAM*. Fun fact: Lee's original professional name was Walter Busterkeys.

I never seriously considered *METAL MACHINE MUSIC* on 8-track for this list despite the fact that RCA correctly marketed it as having "special value!"

1. *HIGHWAY 61 REVISITED* by Robert Zimmerman (1965)
2. *THE BEATLES* (1968)
3. *THE KINKS ARE THE VILLAGE GREEN PRESERVATION SOCIETY* (1968)
4. *THE VELVET UNDERGROUND* (1969)
5. *MORRISON HOTEL* by the Doors (1970)
6. *VINTAGE VIOLENCE* by John Cale (1970)
7. *MAD SHADOWS* by Mott the Hoople (1970)
8. *PLASTIC ONO BAND* (1970)
9. *RAM* by James and Linda McCartney (1971)
10. *NEVER A DULL MOMENT* by Rod Stewart (1972)
11. *EXILE ON MAIN STREET* by the Rolling Stones (1972)
12. *THE KINK KRONIKLES* (1972)
13. *QUADROPHENIA* by the Who (1973)

14. *THE MADCAP LAUGHS/BARRETT* by Roger Keith Barrett (1974)
15. *LODGER* by David Jones (1979)
16. *THE CLASH* U.S. edition (1979)
17. *LONDON CALLING* by the Clash (1979)
18. *FLUSH THE FASHION* by Vincent Damon Furnier (1980)
19. *TAKING LIBERTIES* by Declan Patrick MacManus (1980)
20. *A SHAMELESS FASHION* by Celibates (1981)
21. *BORN IN THE USA* by Bruce Springsteen (1984)

I have been informed by some children in my neighborhood that rock music didn't end in 1984 like I thought but that it allegedly continues to this very day in some watered down form. I'm sure if there had been any good music made in the last three decades I would have heard about it. The cream always rises to the top.

Printed in Great Britain
by Amazon